Homesick

Homesick

Finding Our Way Back to a Healthy Planet

Lyla Yastion

HAMILTON BOOKS
Lanham • Boulder • New York • London

Published by Hamilton Books
An imprint of The Rowman & Littlefield Publishing Group, Inc.
4501 Forbes Boulevard, Suite 200, Lanham, Maryland 20706
www.rowman.com

6 Tinworth Street, London SE11 5AL

British Library Cataloguing in Publication Information Available

Library of Congress Control Number: 2018949741
ISBN 978-0-7618-7050-0 (pbk : alk. paper)
ISBN 978-0-7618-7051-7 (electronic)

∞™ The paper used in this publication meets the minimum requirements of American National Standard for Information Sciences—Permanence of Paper for Printed Library Materials, ANSI/NISO Z39.48-1992.

Printed in the United States of America

to Earth and all Earth-keepers

Living nature is not a mechanism but a poem.

—Thomas Huxley, scientist

One day's exposure to mountains is better than cartloads of books.

—John Muir, naturalist

I would go back to the law of the Inuit, the law of nature. I would live like that while checking e-mail.

—Zacharias Kunuk, Inuit native and filmmaker

Contents

List of Figures

List of Tables

parties must apply directly to Penguin Random House LLC for permission. From *Last Child in the Woods* by Richard Louv, reprinted by permission of Algonquin Books. From *Voluntary Simplicity* by Duane Elgin. Copyright © 1993 by Duane Elgin. Reprinted by permission of Duane Elgin and HarperCollins Publishers. From *Earth in Mind* by David Orr. Copyright © 2004 David W. Orr. Reprinted by permission of Island Press, Washington, DC. From THIS CHANGES EVERYTHING by Naomi Klein. Copyright © 2014 by Naomi Klein. Reprinted with permission of Simon & Schuster, Inc. All rights reserved. Special thanks go to filmmaker Zacharias Kunuk for giving permission to reprint in the epigraph his quote which appeared in "Returning Tundra's Rhythm to the Inuit, in Film" by Clifford Krauss, *The New York Times*, March 30, 2002. All other permissions are acknowledged in chapter endnotes.

Preface

Human-induced climate change is emerging as the most critical issue of the modern era. Ninety-seven percent of climate scientists now confirm that human extraction and burning of fossil fuels, along with rampant deforestation, is causing a rapid buildup of carbon dioxide and other greenhouse gases in air and water. These emissions heat up the planet and may be pushing Earth's capacity beyond the threshold at which equilibrium can be restored. Global warming is sustained by a global capitalist economy dependent upon the fossil fuel industry and agribusiness, both of which are unsustainable. The toxic effects of air pollution, ocean acidification, and soil degradation are harming the health of all species. As ecosystems break down an alarming extinction of plant and animal species threatens the evolutionary role of biodiversity. Scientists warn that in order to avoid catastrophic consequences this issue must be immediately and forcefully addressed.

How did the human species, gifted with the light of reason, get to this precarious juncture? The underlying cause is subtle. We are trapped in a self-inflicted cultural mindset that limits our ability to step back and see what we are doing to ourselves and to the Earth. Especially in the industrialized West we are enculturated into the fallacious belief that the human species, unlike other species, is not bound by ecological laws but has a special right to control and master the natural world. This perilous detour in human cultural evolution arises from the illusion that we are separate from the Earth. Our planetary home is perceived as an object—a commodity—to exploit through technology. Unlike indigenous peoples who feel a visceral connection to Mother Earth we modern humans have a mechanized view of the world. We have forgotten our ancestral bond with the Earth. This forgetting has led to the misuse and abuse of her resources. It is imperative that we reconcile ourselves to the natural world by remembering that we are not *apart from* but *part of* the natural world. Only then is health restored to the Earth. Only then do we achieve a human-induced reversal of climate change.

It seems untenable that such a dramatic shift in worldview can occur; yet humankind has the capacity to adapt to and modify the environment through cultural choices. The maladaptive behavior that threatens all life can yield to common sense through a global rise in awareness. Cultural transformation towards a sustainable future for all species starts with the reawakening by each of us to Nature as provider and partner. As memory of our embedded-ness in the natural world is aroused we begin to experience our inclusion in the web of life that sustains us. This reawakening incrementally induces a radical change in thinking within society and sets in motion a paradigm shift. Cultural institutions are then reshaped to match this new benign worldview.

Homesick is divided into three parts. Part One: Children of the Earth (chapters 1–3) describes the relationship between the human species and Nature and how the response of human societies to their environment can be both adaptive and maladaptive. The effects of maladaptive behavior are investigated and a remedy is offered. Chapter 1 presents the concept of *home*, tracing its expanding circles from family dwelling place to planetary home. The damage human beings are currently inflicting on the Earth through human-induced climate change suggests that we have strayed from home and need to reconnect with our extended family in the natural world. Chapter 2 introduces the two ecological laws of interdependence and reciprocity. When human beings disobey these laws, which regulate both biological and cultural systems, they create an *ecocultural system* which is maladaptive. Scientific evidence is given confirming the reality of human-induced climate change. The idea of a paradigm shift in thinking, triggered by a collective cultivation of awareness, is explored as the antidote to this addictive pattern of exploitation. As the cultural mindset changes a life-centered *ecocentric* paradigm emerges to replace the human-centered *anthropocentric* paradigm. Chapter 3 investigates the ways in which the five basic elements of life—air, fire, water, earth and space—are being contaminated by human actions. Particular attention is given to the element water—both its polluted condition and its absence, drought. The story of trees is told from biological, cultural and spiritual perspectives to illuminate the de-structive power of rampant deforestation which, combined with drought, has been a prime mover in the collapse of societies. Also addressed is the alarming increase in species extinctions taking place on our watch. The backbone of ecological health—biodiversity—can only be restored when human beings recognize—through awareness—the right to life of all species.

Part Two: Departure (chapters 4–6) and Part Three: Return (chapters 7–10) present opposing paths of human cultural evolution. Part Two: Departure employs psychological, sociological and historical analyses to trace the outward, centrifugal movement of human societies from an original bond with the Earth to a growing disconnect from the natural world which has precipitated the current ecological crisis. In dissociating ourselves from Nature we have, through our cultural systems, denied our own identity as members of the Earth community and constructed a mechanized, artificial world where the Earth is exploited for human use. Chapter 4 begins a search for those psychological and sociological factors that have precipitated this disconnect. What caused human beings to replace the original role of steward with the role of predator? Clues are discerned from various sources including archetypal myths of a fall from grace and psychological analyses of the formation of a narcissistic society bent on achieving the narrow aims of ego. A review of Western cultural history from the classical Greek era through the Scientific Revolution reveals that *species arrogance* (Greek *hubris*) was facilitated by a dramatic cultural shift from a God-centered to a man-centered worldview. With the birth of science the cultural symbol for Nature, *anima mundi*—the archetypal *world soul* and embodiment of female energy—was exchanged for a new symbol: the machine. The scientific manipulation of Nature's 'machinery' became the leading tenet of Western 'progress.'

Chapter 5 discusses how the Industrial Revolution and the birth of capitalism solidified this mechanistic paradigm and accelerated the adversarial attitude towards Nature. Capitalism gradually reveals it predatory aspect, described by the Native American word *wétiko* which means *cannibal*. The question is asked, is a society that values a disproportionate distribution of wealth and reckless consumption of Earth's resources an advanced society? What criteria define an advanced society? Alexis de Tocqueville warned that a capitalist democracy which elevates self-interest and ignores service to the community invites a descent into tyranny. As the capitalist ethos progressively morphs into a mechanized and dehumanized culture it is dominated by a narrowing of mental faculties called *technological mind*—a modality of thinking that recalls Herbert Marcuse's *one-dimensional man*. Technological mind arose out of the Cartesian emphasis on rationality. But is it rational to poison one's habitat? The chapter concludes with Naomi Klein's analysis of how *disaster capitalism* is defacing the Earth and accelerating climate change. Chapter 6 applies Klein's thesis to the two unsustainable engines of the modern capitalist system: the fossil fuel industry and agribusiness which, like a double-barreled shotgun, have lethal power to destroy Earth's ecosystems.

Part Three: Return envisions a centripetal journey back to our roots in Earth's loamy soil. In order to achieve this about-face our primary task must be to change the mindset that cripples our ability to see ourselves as anything larger than what Alan Watts calls "isolated egos inside bags of skin."[1] Each of us must realize in experience that interdependence supersedes individual independence because the former reflects the unitive consciousness that generates all life. Chapter 7 begins the return journey with an investigation of the web of life. The ruling symbol of the ecocentric paradigm is a web. This web is examined as it expands from the subatomic level into three dimensions—biological (ecosystems), social and spiritual. Because indigenous peoples, as implicit ecologists, regard the web of life as the animate and sacred body of Mother Earth their philosophy of cooperation with Nature is instructive to modern industrialized societies. Chapter 8 links the idea of a web of life to the perception of Earth as sacred space. A discussion of the Greek concept of *chora* (sacred space) is expanded to describe the belief by indigenous peoples that the whole Earth is chora. Our indigenous heritage is explored with particular focus on the worldviews of the Mbuti pygmies, the Navajo, and the Aranda. The question is posed: does the memory of an intimate relationship with all life forms lie dormant in the modern psyche and if so is it possible to retrieve it? The translation of the shamanic art of soul-retrieval into its modern equivalent, ecopsychology, suggests that it is. When patients are reintroduced to the natural world through sensory awareness they shed their sense of alienation and fear and begin to heal—as Richard Louv discovered in children suffering from what he calls Nature Deficit Disorder or NDD. *Ecology of mind*—a mental framework associated with tribal societies—is curative as well because it remembers interdependence and is careful in the use of the natural world.

The final stretch of *Homesick* begins with Chapter 9 which presents the fork in the road of cultural evolution that humanity now faces. Do we continue to produce the destructive *Technozoic Era*, as ecotheologian Thomas Berry calls it, or do we create an *Ecozoic Era*? Thomas Kuhn's theory of paradigm shifts outlines the process of cultural transformation. A brief sketch of three mentors for the Ecozoic Era—Henry David Thoreau, John Muir, and Aldo Leopold—provide the inspiration for change based in respect for the natural world. Chapter 10 takes us home in mind and heart by outlining the ways in which the main cultural values of the Ecozoic Era—biophilia (love of life) and sustainability—will be stimulated through the practice of awareness and the adoption of a lifestyle of *voluntary simplicity* (Duane Elgin's term). A reformed educational system will teach and disseminate these values which can then be implemented in society—as exemplified, for example, in a sustainable economy. As the positive aspects of male and female energy are integrated and balanced it will be possible to construct what Riane Eisler calls a *partnership model* of society, tailored to the modern age.

We have a choice, a window of opportunity—slim though it may be—to change course as a species. *Homesick* examines that choice using a holistic, interdisciplinary approach. It is hoped that you who read this book will be inspired to adopt a more sustainable lifestyle and work in your lives towards restoring health to our common home, for the sake of our children grand-children, and all life forms. For those of you who are already engaged in sustainable practices may *Homesick* deepen your understanding of the crisis and strengthen your commitment to effective action. As Native Americans remind us, each person is responsible by his or her actions for the health and wellbeing of seven generations into the future.

Part I

CHILDREN OF THE EARTH

Chapter One

Home Sweet Home

To thine own self be true. . . .

—Polonius, *Hamlet* I:3

Over the weekend of April 26–27, 2014 a rash of tornadoes hit the central and southern United States, burrowing out a 200 mile long, half-mile wide, path through Oklahoma, Arkansas and Iowa. Out of at least thirty-one counted, seven tornadoes were deadly, killing seventeen people. On April 28 three more tornadoes struck Mississippi and Kansas. Arkansas suburbs of Mayflower, Paron and Vilonia, a town of 3,800 people, lay at the center of the violence. Back in 2011, when a record 753 tornadoes hit the United States, a tornado passed through Vilonia. On April 27, 2014, the town was revisited—this time by an EF 3 tornado (136+ mph on the Fujita or EF scale of 0–5). The twister flattened houses, cars and trucks, and even a new school not yet occupied by students. Because the warnings were timely and people in this region—known as Tornado Alley—were accustomed to seeking protection in underground storm shelters, many townspeople were able to escape harm. In shelters built into hillsides close to the family home or in larger community shelters people hunkered down, holding hands and praying. Most of the dead were killed inside their homes as the tornado crushed roofs and walls that lay in its path. A man and woman, emerging from a shelter after the storm had passed, saw their home destroyed. Picking through debris for family photos they told one reporter that they had been ready to get married and live in that home, but things were different now; they would have to wait. In Paron, Arkansas, a seventeen-year-old girl crouched with her family under the stairs of their 2-story home as a twister tore away walls and ceilings. The girl survived but she watched as the twister killed her father and two sisters.

This one series of devastating tornadoes joins a lengthening list of extreme weather events that include intense hurricanes, droughts and wildfires. Global warming is increasingly invoked as a major contributing factor. Scientists see a relationship, for example, between the increase in recent years in severe thunderstorms—the environment in which tornadoes usually form—and intense tornado activity. Severe thunderstorms are induced by a rise in atmospheric temperatures. As the planet warms unnaturally from a global economy based upon the extraction and burning of fossil fuels extreme weather events intensify. The devastation wrought in 2017 in Texas, Florida and Puerto Rico by three powerful hurricanes (Harvey, Irma and Maria) reveal a deadly confluence of three climate-related factors—namely, a warming trend in the Atlantic Ocean, higher sea levels along the gulf coast and an atmosphere thick with water vapor. Meanwhile, on the west coast of the United States in drought-prone California wildfires burned out of control, scorching the vineyards of Sonoma Valley and destroying homes in major urban areas like Los Angeles. With nearly 9,000 fires burning across the state, ravaging more than one million acres and killing forty-six people, 2017 became the worst year on record for wildfires.[1]

These events not only disrupt the sensitive network of Earth's ecosystems; they also impact human society. Yet, even in the face of displacement and suffering, people are resilient. The townspeople of Vilonia, for example, have not moved away. In spite of the destruction of their houses this is where family and friends live; this is home and they will build again. Vilonia's stoic response comes from a deep identification of human beings with their homes. Homes hold and shelter our identity as individuals and as families. As such, home is precious. Absent from its familiar comfort we grow homesick. Whatever composition the particular family unit takes, home is the extension of the members' bond.[2] In my grandmother's day, in the 1900s, the family homestead in Dardanelle, Arkansas housed many children, parents and grandparents, maiden aunts and bachelor uncles—over several generations. The homestead was virtually self-sufficient due to the work ethic of the extended family (everybody had chores), plus the sustenance provided by animal members of the household—hogs, chickens, cows, and bees—a vegetable garden and an orchard.

Beyond the homestead was one's hometown. Made famous in Thornton Wilder's play *Our Town*, the hometown widened the circle of home and the sense of security home breeds because almost everyone stayed in that town their whole lives; they were born there, married, had children and died there. Everyone knew everyone (and everyone knew what everyone else was doing). As social patterns changed, eclipsing the extended family and introducing mobility, especially through technology such as the automobile, the concept and reality of homestead and hometown faded.

The Homeless Mind, published in 1973, is a sociological study of the attrition of social patterns that once gave people the feeling of security and rootedness embodied in the idea of home. The authors correlate modernization, its technological advances, social mobility, and a decline of identification with public institutions—especially traditional religion which had provided an anchor of meaning and certainty in the midst of rapid change—with feelings of alienation and homelessness. They write:

> Not only are an increasing number of individuals in a modern society uprooted from their original social milieu, but, in addition, no succeeding milieu succeeds in becoming truly 'home' either. . . . A world in which everything is in constant motion is a world in which certainties of any kind are hard to come by. . . .[3] Modernity has indeed been liberating. It has liberated human beings from the narrow controls of family, clan, tribe or small community. . . . It has provided enormous power, both in the control of nature and in the management of human affairs. However, these liberations have had a high price . . . homelessness.[4]

The authors go on to describe efforts by individuals and groups to resist the dehumanizing influences of modern life through movements that introduce communal substitutes for the old primary institutions. Quilting and bowling clubs, Elks lodges and soup kitchens are succeeded today by new voluntary associations like yoga and martial arts groups, organic farming cooperatives, and various intentional communities. The search for family and community continues, as evidenced by Facebook and other social media, which use the impersonal globalizing force of the Internet in search of a new intimacy.

Beyond one's hometown is a wider circle yet: the state. The strength of this identity—I'm a New Yorker, you are a Virginian—has weakened; but it was a primary factor in the Civil War, compounded by the passionate debate over slavery, which severely tested the ability of residents of Northern and Southern states to move beyond the regional perception of home and see themselves as part of the next circle of potential fellowship: the nation. Could the concept of *union* transcend *yankee* and *rebel* and, as such, create an American nation? Lincoln pleaded for this resolution of conflict when he said in his First Inaugural Address on March 4, 1861:

> We are not enemies, but friends. We must not be enemies. Though passion may have strained it must not break our bonds of affection. The mystic chords of memory, stretching from every battlefield and patriot grave to every living heart and hearthstone all over this broad land, will yet swell the chorus of the Union, when again touched, as surely they will be, by the better angels of our nature.[5]

As the ravages of the Civil War show, an allegiance to home should not be romanticized. There have always been and still are street gangs, family feuds, opposing sides of 'us and them,' from the subjugation of Native Americans, whose home—the American wilderness—was invaded and claimed by European colonists, to the enslavement of blacks working for white masters on southern plantations. Even when the idea of nation is illuminated at times of crisis—as, for example, the attack on Pearl Harbor which galvanized American participation in World War II or the toppling of the World Trade Center in 2001—this larger identification easily deteriorates into false patriotism or jingoism. Other nations become 'the enemy' and where they live—their homes—uncivilized. The 'enemy' or 'stranger' becomes an object to be vanquished. We tend not to see the third reconciling force between opposing sides. Whether the perception of 'other' is based on race, ethnicity, gender, class, religion, party politics or national affiliation there is that which is larger than and unifies the 'us and them' construct. That third force is humanity.

Currently humanity faces a crisis in which an even deeper and more consequential circle of connection is being lost. Our planetary home, which houses and connects all living beings under one roof (the blue sky) and one floor (the earth) is suffering from an ecological crisis greater than wars between nations. The word *ecology* means the science (*logos*) of the house (*eco* derived from the Greek *oikos*) where we live. This house we call Earth is our larger sentient Body. The confrontation between humanity and the Earth body stems from ignoring the unity that binds all organisms to their earthly home. This ignorance could be fatal to all species.

For many of us the warm feelings that arise with the thought of *home* and *family* do not extend into the biosphere but remain localized, retracted into immediate, tactile and familiar relationships. The words *family* and *familiar* are formed from the same root meaning *of the household*. Whereas we rarely allow our own personal homes or even communal structures such as hospitals and schools to fall into disrepair, the pollution of our Earth house is permitted day in and day out. In fact, the pollution of air, water and soil is increasing to such an extent that scientists question whether the threshold nears, beyond which Earth's self-regulating mechanisms to restore balance are insufficient. As a species we are gifted with a cortical brain capacity and neural complexity that allow us to surpass the limitations of instinct. We can choose to defy the design of planetary law. However, by such maladaptive behavior we threaten our own existence. Is it not ironic that we who boast a superior rationality commit irrational acts by polluting the very elements that our bodies and minds require to live?

Biologist James Lovelock tackles the problem of human abuse of our earthly home by introducing us to the Gaia Hypothesis. He uses a metaphor based in Greek mythology that warns humanity of its dereliction of duties. In the Greek myth Earth is Gaia, the Mother of Creation. Gaia loves all her children equally; she provides unceasingly for the whole Earth family. If, however, one life form disobeys Her basic laws that species must be sacrificed for the preservation of other living forms. Lovelock's theory describes Earth as a living organism with self-regulating mechanisms of homeostasis that are shared by all living organisms; in other words, all species by their actions help to maintain the integrity of Earth's ecosystems. The implication that this synergistic relationship between organisms and their environment is intentional, beyond mechanistic reactivity, has been criticized. Critics are skeptical of the teleological implication of the theory. They point to scientific evidence that this 'feedback coupling' between organisms and the environment does not necessarily enhance homeostasis. Nor does natural selection necessarily improve the environment by giving adaptive reproductive advantage to an organism that carries a certain trait; the environment could suffer degradation. In other words, there is not necessarily a direct link between the environment and organic life evolving through natural selection. Nevertheless, the Gaia Hypothesis remains an intriguing theory and, for our purposes, an important scientific assertion of a synergistic Earth community.[6]

How is it that we as a species do not appear to see or feel the gravity of the situation we are creating? The reason is clear: *we do not perceive Earth as home.* Although globalization is the new local, the ardor we feel for those closest to us has not yet expanded to the myriad family members of our earthly home; thus we do not administer the medicines that will cure the sickness of global warming. Earth is resource, property, an object for human use. When use degrades into abuse it is not perceived as such. Yet these acts of abuse are "crimes against Nature;" and crimes are punishable under the law.[7] If we are to survive the word *home* must acquire a grander, inclusive meaning.

John Muir, nineteenth century wilderness advocate and founder of the Sierra Club, wrote in his journal: "there is a love of wild nature in everybody, an ancient mother-love ever showing itself. . . ."[8] Nursed by our hi-tech industrialized cultures we have forgotten this natural impulse that draws us to the land. How did this collective loss of memory come about? How will memory be restored? What needs to be re-membered—literally, what understandings will make us whole again by their fusion? And, most importantly, how do we as individual agents of change galvanize our societies to implement this remembering in our cultural institutions so that we act in keeping with the heart's ancient mother-love?

Fortunately the idea of a primordial cosmic harmony within which humans have a constructive role is still alive in the worldview of indigenous people. It is imperative that we residents of the modern version of home—of technological wizardry and disconnect from Nature—reacquaint ourselves with an ancient wisdom about the real relationships that adhere among living forms. Indigenous peoples remember their kinship with an animate universe. They intuit a spiritual force that adheres between all sentient members of the Earth community.

This ancient wisdom abides at the mystic heart of all religions. For example, in Sufism—the Islamic mystical tradition—*ghaflah* or *forgetting* describes the condition by which humans forget their home in Allah and their connection to other forms of life. The remedy, *dhikr*, means *remembering*, through inner contemplation, this elemental connectedness. Thirteenth century Persian Sufi mystic and poet, Jalaluddin Rumi, voices the predicament of humans who have forgotten who they are and where they came from. He writes:

> A man goes to sleep in the town where he has always lived,
> and he dreams he's living in another town.
> In the dream he doesn't remember
> the town he's sleeping in his bed in.
> He believes the reality of the dream town.
>
> The world is that kind of sleep.
>
> The dust of many crumbled cities
> settles over us like a forgetful doze,
> but we are older than those cities. We began
> as a mineral. We emerged into plant life
> and into the animal state, and then into being human,
> and always we have forgotten our former states,
> except in early spring when we slightly recall
> being green again. . . .
>
> Human kind is being led along an evolving course,
> through this migration of intelligences,
> and though we seem to be sleeping,
> there is an inner wakefulness
> that directs the dream,
>
>   and that will eventually startle us back
> to the truth of who we are.[9]

Only a tectonic shift in thinking, generated by 'an inner wakefulness,' will 'startle us back' and reverse the current outcome of our actions. Only a new cultural ethos that recognizes the pretense of a private existence and embraces unity in diversity can heal the deep, self-inflicted wounds that maim our collective psyche and harm the living species whose homes we invade, whose lives we see as dispensable. This is the mental-emotional shift that will recast the current paradigm of denial and greed.

Because the circles of *home*—from individual to social to national to planetary—weave together as a web, the unnatural abrogation of our household duties as caretakers of this earthly realm affects the harmony of the smaller circles of identification. These smaller circles of family and community become infected with violence, invariably terminating with that inner violence—expressed as neuroses, phobias and other afflictions such as depression—that oppresses the individual psyche which increasingly experiences itself as alienated and fearful.

As we lose conscious awareness of our perennial source of sustenance—the Earth—we do violence to ourselves. This interior chaos in turn spawns violent acts in society—from random shootings to wars, genocide and terrorism. The formation of psychopath, sociopath and totalitarian autocrat are nurtured. When we split from our Larger Body, the Earth, we deny our true selves and shrink into a self-image conflated with personal ego. This is the big lie, says Trappist monk and social critic Thomas Merton; and this lie

brings violence and disorder into our nature itself. It divides us against ourselves, alienates us from ourselves, makes us enemies of ourselves, and of the truth that is in us. From division hatred and violence arise. We hate others because we cannot stand the disorder, the intolerable division in ourselves. We are violent to others because we are already divided by the inner violence, our infidelity to our own truth. Hatred projects this division outside ourselves into society.[10]

Healing these inner and outer divisions requires that we reawaken and remember our original bond with other human beings and with all life forms. The etymological root of the words *whole* and *heal* is the same: the Anglo-Saxon *hal*. Healing makes us whole again. The individual and collective act of remembering starts a process of reintegration that refashions mind to think anew and stimulates heart to feel again an affinity with all life. We are then primed to understand Confucius's definition of self as a network of relationships with the power, through purification of the heart, to change the world. In the 6th c. BCE Confucius wrote words for the modern era; he said: "'If there is righteousness in the heart, there will be beauty in the character; / If there is beauty in the character, there will be harmony in the home. / If there is harmony in the home, there will be order in the nation. / If there is order in the nation, there will be peace in the world.'"[11]

Fifteen centuries later the Neo-Confucian philosopher Chang Tsai (1021–77 CE) extended filial piety and responsibility to identification with a living cosmos. Tsai writes:

"'Heaven is my father and earth is my mother, and even such a small creature as I finds an intimate place in their midst. Therefore that which extends throughout the universe I regard as my body and that which directs the universe I consider as my nature. All people are my brothers and sisters, and all things are my companions.'"[12]

The ethical behavior that harmonizes all circles of relationship is based in the Golden Rule: 'do unto others as you would have them do unto you.' When *hsin* (the individual mind-heart) is purified and returned to its natural state of *jen* or benevolence then the wider circles of identity are clearly known and felt by the individual.[13] This vision of an ecospiritual network of relations is portrayed by a simple diagram.

Since the Industrial Revolution *progress* has been the Western industrial mantra—progress at the expense of Earth's equilibrium. In the modern era the sanctity of unbridled self-interest has so corroded Western culture that the only remaining value may be life itself reduced to individual survival and the

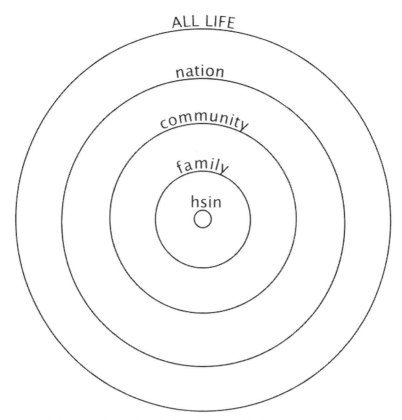

Figure 1.1.   Neo-Confucian circles of relationship by Dominique Medici.
Used with the permission of Dominique Medici.

satisfaction of base appetites. This debilitating condition continues to impoverish humanity's self-image and inhibits communion with an animate planet.

In order for human culture to evolve, there must be a collective realization that a worldview based on material, sensory gratification and overweening ambition is clearly maladaptive. Such a worldview legitimizes actions that violate the elemental ecological laws of interdependence and reciprocity by which all species live. As the American continent was being settled, Chief Seattle of the Suquamish tribe watched with sad resignation the avarice of the white man. He warned his white brothers, saying, "All things are connected. Whatever befalls the earth befalls the children of the earth."[14]

The exploitation of natural resources continues. But the law is tenacious and in time catches up with the miscreant. If the human species is to evolve beyond this misadventure a successful adaptation will not be through technology but through a new way of thinking which technology can then implement. Technology is a material outcome of human ingenuity—a tool that reflects the conceptual universe that guides the inventive mind. For example, the invention of cars, trains and airplanes was a technological feat that greatly accelerated human mobility and the speed with which one could travel from one place to another. The positive effects of advances in transportation, however, have been offset by the build-up of emissions of carbon dioxide in the atmosphere due to the use of fossil fuels as energy source. That this negative effect was not foreseen or corrected is due to an enculturated belief in modern society that we humans have the right to use and develop natural resources without limit because Nature, as an object, was made for us.

The new conceptual universe will favor a biocentric, or ecocentric, mindset that, like Gaia, values the lives of all organisms. When humans awaken from the dream of conqueror and become servants of the land they will act out the Golden Rule. Life will surely change for every species. Reformed and transformed in mind and spirit, human beings will be reconciled with the natural world and rediscover their role in the original harmony.

Albert Einstein wrote of this next evolutionary step. He said:

A human being is part of the whole, called by us universe, a part limited in time and space. We experience ourselves, our thoughts and feelings, as something separated from the rest. A kind of optical delusion of consciousness. This delusion is a prison for us, restricting us to our personal desires and to affection for a few persons nearest to us. Our task must be to free ourselves from this prison by widening our circle of compassion to embrace all living creatures and the whole of nature in its beauty.[15]

In *The Need For Roots* philosopher Simone Weil argues that being rooted in a place, which includes the natural environment and social groupings, is "perhaps the most important and least recognized need of the human soul."[16] Even though we humans are displaced from the Earth, our ancestral home, by our own volition, it is also true that a homing instinct is shared by all creatures, including humans. There are stories of dogs and cats, for example, who get lost and miraculously find their way home. Domestic homing pigeons, bred from the wild rock pigeon, provided an essential messenger service during World War II, carrying messages from the front to headquarters and back again at an average speed of 50 miles per hour. Recently Dr. Manuel Leal, a biologist at the University of Missouri, discovered that ordinary lizards—anoles—can find their way home. [17] Leal was studying how three different species of anoles shared a tree trunk home in the Puerto Rican rainforest by occupying three different niches—the bottom, middle and upper parts of the trunk. By analogy, imagine a tall apartment building divided into three sections. Leal wondered whether the anoles midway up the trunk would take advantage of a larger territory if it were made available to them. So he removed the anoles who occupied the lower section of the trunk, to allow the 'upstairs' neighbors to move down, and deposited these lower section anoles about twenty-five yards into the dense rainforest. They came back to their tree trunk home. So he tried to trick these canny anoles by ruses such as gluing magnets to their heads to prevent them from using the Earth's magnetic field to sense the right homeward direction. Still these homing lizards returned. After all strategies to obstruct their homeward journey had failed Dr. Leal had to admit that science was stymied by a mystery born of instinct and persistence.

Are we human beings as persistent to return home as these tiny creatures? Persistence is necessary; but the first step in the journey must be the realization that we have indeed left home.

Chapter Two

Setting the Stage

Something is rotten in the state of Denmark

—Marcellus, *Hamlet* I:4

Human beings have long regarded themselves as part of a greater whole. That whole begins with the natural world of plants, animals, sun, moon and rain—indeed, Earth as a living organism—and extends to the mystery of the universe. From the emergence of *Homo habilis* or Stone Age Man at the start of the last Quaternary or Pleistocene glaciation some 2.4 million years ago, Earth has been perceived as our planetary home.

Since her birth, some 4.5 billion years ago, Earth has sustained life in all its myriad forms. For the human species that sustenance has extended beyond provisions for the body to include mental-emotional stability and spiritual consolation. Indeed, for traditional cultures, such as Native Americans, Earth has always been more than just a source of food and shelter. The Lakota Sioux, for example, define Earth as mother, *Maka Ina*, and all creatures as kin. All life forms are addressed alike with the words: *mitákuye oyás'iŋ* which means *all are related*. A tribal member is morally obliged to align his or her actions with this statement of unity. All beings are animate; all beings have a spiritual essence or *ton* which connects them to each other. This philosophy of an animate, ensouled world—called *animism* by anthropologists—is a cultural given for many indigenous peoples.

The relationship with the natural world may be experienced as love, fear, affection, anger, gratitude—in fact by all the emotions which may arise between human beings; but a relationship does exist, and the health of that relationship is based on the perception and conception of a primordial bond, a living wholeness in which the whole is intuited as greater than the sum of its parts. The 'new physics' of quantum mechanics has simply corroborated what our earliest ancestors, as implicit ecologists, have always intuited: there is a network of relationships, a web that characterizes and joins all forms at physical, psychical and spiritual levels. The living thread of this web is energy—known to a tribal member in Polynesia as *mana*, to a Taoist as *ch'i*, to a Hindu as *prana*, to the modern scientist as *the quantum field*. Physicist David Bohm joins physics to spirituality when he states that the universe is "'a sacred web of relations.'"[1]

But that intuition of unity in a world of diverse material forms, that centuries-old feeling of connection to the natural environment, is being lost. Thus we commit daily acts of abuse against the interconnected web of life. The journey homeward will only begin with a clear acknowledgement that we have, as a species, mentally disconnected ourselves from our home base—the Earth. In this chapter we anticipate the homeward journey by familiarizing ourselves with Nature's ecological design to which human societies have for centuries adapted. Then, by studying the mounting evidence of a clash between how the Earth naturally retains balance and how human beings are obstructing that balance, we discover the culprit of this tension: a behavioral pattern, deeply en-grained in modern society, by which humanity plays out its assumed privilege to dominate the natural world. In order for us as a species to take on a more propitious role in the evolution of the planet, this behavioral pattern must be dissolved. The solution is at hand. As we cultivate awareness of the environ-mental crisis, which we have helped to create, that same awareness becomes the agency whereby the crisis is defused and the Earth healed.

HOW NATURE WORKS

It is important to realize that, for better or worse, our relationship to the natural world cannot in fact be severed because the universe is constructed as a network which is governed by two ecological laws: interdependence and reciprocity. These two laws are in constant play. Take for example the rela-tionship between oak tree, soil, and squirrel. The oak tree clings to the fertile forest soil, storing water through its roots so that the soil doesn't dry out for the many microorganisms, nematodes, earthworms and fungi who live in it. The oak tree is giving oxygen through its leaves to birds and other animals who repay the oak tree with the carbon dioxide it needs to live. The squirrels in particular are interested in the oak tree's progeny—acorns—which they eat and bury in holes in the ground which serve not only as a winter pantry but also as a propagation site for the oak tree since, as often as not, squirrels forget where their loot is buried.

The forest environment described above is one of many ecological *niches* which are called home by groups of plant, animal and mineral species. Lakes and meadows, oceans and mountains, deserts and swamps—these are examples of other habitats that attract and support a select group of flora and fauna adapted to those environments. These homes and their residents, which are called *a community of interest*, are *ecosystems*. Biological ecosystems operate through the laws of interdependence and reciprocity. But these laws regulate cultural systems as well. The health of a culture is determined by how well it adheres to the two laws in social, economic and political spheres of action. In fact, the ecological and cultural systems interlock and impact each other, forming a greater whole: *an ecocultural system*. Over time the mutual impact between the natural environment (*eco*) and human beings (*anthropos*) through their cultures greatly determines the longevity of that ecocultural system.

The first step in a people's interaction with the natural habitat is their observation of and adaptation to the biotic environment. Basic needs must be satisfied: food and a way to procure it, water, and shelter. The simplest and oldest means of livelihood is hunting and gathering—a subsistence economy identified with indigenous peoples. But the diversity of what is hunted and gathered, plus possible supplementary activities such as gardening (horticulture), fishing, or raising livestock (i.e., nomadic pastoralism) will depend upon a network of geographical features such as terrain, climate, soil fertility and arability, rainfall, and access to water. The main adaptive tool is the formation of a cultural system that fits the environment and may even modify it in ingenious ways through technology. For example, in the treeless terrain of the Arctic the indigenous Inuit people had to invent a seaworthy vessel not made of wood to traverse the frigid waters in search of their main dietary staple of fish and sea mammals. They came up with the kayak, a lightweight boat made from sealskins.

Some cultural adaptations to the physical environment seem paradoxical. For example, the Winnebago tribes of Minnesota never mined vast surface ore deposits, not for lack of technology but for lack of interest. From the modern Western perspective, focused on material gain, this neglect seems foolish. For indigenous peoples land is not owned but on loan from the Creator; the inner parts of the Earth are the Mother's organs and thus inviolate.

There are three key questions to be asked in studying a people's relationship to their environment. First, how is the society using or misusing resources at its disposal? Secondly, what worldview motivates and defines the use of these resources? And finally, what environmental (and other) stresses does the society face and how does it respond to these stresses? The main stress faced by the Inuit people, for example, is the harsh Arctic climate.

Through subsistence fishing and hunting, supplemented by a diet of grasses, tubers, seasonal berries and seaweed they have been able to survive for centuries. The Inuit traditionally lived in icehouses and wore warm animal skins sewn together with animal bones as needles and sinew as thread. Nurtured by an animist worldview the Inuit invoked the powers of Nature, particularly the Sea Goddess, to provide them with game.

In modern times two intertwined stresses challenge the Inuit: climate change and the drive by oil companies to drill in the Arctic. As the waters of the Arctic warm and ice melts due to climate change, rising seas endanger Inuit coastal villages which are sinking into the water due to erosion. In remote Kozebue, Alaska, a coastal city in the Northwest Arctic Borough, the tribal council of the Inupiaq—an Inuit group whose native villages border Kozebue Sound—is concerned that the climate crisis is disrupting their way of life. Even as wind turbines are being installed on the tundra to help cut fuel costs for all Kozebue residents it is clear that oil and gas development may provide economic relief for everyone in the transition to a renewable energy future. In fact, a 2013 management plan enacted by the Obama administration opens up the potential leasing of 11.8 acres of the National Petroleum Reserve which consists of almost 23 million acres of tundra, wetlands and coastal lagoons. Both the reserve and the nearby Arctic National Wildlife Refuge provide habitat for a rich variety of wildlife including migratory and aquatic birds, caribou, whales, seals and polar bears. In order to protect wildlife the plan outlaws drilling in certain special areas—a decision lauded by environmental groups and native villages. However, this hard-won compromise is now in jeopardy as the Trump administration is not only ordering a full-scale implementation of the 2013 plan but also seeks to develop the restricted areas. A wholesale development of drilling sites in the region could have dire effects on the ecocultural system—not the least of which is a possible major oil spill. Still reverberating in our collective memory are the Exxon-Valdes disaster in March 1989 when an oil tanker rammed into the Prince William Sound Bligh reef releasing 260,000 barrels of crude oil into the frigid water and the explosion of the BP Deepwater Horizon platform in 2010 which killed eleven men and released 3.19 million barrels of oil into the Gulf of Mexico, killing wildlife and damaging coral reefs.[2]

The relationship between humans and the land can—as historical records reveal—move from being functional and healthy, to being dysfunctional and unhealthy due to a shift in cultural worldview. In other words, while conservation of resources is the natural and intelligent response to survival, the relationship between ourselves and the land can be severed *in the mind*. Cultural systems are then designed to reflect and teach that severance. When we *think* we are free to do what we want with the environment and perceive its inhabitants—human and non-human—as objects, then a master-slave relationship is created.

Each thought is a vibration, a pulse of energy. When feelings enter the mix a thought becomes an attitude and the action that follows announces that attitude. When a person litters the roadside by casually throwing the residue of a fast-food lunch out the car window that person's attitude about the Earth, what he or she thinks and feels about the Earth, is revealed. The thought 'the Earth is my garbage can' is accompanied by a feeling of indifference. This banal thought vibration is generating our escalating ecological crisis. It was political theorist Hannah Arendt who coined the phrase "the banality of evil."[3] After the trial of Holocaust perpetrator Adolf Eichmann in 1961 Arendt wrote *Eichmann in Jerusalem: A Report on the Banality of Evil* in which she posed the question as to whether such evil acts as Eichmann's were deliberate and therefore radical in nature or evidence of a tendency in human beings to act mindlessly in a conformist, habitual manner in obedience to higher authority figures or mass opinion. The robotic routinization of immoral actions, which she termed the banality of evil, persists when a conscious evaluation of their consequences is absent. Although an act of littering the Earth is not comparable to the torture of human beings does not the same attitude of indifference demonstrate a disregard, even a contempt, for life in any and all its forms?

WARNING SIGNS

Since 1950 a confluence of human activities has put excessive stress on the natural world causing reactive disturbances in Nature's equilibrium and upsetting the balance in the ecocultural system. Because of the ecological law of interdependence these individual stresses are interrelated, exacerbating the impact of each one upon the natural world. Moreover, these environmental stresses are rebounding back onto human health and wellbeing: this is the law of reciprocity. We reap what we sow. Increased levels of diabetes, obesity, mutant viruses, mental illness and suicide indicate this law at work.[4]

The source of a major stress on the environment is the counterpoint between a spike in human population and the extraction and burning of fossil fuels (coal, oil, and natural gas) to provide energy for home and commercial use, industrial and agricultural production, and transportation. As of February 2018 the global population reached 7.6 billion, a steep climb from the 1950 level of 2.5 billion; yet, according to the most recent global estimates by the World Bank of people living in extreme poverty (2013), 767 million people live on less than $1.90 per day.[5] This statistic reflects the inequities of a capitalist system skewed to favor the wealthy. About 10,000 years ago—400 generations ago—the global population was estimated at two million. This point in time marked the emergence of the Agricultural Revolution in the Middle East where the geography of fertile soil and pure rivers predated current desert conditions. Today the drain on the world's natural resources to feed an unsustainable 7.6 billion people, combined with inequitable food distribution and the looming probability of famine along with water shortages, create conditions that English cleric and philosopher Thomas Malthus warned of in his 1789 essay on the dangers of excessive population growth.

As a consequence of the Industrial Revolution, which we are still acting out, global emissions from the burning of fossil fuels increasingly fill the atmosphere with excessive amounts of carbon dioxide (CO_2) and other greenhouse gases such as nitrous oxide (N_2O), ozone (O_3), and methane (CH_4). Although China has surpassed the United States in carbon emissions as of 2014 the United States, with 4 percent of the world population, is responsible for close to a third of excess CO_2 emissions. [6] The United States has been utilizing fossil fuels far longer and in greater amounts than China which has four times as many citizens.

The build-up of greenhouse gases in the atmosphere to unhealthy levels produces two major effects: pollution, which causes an increase in respiratory and other physical ailments, and a rise in air temperature which overheats the planet. An example of the first effect is the coal-generated air pollution that is sickening the Chinese population. According to a World Bank study, only 1 percent of the 560 million urban residents in China breathe air considered safe by European Union standards. [7] As of January 2017 China canceled plans to construct more than 100 coal-fired power plants and, instead, is encouraging the development of renewable wind, solar and nuclear industries.

The inordinate warming of the air manifests as the Excessive Greenhouse Effect. When greenhouse gases keep to their natural ratio they provide, along with water vapor, a life-sustaining blanket of warmth known as the Greenhouse Effect. These beneficial gases prevent solar heat from escaping and maintain a balance between incoming sunlight that heats the planet and outgoing heat radiation that cools the planet. Earth keeps itself at a constant 0 degrees Fahrenheit—in the stratosphere, that is. The lower atmosphere and surface of the Earth are warmer than the stratosphere, which is why we can get away with wearing just a wool coat in winter or a t-shirt in summer. When Earth recognizes that it is radiating too little heat into space it will warm up in order to radiate more heat into space; or conversely it will radiate less heat to retain its correct surface temperature. By analogy, our bodily metabolism is designed to keep a core body temperature within set boundaries (97.7–99.5 degrees Fahrenheit). This internal thermoregulation is an aspect of homeostasis. On a hot summer day the body sweats; we wear light clothing. On a cold winter day the body shivers, alerting us to the need to put on the down coat, hat and mittens.

When greenhouse gases accumulate from the burning of fossil fuels and are trapped in the atmosphere the overall warming on land and in water increases, creating an Excessive Greenhouse Effect. Water vapor warms the atmosphere too much, the temperature of the air rises too much, seas heat up and slowly rise, and the Earth has trouble radiating all this heat into space to restore equilibrium. In like manner, if the human body is exposed to temperatures of 131 degrees or above, thermoregulation fails and hyperthermia occurs with lethal effect if exposure exceeds a few hours. One of the worst heat waves to hit India in April–May of 2015 killed more than 2,400 people; then in May of 2016 another heat wave hit, with a record high temperature of 123.8 in the state of Rajasthan. [8] The situation was compounded by a record drought. Global warming is suspected as a causal factor in both the severe heat and the drought.

Oceanographer Dr. Charles Keeling has studied the history of Earth's natural cycles of cooling and warming in which the level of carbon dioxide (CO_2)—the primary greenhouse gas—varied during geologic ages. For example, in the Carboniferous Period 400 million years ago plants were the dominant life form due to an abundance of CO_2 in the atmosphere. Keeling

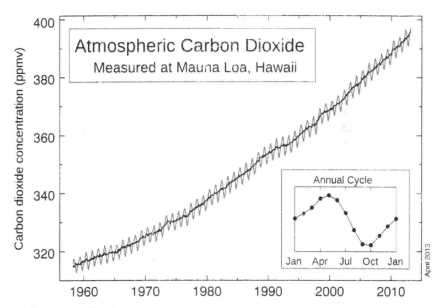

Table 2.1. Keeling Curve.
Courtesy of Mauna Loa Observatory staff, Narayanese, Sémhur and NOAA.

measured the rise of CO_2 in the atmosphere from 1800 to 2006. He saw a definite correlation between the rise of CO_2 and the rise in air temperature. The graph of his findings shows a steady increase of parts per million of carbon dioxide.[9] The over-all synchronous pattern points to an Excessive Greenhouse Effect and highlights the dangers that global warming poses to the health of all species.

The average global temperature continues to rise. Four agencies around the world, including the National Oceanic and Atmospheric Administration (NOAA) and the National Aeronautics and Space Administration (NASA), have kept records of global temperatures since 1880. According to a combined study by NOAA and NASA ten of the warmest years on record occurred since 1998 with five of those years occurring after 2010.[10] All agencies document a long-term warming trend linked to the burning of fossil fuels and deforestation. In fact, a remarkable event occurred on December 30, 2015: the temperature at the North Pole rose to 35 degrees Fahrenheit! Never before have above freezing temperatures been witnessed at the North Pole between December and April.

As human activities disturb the world's ecosystems the Earth responds, seeking equilibrium. The feast or famine of weather extremes—prolonged drought or heavy flooding, for example—replaces more moderate shifts. Tornadoes multiply; hurricanes become fierce. Scientists conclude that a major factor in both Hurricane Katrina in 2005 and Hurricane Sandy in 2013 was the rising temperature of the ocean. Just as the air warms and becomes polluted due to human interference so do the oceans warm, rise, and become acidic due to the water's absorption of excessive carbon dioxide. People who live in coastal cities around the world are at risk. In Miami, for example, the sea line has risen five inches in five years forcing salt water to leak through storm drains into the streets. Oceans have risen about eight inches since 1880—a year often used to mark the acceleration of the Industrial Revolution. The rise in sea level kept pace with the increase in global temperatures of about 1.8 degrees Fahrenheit.[11] An alarming reminder of the lethal combination of rising seas and extreme weather events was the meltdown of Japan's coastal Fukushima Daichi nuclear plant in 2011 after a violent earthquake and tsunami damaged the structure. Nearly 19,000 people lost their lives. The question remains: to what extent was global warming a causal factor in the rising sea level and intense storm surge associated with the meltdown.

Because the Earth is a global ecosystem each piece of the puzzle, as it were, is contiguous to every other piece and influences its behavior. As air and water warm due to climate change so the melting of polar ice accelerates. In 2008 the Ward Hunt Ice shelf in Northern Canada fell into the Arctic Sea. Six years later a NASA report showed the inevitable loss of the Pine Island Glacier ice shelf in West Antarctic. NASA's GRACE satellites reveal glacial ice loss in Greenland at a staggering 286 gigatonnes each year since 2002.[12] In temperate regions glaciers are also shrinking. For example, the shrinking of Sperry Glacier in Montana's Glacier National Park could severely affect Western states where at least 80 percent of the water supply comes from the mountains.

Of particular concern to climate scientists is the possibility that the global thermohaline circulation of ocean water, known as the Great Ocean Conveyor Belt, might halt if seawater continues to warm, freshen and expand. Just as blood circulates in our bodies, transporting food and oxygen to maintain each cell's metabolism, so the Earth's body is kept healthy by a circulatory system of waterways.

The Arctic's salt water—which is denser and heavier than fresh water—normally drives the Conveyor Belt by sinking down and flowing southward, thereby influencing regional climates. The thawing and retreating of sea ice in the Arctic could disturb or even halt the rhythm of this great system as ice melt adds fresh water to the saline ocean, making it more buoyant. This change in composition is called a *freshening* of the North Atlantic. As fresh

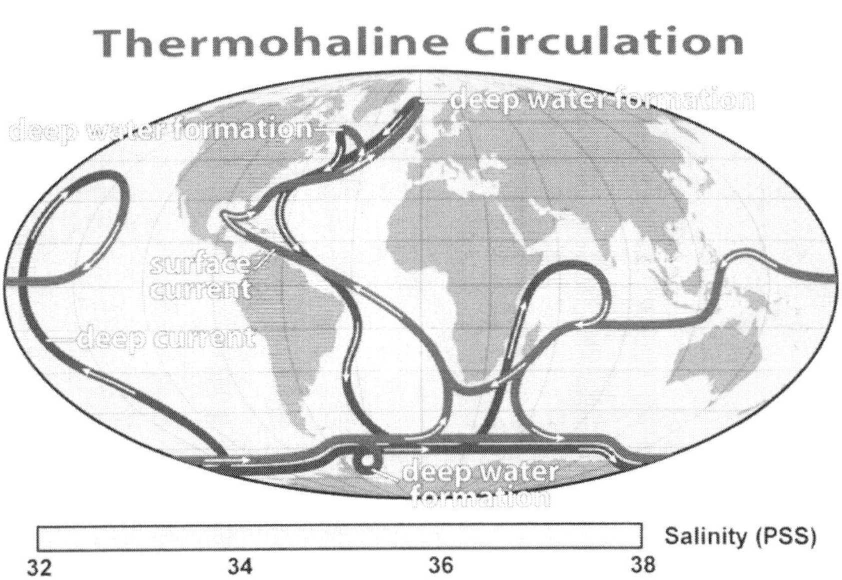

Thermohaline Circulation

Salinity (PSS)

32   34   36   38

Figure 2.1.   Great Ocean Conveyor Belt.
Courtesy of NASA.

water displaces saltwater at the Arctic hub of this circulatory system the surface of the water loses the necessary force to drive the Conveyor Belt. Normally the movement of the Conveyor Belt conveys heat into the atmosphere so that, for example, the Gulf Stream current from the Gulf of Mexico moves towards England, delivering warm, moist air. If the circulation were to slow or stop northern Europe would be snowed in.

Scientists propose that at the end of the last ice age melting ice sheets triggered a sudden halt in the Conveyor Belt, plummeting the world into a thirteen hundred year period of ice-age conditions called the Younger Dryas Cooling. If polar ice continues to melt we could be looking at another deep freeze. A June 2012 report in the journal *Nature Climate Change* explains how global warming could slow down the Conveyor Belt—and thus the Gulf Stream flow—leading to a precipitous sea level rise and the inundation of cities on America's eastern coastline. Hurricane Sandy's fury may be a grim precursor.[13]

According to Greek mythology Zeus wanted to find the home of his Grandmother Gaia, the Earth Goddess. He sent two eagles, one from the east and one from the west and where they crossed, at Delphi, a sanctuary was established to mark the site of Gaia's navel or omphalos. This sacred site was dedicated to Apollo and served as a center of prophecy through a resident priestess' visions. Two of the 147 maxims inscribed at the Delphic Oracle embody the Hellenic ideal of a measured life: *Know thyself* and *Nothing to excess*. When the meaning of *thyself* shrinks to ego and ego's desires replace the virtue of moderation then sickness occurs. Just as the physical body becomes sick from overeating and unhealthy food so the global body of the Earth, on whom all bodies depend, becomes sick when human societies exceed their natural limits by polluting air and water. The outcome is ecological imbalance. Witness, for example, the 5.25 trillion pieces of plastic debris which litter the world's oceans. Scientists predict that by 2050 the oceans will contain more plastic waste than fish.[14]

PALE BLUE DOT

In 1994 the eminent astronomer Carl Sagan was contemplating a photo of Earth taken by Voyager 1 outside the orbit of Neptune. Earth appears as a tiny speck which at the moment the photo was taken was lit by a sunbeam in the inky blackness of space. From this contemplation Sagan went on to write about the relationship between humanity and the Earth in his best-selling book *Pale Blue Dot*. It is clear that he marvels at the creative power of the human intellect and will displayed in the remarkable space adventures of Apollo 17 and the Voyager Project. But his enthusiasm is measured alongside a healthy apprehension that arises from his understanding of how human beings perceive their role in the universe. Early in the book he describes the "pale blue dot"—Earth—as the home of countless generations of human beings whose character ran the gamut from moral to immoral, whose cultures espoused various ideologies and built diverse economic, social and religious systems that fostered both happiness and suffering. All of human history has taken place on this small, insignificant globe surrounded by a vast cosmic ocean of space. Here humans have fabricated an image of themselves as masters, imagining their own greatness. Yet, says Sagan, this "folly of human conceits" is betrayed by the photo of Earth as a distant and lonely pulse of life.[15] We can, he says, gain insight from looking at the pale blue dot because it teaches us to reevaluate who we are and what our position really is in the universe. It can guide us in creating a new ethos of compassion towards one another and responsibility towards the only home we will ever know.

Sagan's prescient evaluation of both the brilliance and recklessness of human invention may have roots in his witnessing of prior events that exposed human fallibility and the dangers of an inquisitive mind without a moral compass to set limits. In the late 1970's, for example, scientists noted a widening hole in the ozone layer in Antarctica. They found the culprit: a group of halogenated hydrocarbons—chlorofluorocarbons or CFCs—which were causing ozone depletion in the stratosphere. These compounds, hailed as a brilliant alternative to ammonia and other refrigerants, were allowing harmful wavelengths of ultraviolet radiation into the Earth's atmosphere as well as causing illness through leakage. Finally, in August of 1987, the major industrialized nations took action, signing an international treaty called the Montreal Protocol banning CFC use. In response the refrigerant industry reinvented their products by exchanging heat-trapping hydrofluorocarbons (HFCs)—which are supergreenhouse gases—for the outlawed CFCs. Since 1995 the amount of HFCs in the atmosphere has risen by over 5 Mt (metric tons).[16] It was not until October 2016 at a meeting in Kigali, Rwanda that the global community of 170 nations reached a deal to phase out HFCs used in aerosols and air-conditioners. The legally binding Kigali accord has not been easy for nations with very hot climates to accept. In India, for example an air conditioner is not only a lifesaver when temperatures soar but also a sign of upward social mobility. The solution to such ecocultural considerations adds another layer to the negotiating process.

The success of the Montreal Protocol galvanized efforts to control emissions of greenhouse gases. The aim of the 1992 Earth Summit in Rio de

Janeiro was to press the international community to agree on setting limits for fossil fuel use. Indeed, by 2000 an Earth Charter was composed giving elegant language to the need to consider the health of the whole planet and every organism in it. However, practical steps to curb carbon emissions were not taken. Under the auspices of the United Nations Framework Convention on Climate Change (UNFCCC) successive meetings of the major industrialized nations, beginning with the Kyoto Protocol in 1997, tried but failed to yield agreements to wean global industries from fossil fuels and prevent the atmosphere from warming more than 3.6 degrees Fahrenheit (2 degrees Celsius) above the pre-industrial average which would send the planet into catastrophic mode.

Finally, an international negotiation by 195 nations in Paris in 2015 yielded a legally non-binding agreement to curb carbon emissions with a conference in Marrakesh, Morocco set for November 2016 to work out practical details of implementation. Nations participating in the Paris Agreement reconvened at a follow-up conference in Bonn, Germany in November 2017 where they recommitted themselves to fulfilling their pledges. In attendance were also representatives from a diverse group of American cities, states, and businesses. In defiance of the Trump administration's withdrawal from the Paris Agreement this coalition, called America's Pledge, is bringing together citizens from the public and private spheres to accomplish the Obama administration's pledge to reduce carbon emissions at least 26 percent below 2005 levels by 2025.[17]

The main obstacle to any concrete global transition to renewable clean energies continues to be the belief that economic hardship will result from a job market overhaul—a belief backed up by the corporations that benefit from the extraction and burning of fossil fuels. It is true that coal miners in West Virginia, for example, will lose their jobs, but a 'New Deal' program that retrains workers for the new economy could be set up, with some type of federal subsidy for wages lost in the interim. Data showing an increase in renewable energy initiatives during the Obama administration demonstrates that an economy can change to benefit everyone.[18] It has also been assumed that transitioning to renewable energy options would be costly. However, a research group called the Global Commission on the Economy and Climate released a report in September 2014 that countered this assumption, citing fewer health problems from a reduction in air pollution, reduced medical costs, and lower prices of renewable fuel as factors that would not only offset initial costs but possibly save money over the long run.[19]

James Hansen, climate scientist and former director of the NASA Goddard Institute for Space Studies, has issued persistent reminders about the seriousness of global warming since his appearance before a Congressional committee in 1988. In a 2013 speech, in which he accepted the Ridenhour Courage Prize, Hansen reiterated his earlier warnings regarding excessive amounts of carbon dioxide in the air. He advised immediate decarbonization through joint measures of a carbon tax on industry, cap and trade, and investment in renewable energies. The maximum acceptable limit, said Hansen, is 350 ppm (parts per million), a level that was passed some time ago. In fact, from 2006 to 2015 carbon emissions rose from 385 ppm to an alarming 400 ppm. Before the Industrial Revolution carbon dioxide levels were at 280 ppm. The planet has warmed 1.4 degrees Celsius since the late nineteenth century. According to an ominous report issued by the World Meteorological Organization in October 2017, the amount of CO_2 in the atmosphere climbed to 403.3 ppm in 2016, while a further spike to 408 ppm has been verified by NASA as of June 2018.[20] Although El Nino conditions, in combination with fossil fuel use and deforestation, are said to have contributed to this rise in CO_2 the increase, accompanied by a disturbing rise in methane, approaches a level characteristic of the planet's atmosphere 800,000 years ago!

The United Nations Intergovernmental Panel on Climate Change (IPCC) affirmed in 2013 the consensus among scientists that global warming is real, that humans are largely responsible through the burning of fossil fuels, that sea levels will rise dramatically by the end of the century accompanied by tidal flooding, and that aggressive action to reverse this ominous global trend is essential. A similar diagnosis of the baleful effects of human-induced climate change was reached in both the 2014 and 2017 National Climate Assessments issued by thirteen federal agencies that include NOAA and NASA.[21]

In order to keep warming temperatures below 3.6 degrees Fahrenheit the IPCC panel in 2013 recommended a global 'carbon budget.' No more than one trillion metric tons of carbon could be burned and released as CO_2—in a timeframe that began with the Industrial Revolution; we have already depleted about 52 percent of that budget.[22] In other words, the bulk of fossil fuel reserves must remain in the ground. This act of economic restraint would go against every cultural nerve ending. Motivated by a worldview based in conquest of Nature multinational companies are already at work researching new technologies to extract deeper layers of fossil fuels. If the acquisitive instinct wins over common sense then we could in short order commit ecocide which is suicide writ large. In a prescient 1938 essay French author Jean Giono writes: "'It would seem by some chemical kind of justice, nature when driven to self-contradiction and the anti-natural, makes its offshoots [we humans] work for their own destruction.'"[23] Lao Tzu, legendary founder of Taoism, had a similar premonition in the 6th c. B.C.E. He wrote, in his classic work, *Tao Te Ching*:

> The world is sacred.
> It can't be improved.
> If you tamper with it, you'll ruin it.
> If you treat it like an object,
> You'll lose it.[24]

REDISCOVERING THE BALANCE

Now that the scientific consensus of human-induced climate change is established we are faced with a human-induced recalcitrance to refashion the cultural perspective in which Nature is perceived as an object for human use. While human development of Nature's resources through technology is part of our participation in Nature, the perennial question remains: what should we do with what we are given? If, for example, companies practice sustainable forestry, removing only those trees deemed necessary by society to build homes or communal structures while replanting saplings where possible, this satisfies both human and environmental needs. But if a developer razes a forest for profit to construct more strip malls and other eyesores of suburban sprawl with no sense of measure in the use of Earth's bounty—in other words, if we take indiscriminately without giving back and without considering the consequences of our actions—is this not a transgression of the laws of Nature which subsume laws pertaining to the human species? As long as we think of ourselves as separate from and better than other life forms we will overreach and waste what is given; we will neglect to use the gifts of discrimination and reason which define our species. The battle royal is not between human civilization and Nature; the battle is internal, within our minds. Do we follow the impulse of hubris or the voice of reason that advocates a wise use of Nature's resources? Surely for the good of our planetary home Sagan's warning in 1994 about the folly of human conceits must be heeded.

A salutary example of rediscovering the balance between human use of the natural environment and ecological health is the work of architect, designer and author William McDonough who is an advocate of sustainable architecture. McDonough's firm, McDonough Partners, acts as consultant for companies, governmental agencies and other organizations who want to restructure their buildings to meet new environmental standards. Its website advocates a philosophy that "reframes design as a beneficial, regenerative force—one that seeks to create ecological footprints to delight in, not lament."[25] McDonough also created an information database of the world's woods that is dedicated to sustainable forestry. Builders are encouraged to substitute when possible one of the lesser-known woods on the list to preserve trees endangered by deforestation.

Sustainability is the route towards balance because its precepts and practices reacquaint us with natural law. Bill McKibben, eco-activist and co-founder of the environmental organization 350.org, has been crusading for a reduction in carbon emissions through sustainable practices since the late 1980's. His seminal book, *The End of Nature*, is an impassioned, dystopian account of the danger of losing contact with the natural world as a subject to whom we, as subjects, are related. McKibben explains that if sustainability is not embraced natural processes like respiration, growth and decay will not end but what will end is the idea and evidence of Nature as a wild, grand, complex, intricate ecosystem. Until modern times Nature stood apart, protected from extreme human intervention by our perception of its ultimate mystery and god-like power. McKibben argues that this relationship has been severed. He writes:

> An idea, a relationship, can go extinct, just like an animal or a plant. The idea in this case is 'nature', the separate and wild province, the world apart from man to which he adapted, under whose rules he was born and died. . . .[26] But now the basis of that faith is lost. The idea of nature will not survive the new global pollution. . . . We have changed the atmosphere, and thus we are changing the weather, we make every spot on earth man made and artificial. We have deprived nature of its independence, and this is fatal to its meaning. Nature's independence is its meaning; without it there is nothing but us.[27]

Nature cannot be replicated by man. It can only be replaced by something smaller and artificial, something created in man's image. McKibben defines the agent of that replacement as technological advances in biotechnology and macromanagement, with humanity as the new deity. When, for example, much of Nature's leafy progeny is dead from deforestation and disease neat rows of genetically engineered drought and heat resistant cookie-cutter trees will serve as a paltry substitute for the rich diversity of tree species that still fill the forests of the world. This bogus 'nature' will be reflective of the human ego.

BREAKING A PATTERN

Humanity is caught in and habituated to a vicious, unregulated cycle of actions and reactions, a behavioral pattern based in greed that sustains a dysfunctional ecocultural system. The cycle is robotic in its self-perpetuation: fossil fuels are extracted and burned to produce goods to satisfy consumer needs and desires in a growing global population; a growing consumer base then requires the extraction and burning of more fossil fuels to generate more production to satisfy more consumers while increasing corporate profits. . . .

Exploitation rather than conservation of natural resources is a violation of Nature's rights as a living organism. This thievery is inspired not by need but by desire, by wanting more—which leads to actions that are wanton. Breaking this pattern is like breaking an addictive habit. As former vice-president Al Gore bluntly remarked: "'our civilization is addicted to the consumption of the Earth itself.'"[28] When an ethos of conquest and profiteering rather than stewardship becomes the status quo and cultural inertia sets in it would appear that the corporate view of Nature as an exploitable object is irrevocable. Nevertheless, counter-cultural voices for a sustainable future continue to invoke the ancient worldview of an animate Nature as they advocate human compliance to ecological laws.

At Alcoholics Anonymous meetings the addict always prefaces his or her progress report to the group by admitting addiction as a fact of life. We in the industrialized world have made choices that show an addiction to all the creature comforts we enjoy—from our cars to the computers, washing machines, smart phones, televisions and other mechanical devices that power our homes and businesses. But the source that generates that continuous stream of energy is the power plant that uses coal, oil or natural gas. In order for the collective global body of addicts—the human species—to admit the serious risk of continuing to use fossil fuels to feed our lifestyle habits scientific facts regarding climate change must first be recognized and accepted. During a speech at the 1963 March on Washington Martin Luther King used the words *the fierce urgency of now* to awaken America to the injustices of racial discrimination and violence. These words are also applicable to our current violence against the Earth. If we heed these words we might have the will power to leave the remaining fossil fuels in the ground and redirect our energy pursuits in a more sustainable direction.

Although the current mindset appears to have a stranglehold on free will, we can *change our minds*. In fact, a 2017 Gallup poll shows that the percentage of Americans who worry about global warming has risen to 50 percent, up from 37 percent in 2015.[29] Psychiatrist Robert Jay Lifton calls this shift in mindset a "climate swerve."[30] In spite of the current administration's regressive denial of climate change a growing number of Americans either experience directly or watch on cable news the human and environmental toll of extreme weather events. They want the Paris Agreement to work. As an apocalyptic dread of future devastation grips the collective consciousness there is a growing public conviction, says Lifton, that the fossil fuel economy is immoral.

When enough individuals profess an affirmation of life in all its forms then a new energy matrix constructs itself. Scientist Rupert Sheldrake has called this subtle expansion of worldview *morphic resonance*. It is the precedent for, as physicist and philosopher of science Thomas Kuhn named the revolutionary process, a *paradigm shift* in consciousness. The anthropocentric perspective, which places the human being (*anthropos*) at the center, yields to an ecocentric perspective.[31] The Earth becomes the center of perception and the source of a larger identity.

We may feel that the solipsistic worldview which now envelops the globe is not penetrable by individual effort. Indeed, for the individual to enact change small groups and organizations must form around committed individuals. In time, movements sprout from these organizations. The liberation movements of the 1960s serve as an incisive example. The civil rights, women's liberation and gay rights movements, and to some extent the green movement which was then in its infancy, gradually changed minds and directed the cultural ethos towards tolerance and equality which manifested in new laws. Notwithstanding a backdrop of resistance those Enlightenment ideas continue to percolate in practice, energizing movements for social justice but also for climate justice—for the rights of the living planet that is our common home.

So, we ask, what is the first step in effecting cultural change towards a sustainable future? That step is a humble and seemingly inconsequential one— the cultivation of awareness by the individual. A group is only as powerful as the individuals that form it; a cultural revolution starts with each of us. As the practice of awareness grows like leaven in society it has the potential power to transform that society.

The work of humanist psychologist Carl Rogers exemplifies this idea. Rogers views awareness as the key element in the therapeutic work of becoming fully human. In the clinical dialogue between therapist and client it is awareness, he says, which prompts the client to develop a liking for himself and a caring concern for others. In opposition to the Hobbesian image of man as instinctively incorrigible and selfish, and even contrary to Freud's preoccupation with the seductive powers of man's bestial id, Rogers believes that man is basically good and that, with awareness as his psychic tool, a person "comes to *be* what he *is*."[32] By extension, society comes to be what it truly is.

Awareness, or mindfulness, is the cutting tool of the transition from an anthropocentric to an ecocentric perspective. A perceptual universe limited to humans yields to a wider familial circle that reaches into the biosphere. Awareness of the facts, which emboldens transformative action, requires a willingness to be informed by the facts and to let go of ideas, opinions and biases that distort perception and distract the mind from the matter at hand. And that matter is the Earth herself on which and by which we live. Psychologist Charles Tart describes perception itself as a "simulation of reality" based in habitual, conditioned responses in the mind to sensory stimuli.[33] We

operate according to a "consensus consciousness" molded by cultural preferences and presuppositions that appear normal and true.[34] The illusion of being
separate from what is around us is a particularly potent trans-cultural 'truism'
that hides the reality of the web of life. The current collective inability to
implement a new worldview that reflects and empowers this *real* world is
preserved through an unconscious process known as *perceptual defense.* Tart
defines perceptual defense as "a form of defense mechanism that works to
keep us unaware of events in the outside world that would arouse unpleasant
or unacceptable emotions."[35]

In a short, intriguing essay by transpersonal psychologist Arthur Deikman,
called "The Meaning of Everything," the author defines awareness as "the
ground of our conscious life, the background or field" in which thoughts, images and sensations appear.[36] In other words, there is a distinction between
awareness, which is non-localized and extends throughout the universe as
the organizing force of this huge biosystem, and the mental contents of one's
personal awareness. Naturalist David Abram refers to this distinction when he
says, "one's own awareness is born of a rift within a more primordial anonym-
ity."[37] While walking at dusk through a forested valley Abram remarks: "The
full-bodied alertness I now felt seemed no more mine than it was the valley's;
it seemed a capacity of the land itself that had been imparted to my body."[38]

Awareness is not within us; we are within awareness. Whenever we claim
this universal awareness or consciousness as our own separate possession
the experience of oneness disappears; the illusion of separation takes over.
Suffering is inevitable because perception will reflect and confirm the mental
fantasy of an ego isolated from its brethren. Yet rest the mind momentarily in
naked awareness and the potential for release is reintroduced. Perception is
undressed, the fantasy collapses, and we 'see.'

All created beings possess awareness at some level. In the biosystem, says
Deikman, boundaries are illusory. The awareness of a tree, for instance, does
not differ from our own. But the human capacity *to be aware of being aware,*
to know awareness, is the reflective consciousness that bestows on *Homo sapiens* the unique potential for evolutionary growth. Therefore, says Deikman,
"the individual person is the means whereby reality articulates itself."[39] It is
this pure witnessing that prompts the sage who wrote the ancient *Kena Upanishad* to inquire: "What has called my mind to the hunt? . . . What has made
my life begin? . . . It lives in all that lives, hearing through the ear, thinking
through the mind. . . . It lies beyond the known, beyond the unknown."[40]

In modern society the razor's edge of this primal awareness is dulled. Our
minds run on automatic, cluttered with random thoughts, conditioned and
crusted over with presuppositions, assumptions and prejudices. By means of
machines we have made life easy and efficient but also dangerous as mind

becomes mechanized as well. Only awareness can make us sensitive to the moment-to-moment condition of the mind and strengthen the ability to stay present which is crucial to remedying the condition of the world. Having removed ourselves conceptually and emotionally from the living Earth and from the depth of our own minds (the two are related) we race through life oblivious to the fact that we have lost touch with the one tool—awareness—which both liberates the mind from habit and initiates a path towards survival, not only our own survival as a species but the survival of the Earth Mother whose embrace we no longer feel.

In 1969, in his explosive essay *Eco-Catastrophe*, ecologist Paul Ehrlich imagines a scenario of massive destruction caused by a combination of the rampant use of toxic pesticides in agriculture, a population explosion, and competition between nations for resources in UDCs (underdeveloped countries). Ehrlich's words could be written now, except that Ehrlich would have included human-induced climate change which in the 1960's was not yet realized. Towards the end of the essay Ehrlich writes:

> Indeed, Western society is in the process of completing the rape and murder of the planet for economic gain. And, sadly, most of the rest of the world is eager for the opportunity to emulate our behavior. . . . Man is destroying the life support systems of the Spaceship Earth. The situation was recently summarized very succinctly: 'It is the top of the ninth inning. Man, always a threat at the plate, has been hitting Nature hard. It is important to remember, however, that NATURE BATS LAST.'[41]

The scenario which Ehrlich envisions does not have to occur. It is still possible to learn from and imitate simpler societies where the interconnectedness of life forms is acknowledged, thus mandating a measured use of Earth's resources. We need to reacquaint ourselves with this alternative perspective so that the elements of life—air, fire, water, earth and space—remain healthy and balanced. We have a choice as to the light by which we live.

Chapter Three

An Elemental Disturbance

God hath given you one face but you make yourself another

—Hamlet, *Hamlet* III:1

In the web of life all organisms are made of the same five elements: air, fire, water, earth (soil), and space. Each species is the Earth writ small, including the human species. Our bodies are roughly 70 percent water; our lungs breathe air with the help of trees; our hearts are the fire of the Sun pumping blood to all the cells; our flesh is the flesh of the earth. Human nature is embedded in Nature. When we pollute air and water with excessive amounts of greenhouse gases, and contaminate the soil with pesticides and herbicides, we defile the food we eat, the air we breathe, the water we drink. We pollute and contaminate ourselves, along with other species like bees, birds, trees, and fish who innocently absorb the poisons. We live in an interconnected energy field. In losing intimacy with Nature as our extended living Body and Intelligence—and thereby educating our children to value machines over living Nature—are we in danger of losing our humanity? The severing at birth of the umbilical cord that connects mother and child enables the child to become an independent being; but subtly the connection between mother and child is never lost. Humans evolved into their own unique species with a neurological complexity superior to other species, but remembrance of their connection to Mother Earth and the five elements is vital to survival.

A thin strip of life-enhancing biosphere surrounds the planet Earth. In each biotic environment on Earth ecosystems develop that combine the five elements in ways that promote life. The flora and fauna peculiar to a certain environment exhibit instinctual patterns that match behavior to that environment in a continual process of adaptation. Humans adapt to the natural environment as well, but they use a combination of instinct and culture. By instinct birds migrate south to find shelter in a warm climate. People seek shelter too, prompted by instinct but reliant on culture to attain their goal. They choose materials from the Earth like thatch, adobe, brick, stone, wood, concrete block made of sand, gravel, and cement and even vinyl—a plastic made from crude oil and chlorine. Then, with an eye to climate and inspired by imagination, human beings construct houses.[1]

When human beings make choices that maintain and enrich the total eco-cultural system then not only are the basic needs of human populations met but the needs of other species are met as well; the web of life is balanced and vigorous and the culture itself endures in a healthy way. If those choices are maladaptive then the elements become destructive of life. For example, carbon is the basic element of life. The exchange of oxygen and carbon dioxide between human and plant enables each life form to live. When carbon as carbon dioxide exceeds its limit both in the atmosphere and in the oceans because humans choose to procure energy through the extraction and burning of fossil fuels then the element of life becomes the element of death. According to Josep G. Canadell, an Australian climate scientist who runs the Global Carbon Project, human beings are pumping close to forty billion tons of carbon dioxide into the air every year, a staggering amount which, says Canadell, may now be beyond the capacity of the natural sponges of air and ocean to absorb.[2] The result: global warming.

At the Peoples' Climate March in New York City in September 2014 one of the signs held aloft by a marcher read, to the accompaniment of appropriate photos: *How do we tell our children we did it for the economy/When we can't breathe the air/We can't eat the food/We can't drink the water?*

The treatment of the elements by human societies has been relatively benign throughout history, allowing ecosystems to persist independent of human interference. For example, the Makuna tribe of the Columbian jungle traditionally align their actions to the belief that humans live only through respecting and negotiating with the natural world. Their lifestyle is ecologically sound. The river gives fish and the soil gives vegetables and fruits when the people relate to these sources of nourishment as kin and reciprocate the gifts through ceremonial rituals of thanksgiving. The Makuna believe that they were born in the river and then came onto land; that, in fact, the fish are people wearing fish clothing. It is important, the elders tell the children, not to fish at Thunder Rapids because this sacrilege will kill you. The warning hides an implicit understanding of biology and conservation. The elders know that this location is the fishes' spawning ground and that overfishing here will deplete an important resource and offend the fish spirits. At the annual Peach Palm festival masked tribesmen dance all night to summon the spirits of the fish people into their bodies while the whole community thank the spirits by feeding them with prepared delicacies so that they in turn will be fed. The Makuna shaman teaches: "take it [food] and it will kill you; ask and it will feed you . . . Life is a gift and a sacrifice . . . life is prayer; everything consents to be sacrificed . . . the human task is to negotiate with the spirits."[3] The shaman concludes by contrasting Western knowledge with tribal wisdom. He says: "Knowledge cuts things up; wisdom makes them whole."[4]

In order to explore the ways in which human-induced climate change is disturbing the physical elements of planetary life this chapter will focus on four themes: the element water, and its absence—drought; deforestation, which exacerbates the build-up of carbon emissions released by the burning of fossil fuels; the frequent combination of drought and deforestation in past instances of ecological deterioration; and, finally, the impact of elemental disturbance upon living species around the globe.

WATER

Scientists predict that pure, fresh drinking water may be the most valuable resource of the future. As a result of global warming drought is turning large swaths of Africa, Australia, South America and even the United States into parched land. Lakes are drying up and rivers are shrinking. In July of 2016 Lake Poopó in Bolivia finally succumbed to years of water diversion, drought and deadly warming of the lake due to climate change. The indigenous fishing families lost not only their livelihood but their parents, for they view the lake as mother and father. A salty dry expanse littered with dead fish replaces the healthy waters of centuries past. In Cape Town, South Africa, considered one of the greenest cities in the world, a confluence of drought, population growth and climate change is creating a potential catastrophic water shortage. After a record three year drought water levels have fallen so low that the government warns of a Day Zero when all taps in homes and businesses will be turned off until the rains come.

In the American West the Colorado River, which encompasses 1,450 miles, is shrinking. This river provides water to one in eight Americans and supports one seventh of American crops through the construction of a series of dams such as Glen Canyon dam that created Lake Powell. It took seventeen years for the Lake Powell reservoir to fill; nineteen years later the water level continues to sink due to overuse and prolonged drought. More than 160 billion gallons of water evaporate off Lake Powell each year lowering the reservoir by four inches each month.[5] It is becoming clear to those in charge of the Colorado River Storage Project, begun in 1956, that dismantling the dams may be required.

After six years of unrelenting drought, which greatly reduced the state's water supply and led to intensified wildfires, California finally experienced a winter in 2016–17 that produced more rainfall than the state has had in twenty years. However, the snowpack in the Sierra Nevada Mountains, which yearly accounts for 60 percent of the state's water infrastructure, is shrinking and will continue to shrink as the climate continues to warm. Furthermore, climate scientists, led by Dr. A. Park Williams of Columbia University, have concluded that evaporation of moisture from the soil because of warming air temperatures will exceed any increase in rainfall.[6] This situation is compounded by the overpumping of groundwater from wells in Central Valley, a major American agricultural region. The steady depletion of the groundwater supply that originates deep in the valley's vast aquifer may keep the farmers in business for now, but it hastens the time when—like an exhausted bank account—there is no more water to grow the crops.

The plight of Central Valley highlights another ominous sign that climate change is impacting the Earth's water systems: the worldwide depletion of major aquifers. The fertile plains of Kansas, for example, are turning to dust as intensive farming, combined with drought, drain the great High Plains Aquifer that stretches from southern Wyoming into Texas. If the groundwater from this aquifer runs out its refill would require hundreds, maybe thousands, of years of rainfall.

From rivulets of rain and melting snow to creeks, rivers and seas where water evaporates back into the atmosphere, global networks of waterways resemble the circulatory systems in animal and plant bodies. Jack Vallentyne, aquatic ecologist and teacher who helped rid the Great Lakes of laundry detergent phosphates, explains: "'If water is the blood of Mother Earth and soil the placenta, river courses are veins, oceans are compartments of the heart and the atmosphere is a giant aorta.'"[7]

The threat to freshwater comes from a combination of factors including prolonged drought, deforestation which can lead to desertification, agricultural run-off of pesticides and chemical fertilizers high in nitrogen, pollution from coal ash and oil spills, and methane leakage from hydrofracturing which just happens to also require vast amounts of water. These stresses to the element water are also linked to population growth. In Texas, for example, the population has been increasing each year—and so has the need for water. Current drought conditions in populated areas are affecting people and wildlife, creating a competition for available freshwater. The endangered 5-foot tall whooping crane and sandhill crane spend winters in the salt marshes of the Arkansas National Wildlife Refuge on the Texas coast before migrating north to breed. These salt marshes are freshened from the Guadalupe and San Antonio Rivers which in turn are fed during droughts by the Edwards Aquifer which provides drinking water for San Antonio, the seventh largest city in the United States. When the supply of freshwater diminishes the salt marshes get too salty, killing the blue crabs which are the cranes' main food source. When these birds migrate to northern climes via the Central Flyway they stop over at the great Platte River in Nebraska to rest and feed on waste corn in the farm fields. Some 600,000 sandhill cranes arrive in late February followed by their whooping crane buddies. But the Platte River is shrinking by nearly 70 percent as dams block the flow so that the water can be harnessed for drinking, irrigation, and electricity for human beings.

Once an ecological problem becomes chronic it is difficult to reverse the downward spiral. This fact is evident in the case of the Great Lakes, which supply drinking water for forty million people. It is estimated that 180 invasive species have entered the Great Lakes. When non-native plant or animal species enter and infest an ecosystem that system is thrown off balance. The sea lamprey, a parasitic jawless fish that preys on commercial fish species, came into the Great Lakes in the 1800's through shipping channels. It has been difficult to eradicate. Eurasian water milfoil, a freshwater aquatic plant introduced into North American lakes in the 1940's, chokes out other plant-life and imperils lower food-chain marine life with an eventual impact on the fish population. Lake Erie, in particular, remains an endangered lake due to invasive Zebra mussels, goby, grass carp and algal blooms that keep spreading as these phytoplankton eat excess phosphates in the water. In the middle of the lake is a low-oxygen dead zone due to hypoxia which occurs as a consequence of algae consuming oxygen when they die. This process, called eutrophication, deprives fish and other aquatic animals of the element (oxygen) they need to live. Much of the deterioration of the lake is being caused by pollution from nutrient overload, especially nitrogen and phosphorous from chemical fertilizer run-off and animal waste from factory farms. An active coal plant spewing pollutants into the water sits on the edge of the lake.

An ominous new bloom of algae bacteria at the western end of Lake Erie, which supplies drinking water for Toledo, Ohio, was identified in August 2014 as cyanobacteria. People have been warned not to drink the water due to a toxin called microcystin produced by the bacteria which at high doses can cause liver failure. It was the ancestors of cyanobacteria who transformed the planet's atmosphere some three billion years ago by engineering a unique process called photosynthesis. Ironically, the identified 'toxin' in Lake Erie is the very evolutionary adaptation that protected the ancient cyanobacteria from excessive radiation so that they could go about their revolutionary work that allowed the animal kingdom to emerge. Now, as huge amounts of agricultural nutrient run-off pour into lakes and rivers worldwide and the climate warms, cyanobacteria are multiplying exponentially. Water is life. Whereas the body can survive the lack of food for about three weeks, three days is the limit for water deprivation. The ancient Chhãndôgya Upanishad says simply: "The finest quality of the water we swallow rises up as life."[8] The following Sufi tale involves water. It is instructive on several levels, but at its simplest the story reminds us of the respect due to the element water on which we depend.

Once upon a time Khidr, the teacher of Moses, called upon mankind with a warning. At a certain date, he said, all the water in the world which had not been specially hoarded, would disappear. It would then be renewed with different water which would drive men mad. Only one man listened to the meaning of this advice. He collected water and went to a secure place where he stored it, and waited for the water to change its character. On the appointed date the streams stopped running, the wells went dry, and the man who had listened, seeing this happening, went to his retreat and drank his preserved water. When he saw, from his security, the waterfalls again beginning to flow, this man descended among the other sons of men. He found that they were thinking and talking in an entirely different way from before; yet they had no memory of what had happened, nor of having been warned. When he tried to talk to them, he realized that they thought that he was mad, and they showed hostility or compassion, not understanding. At first he drank none of the new water, but went back to his concealment, to draw on his supplies, every day. Finally, however, he took the decision to drink the new water because he could not bear the loneliness of living, behaving and thinking in a different way from everyone else. He drank the new water, and became like the rest. Then he forgot all about his own store of special water, and his fellows began to look upon him as a madman who had miraculously been restored to sanity.[9]

At a spiritual level the story could be interpreted thus: the preserved water symbolizes a time when humans lived a pure, virtuous life in harmony with the cosmos. The changing quality of the water implies that the culture devolved due to a coarsening of consciousness, a pollution of the mind. Man trespassed the law and so his purity, represented by the pure water, is taken away. The new water may not look different from the old water, just as the sparkling of a lake's surface does not reveal underlying eutrophication, but this new inferior water is erasing memory of the former harmony. Only one man listens to the master's teaching and heeds the warning (as did Noah in the biblical story, which features a flood). For a time he holds onto the memory of a virtuous life by hoarding a supply of the pure water, but the desire to conform and ease his solitary lifestyle overtakes this initial obedience. He accommodates to the acceptable norm and falls into a sea of unreflective mob-consciousness.

The Oceans

An investigation of the Earth's vast oceans reveals the extent to which marine life must develop precise adaptations in order to survive. For example, a barnacle must maintain an attachment to its rock home through the terrors of breaking waves and changing tides at the shoreline. By means of a streamlined conical shape and the secretion of a strong 'glue' that joins its body to the rock surface the barnacle can withstand turbulent surf. The much greater struggle occurs in the larval form when the barnacle tissues are being formed and its vulnerability is pronounced.[10]

When human-induced climate change is introduced into the ocean environment the fragility of some organisms in coping with this added stress is accentuated. For example, in 2009 a non-profit organization, Tara Oceans Expedition, inaugurated an international three-year expedition to study the ecological status of microbial life in the world's oceans. Scientists, artists, journalists and crew members from forty countries signed up and set out aboard a 100-foot schooner. Over a three-year period scientists collected data on a profusion of plankton species, some of which are sensitive to ocean temperature changes. For millennia these genetically diverse viruses, bacteria, amoebas and paramecia have collaborated and battled in the absorption of carbon dioxide, the breaking down of waste, the making of oxygen (they provide half of the oxygen produced each year on Earth through photosynthesis), and the mutual feeding off each other through the predator-prey relationship. As the baseline of all marine food chains these microbial organisms are vital to the health of the oceans. By their dance these beings have, up until now, ensured planetary health, but scientists fear that rising water temperatures due to climate change will adversely affect a percentage of these tiny keepers of the ocean ecosystem, throwing the entire system out of balance.

Just as the concentration of carbon dioxide in the air continues to rise so also the oceans, by absorbing this gas, become warmer and more acidic through a lowering of the pH. The entire Antarctic ecosystem is threatened, for example, by the death of krill eggs in the Southern Ocean due to excessive carbon dioxide in the water. The decline of krill is also related to commercial trawlers that scoop up schools of krill to feed farmed fish. About the size of your little pinkie and similar in shape to a shrimp, this tiny crustacean is one of the most abundant animal species on Earth, providing its flesh as prey for most marine life, including whales, seals, squid, fish, sea birds and penguins. Dr. Linda C. Weiss, an aquatic ecologist, has found that many marine organisms depend on certain chemical changes in the water to indicate food sources or warn of dangers. Ocean acidification has upset these signals so that many fish, for example, can no longer detect predators.

The trend in all ecosystems is toward increasing maturity. However, like a finely tuned athlete's body, the more mature an ecosystem becomes the more fragile and vulnerable it is to potential harm from outside. Maturity implies complexity; the interdependent parts of a mature ecosystem act and react in consort. For example, coral reefs worldwide, and the organisms they support like crustaceans, fish and worms, are fast becoming victims of the dual effect of ocean acidification and warming waters. Water pollution from nitrogen-rich fertilizer run-off and overfishing of herbivorous fish who normally graze on algae that grow on reefs compound this stressful scenario. It is estimated that one-third of the world's coral reefs are already damaged and, if the current plight continues, about half of remaining reefs will be gone by 2030.

Coral reefs are the *rainforests of the sea*. A coral consist of animal, vegetable and mineral parts. The coral polyp—the animal part—is related to the jellyfish. It possesses many little mouths that drink in nutrients. Thousands of polyps can occupy one branch!

Algae, the vegetable part, cohabit with the coral polyp, providing it with food through photosynthesis. The third part—a calcium carbonate mineral structure—serves as a protective home for the symbiotic pair. When excessive carbon dioxide dissolves in the water it forms carbonic acid which eats away at the carbonate ions used by the polyp in reef calcification. The polyp's mineral skeleton is thereby weakened.

Warming waters encourage coral 'bleaching' by inducing the algae to produce excessive oxygen radicals, to which the polyp reacts by evicting the algae, turning itself white. For example, in late summer of 2014 coral reefs in the Gulf of Mexico off the Florida Keys experienced a devastating bleaching event due to soaring water temperatures in July (84 degrees F.) and August (87 degrees F.).[11]

Unnatural warming of the water also affects the coral reproductive cycle. Normally coral polyps eject both eggs and sperm in a mass spawning ritual that fills the water with millions of white, pearl-like organisms—a snowstorm at sea. Climate change disturbs this primordial lovefest which normally coincides with seasonal warming of the waters and the lunar cycle.

One of the most prolific coral reefs, the Great Barrier Reef, is at risk of being added to the United Nations List of World Heritage in Danger sites. This 1,400 mile natural wonder stretches along most of the coastline of the state of Queensland, Australia. It has lost over half its coral cover in the past twenty-seven years from bleaching, but also from inland mining of the vast deposits of coal in the Galilee Basin. At Abbot Point port, a major dock for coal loading, three million cubic meters of silt laced with chemicals were dumped into

Figure 3.1.   Close-up of polyps.
Courtesy of Nazir Amin, taken at Panglima Abu, Perhentian Island, Malaysia.

reef waters in one year. When the Queensland government suggested that the 'dredge spoil' could be dumped instead on nearby wetlands to minimize risks to the reef an outcry erupted from conservationists who countered that wetlands, which are habitat for a host of species in the food chain, are being summarily destroyed around the globe.

The serious plight of coral reefs has captured the attention of scientists such as Dr. Mary Hagedorn, a reproductive physiologist with the Smithsonian Institution. She is combing the reefs of Australia, the Caribbean and Hawaii, collecting and freezing coral sperm. Rather like a seed bank, her sperm bank already contains one trillion frozen sperm, enough to fertilize 500 million to one billion eggs, plus a repository of frozen embryonic cells, some of which have the potential of stem cells to grow into adult corals.

In pristine conditions the distribution, balance and interplay of elements upholds Nature's equilibrium and fosters fecundity of life. Earth as a body rebounds from imbalance as do our bodies from sickness—unless the disease is too serious. An analogy is instructive. Our DNA tells each cell what to do as part of a community of cells that serve the whole body. When malignant cancer cells form and multiply they do not behave according to the genetic program; in time they consume the very body that supports them. Humanity is currently entrapped in a behavioral pattern that constitutes a disease which infects the world and endangers all life. That disease is called *species arrogance*. In a powerful description of this condition (which the Greeks called *hubris*) David Abram writes:

> Do we really believe that the human imagination can sustain itself without being startled by other shapes of sentience—by redwoods and gleaming orchids and the eerie glissando cries of humpback whales? Do we really trust that the human mind can maintain its coherence in an exclusively human-made world? . . . The abrupt loss of rain forests and coral reefs, the choking of wetlands, the poisons leaching into the soils, and the toxins spreading in our muscles compel us to awaken from our long oblivion, to cough up this difficult magic that's been growing within us, swelling us with pride even as the land disintegrates all around us.[12]

A contemporary translation of the ancient *Tao Te Ching* corroborates Abram's warning:

> In harmony with the Tao
> the sky is clear and spacious,
> the earth is solid and full,
> all creatures flourish together,
> content with the way they are,
> endlessly repeating themselves,
> endlessly renewed.
>
> When man interferes with the Tao,
> the sky becomes filthy,
> the earth becomes depleted,
> the equilibrium crumbles,
> creatures become extinct.
>
> The Master views the parts with compassion,
> because he understands the whole.
> His constant practice is humility.
> He doesn't glitter like a jewel
> but lets himself be shaped by the Tao,
> as rugged and common as a stone.[13]

Trees

As deforestation, urban development and suburban sprawl obliterate green spaces from our communities the vacant lots and woodsy areas which used to stimulate the imagination, particularly of children, are disappearing. Manicured lawns and cement playgrounds are no substitute for wild, wooded places in Nature. Before the video game and computer craze brought children indoors, and parents grew wary of the unkempt outdoors as a dangerous place where their offspring could get hurt or even abducted, children naturally gravitated to trees for climbing, for stowing away secret messages in a tree's hollows, or for making a tree house with dad's help.

Trees are central to the exploratory instinct. They are also perceived as companions and teachers. Native Americans regard the *tree people* as kin who speak and impart their wisdom to receptive human beings. In the *Lord of the Rings* trilogy by J. R. R. Tolkien trees talk and move within a landscape of magic and wizardry, personified by the wizard Gandalf. The Ents (treelike anthropomorphic beings) and Huorns (human-like trees that speak and move) uproot themselves from the primeval Fangorn Forest to fight the evil wizard Saruman. Later, in defeating the dark king Sauron in the War of the Ring, the armies of Prince Aragorn hold aloft the holy banner of Gondor that pictures a white tree surrounded by stars. Crowned as King Elessar, Aragorn is told by Gandalf that the age of men has begun and will flourish if Aragorn uses his reign to preserve the good. The new king replies that the Tree in the Court of the Fountain is still withered and barren. He asks Gandalf for a sign that guarantees continuity of a new age of peace and plenty. Gandalf leads the king to a barren waste in the mountains where, out of the snow, a healthy sapling grows bearing white flowers on its crown. Aragorn gently lifts the wondrous sapling from the earth and transports it to the Citadel where he plants it by the fountain, after reverently uprooting the withered tree and laying it to rest.

Poets have long been inspired by trees as living works of art. The poem by Joyce Kilmer that begins "I think that I shall never see a poem as lovely as a tree" was once a staple recitation choice in elementary schools. Ee cummings begins a poem of thanksgiving to God by saluting "the leaping greenly spirits of trees."[14] John Muir compares trees and humans, while taking a jab at human bouts of melancholy, when he says: "I never saw a discontented tree. They grip the ground as though they liked it . . . and go wandering forth with every wind, going and coming like ourselves. . . ."[15] In the poem "Tree at My Window" by Robert Frost the poet takes refuge in a comparison of his own mental agitation with the struggle of a tree to weather 'outer' storms. He writes:

Tree at my window, window tree,
My sash is lowered when night comes on;
But let there never be curtain drawn
Between you and me.

Vague dream head lifted out of the ground,
And thing next most diffuse to cloud,
Not all your light tongues talking aloud
Could be profound.

But tree, I have seen you taken and tossed,
And if you have seen me when I slept,
You have seen me when I was taken and swept
And all but lost.

That day she put our heads together,
Fate had her imagination about her,
Your head so much concerned with outer,
Mine with inner, weather.[16]

In her memoir, Buddhist scholar and environmental activist Joanna Macy describes a maple tree which became her best friend, mentor and alter-ego during childhood summers spent at her grandfather's farm. The great tree stood in front of the main house and she would climb it regularly, sitting in the branches to survey the world—and herself. She describes a mystical experience of communion with this nonhuman other whose presence, she says, protected her and taught her the value of solitude. She writes:

I only went there alone. It was a place to be quiet, a place to disappear into a kind of shared presence, the being that was tree and me, with the light coming through. The light is what I remember most of all; high and wide around me, it shaped a luminous, breathing bowl. It danced through the leaves, glowing them green and gold. It stroked the limbs with flickering shadows. When I sat very quiet, the play of light seemed to go right through my body, and my breath was part of the maple's murmuring. . . . She let me glimpse a wild serenity at the heart of my world.[17]

A spiritual relationship between humans and trees is embodied in many religious traditions. The Tree of Good and Evil and the Tree of Life in the Garden of Eden offer contrasts for human choice. In the *Egyptian Book of the Dead* twin sycamores are described as standing at heaven's gate in the east where the sun god Ra emerges every morning. Sycamores were planted at burial sites and used to build coffins to aid the dead in their return to the womb of the maternal tree goddess. Sacred trees were planted on the ramping terraces of Mesopotamian ziggurats and in the Hanging Gardens of Babylon. Sacred groves of ash in ancient Greece were dedicated to Apollo while the oak tree was identified with Zeus. A special oak tree served as an oracle at the sanctuary of Zeus in Dodona; the rustling of its leaves were believed to be the voice of Zeus whose messages were deciphered by temple priestesses. In the Christian tradition a tree was the place of Jesus' sacrifice, while the evergreen tree became a symbol of his resurrection. Buddha was enlightened under a bodhi tree. The annual ritual of the Plains Indians—the Sun Dance— is celebrated around a sacred cottonwood tree which is felled amidst prayers of thanksgiving, then ceremoniously carried to the center of a sacred dancing circle where it is inserted in the ground.

The affinity that humans feel towards trees, whether conscious or subconscious, is a deeply felt affinity which, though manifesting at psychological and spiritual levels, is embedded in the basic biological cycle that plants and animals share. The axiom that 'trees are the lungs of the planet' is not really accurate. Trees (and all vegetation) are one lung and animals, including us, are the other lung. Trees inhale the animal waste of carbon dioxide and animals inhale the tree's waste, oxygen. This great carbon/oxygen cycle of exchanged nourishment and waste is an example of the reciprocity essential to life. In order to stay alive the human being is utterly dependent upon the tree as partner.

Looking at this cycle more closely we learn that as trees breathe in CO_2 they have the ability to break the bonds between the two oxygen atoms through the capture of sunlight which ignites a chemical reaction called photosynthesis—the synthesizing of photons. They then use the free carbon as a raw material to make their carbohydrate bodies while storing extra carbon in their root systems. The ability of trees to absorb and store carbon makes a forest the most significant carbon sink and the most effective weapon against global warming. Trees absorb between one-third and one-fourth of the world's total carbon dioxide emissions.[18]

The trees' waste, oxygen, is our lifeline. Yet we humans are creating an overload of carbon in emissions that stretches the ability of trees to restore balance in our shared biological cycle. The resultant global warming invites raging wildfires that consume trees and release the stored carbon into the air as carbon dioxide. As this gas increases in the atmosphere global warming accelerates in an ominous feedback loop.

Trees also have the capacity to store water in the ground, keeping the soil integrated, moist and fertile from the annual loss of leaves. As loggers chop down trees to make way for crops or pasture for beef cattle the soil is degraded, the water cycle is disturbed, and the specter of desertification looms. Trees are the homes of wildlife including birds, squirrels and insects so deforestation destroys wildlife habitat as well.

As a result of global warming old-growth trees like giant sequoias, redwoods and bristlecone pines are becoming sick from drought and insect infestation. The coastal redwoods drink in fog through their needles; this absorption of water-drenched air accounts for 40 percent of their water intake. But the daily fog that rolls in from the warming waters and warming air of the California coast has been diminishing—by as much as three hours a day over the last century.[19] In the central and southern Sierra Nevada Mountains in California a lethal stew of stresses including drought, soaring summer heat, insufficient forest management, and assault by bark beetles who thrive in warmer winters are threatening the pine trees with extinction. According to the U.S. Forest Service, from 2010 to 2016 more than 102 million trees in the state succumbed to this assault, with most tree deaths occurring in the Sierra Nevada.[20] Some of these individuals are 5,000 years old. Sequoias come in a close second in longevity with some trees reaching a ripe age of 2,000 to 3,000 years. The Sierra Nevada Mountains are the only place on earth where sequoia can be found. None of these great tree species were built to withstand a dry and warming climate, now stretching into decades. To help save seedlings of stressed tree species conservation biologists are moving them north into Canada's mountainous regions, a procedure known as *assisted migration*.

In Canada trees are not faring much better. The vast Canadian boreal forest, rich in virgin coniferous trees, covers one billion acres in the provinces of Northern Ontario, Quebec, Saskatchewan, and Alberta. This forest, which comprises one-quarter of all global forests, acts as a repository of carbon trapped in peatlands and is one of the largest sources of surface freshwater in the world. Its numerous wild rivers flow into northern oceans, driving oceanic currents and creating marine fisheries. Yet its trees are being chopped down at record speed in order to drill for vast amounts of tar sands crude oil. An environmental campaign called Boreal Birds Need Half is pressing for half of the forest to be preserved for the myriad flocks of migratory birds that call this place home.

Boreal forests worldwide are also dying from an increase in wildfires. In May 2016 a raging wildfire in the Canadian boreal forest spread into Fort McMurray, claiming most of the city and imperiling the lives of 90,000 residents who fled the towering flames. Global warming is suspected as a primary cause in these wildfires due to a confluence of interrelated factors: warming temperatures which encourage the deadly formation of lightening, persistent drought, premature snowmelt leaving forests dry as fire season arrives, and insect infestation.

Rainforests are also under siege. Once covering 14 percent of the Earth's surface, rainforests now cover only 6 percent with one and one-half acres continuing to be lost every second due to deforestation.[21] With the disappearance of rainforests 137 native plants, animals and insects suffer extinction daily. In the Amazon alone 20 percent of the rainforest is already gone and the rest is disappearing at a rate of 20,000 square miles each year. As the Amazon rainforest shrinks so does its richly diverse but very specialized array of plant and animal species (there are at least 1300 species of birds).

Rainforests are second only to the oceans in providing an important source of atmospheric water vapor through the process of transpiration. One mature tree can release about 200 gallons of water each year; this outflow translates as rain.[22] A perennial mist hangs over rainforests keeping them warm and humid—ideal conditions for two-thirds of the world's plant species.

Brazil features as a major player in deforestation. Agribusiness giants, cattle ranchers, and multinational logging companies are rapidly denuding the landscape, exposing the landscape to drought conditions. The worst drought to hit Brazil in eighty years combined with the stripping so far of 80 percent of rainforest along the Serra da Cantareira watershed that feeds six reservoirs. As these reservoirs dry up so does the supply of freshwater to the twenty million people who live in São Paulo.

The Brazilian government has a mixed record on environmental conservation. In March of 2018 the Brazilian Supreme Court upheld a governmental relaxation of environmental laws, leading environmentalists to fear that illegal deforestation will spike, even as it had fell during a federally imposed monitoring period between August 2016 and July 2017. Supporters of the decision argue that a balance must be set between rainforest conservation and opportunities for economic growth. Brazilian law requires each landholder to leave intact at least half of the forest on his property. At the same time farmers are encouraged by the government to raze thousands of acres to create highly profitable soybean fields. One farmer was offered a yearly cash payment to leave his forest standing by a local environmental group. The farmer was torn between a desire to combat climate change and the need to feed his family. In forty years, if logging and clearing continue at the present rate, there will be no rainforests left—and little rain.[23]

Moreover, the effect of deforestation on once fertile soil is a deficit that cannot be made up in quick time because it takes 200 years in wet tropical areas to create one centimeter of good soil that can sustain crops.[24] Deforestation also deprives indigenous peoples of their livelihood and traditional way of life. In Brazil, for example, the survival of the Yanomami tribe, whose home in the rainforest dates back centuries, is threatened by miners both local and foreign who cut down trees and pollute the waters in search of gold. Much of the lowland forests of the Malay Peninsula, Borneo, Solomon Islands, Sumatra, the Philippines, New Guinea and Madagascar are being eradicated—a scenario reminiscent of the plague of locusts that decimated the earth in biblical times. The ecosystem of Madagascar, for example, is home to plant and animal species found nowhere else on the planet, including the endangered Sifaka lemurs. With 90 percent of its rainforests gone, the budding eco-tourism industry of Madagascar, which could provide many jobs in a poor and overpopulated country, is losing its main attraction.

There are some signs that humans are awakening to the looming crisis caused by deforestation. For example, the Green Belt Movement, founded by the late Wangari Muta Maathai (for which she won a Nobel Peace Prize in 2004) combined political, economic and social aims with ecological practices to reverse the cycle of poverty and raise the status of women in Kenya. Because of drastic deforestation and resulting soil erosion farmlands were not providing sufficient crops to nourish families, nor was there the wood necessary for cooking. Farming and collecting firewood was traditionally women's work, so the Green Belt Movement combined reforestation with steps towards economic renewal and social justice by giving women jobs planting trees. Today Maathai's grassroots movement has produced over fifteen hundred tree nurseries.

Coinciding with the UN Climate Summit in September 2014 some major companies moved ahead of governments to curtail business activities associated with deforestation. Forty companies, including Nestle, Kellogg, Cargill and Unilever are pledging to cut tropical deforestation in half by 2020 and stop altogether by 2030. This is especially crucial in Indonesia where palm oil, an ingredient in many products, is harvested through rampant deforestation.

One of the most inspirational accounts of an individual fighting a cultural system that favors corporate profit above regulatory action in regards to deforestation is Julia Butterfly Hill's book, *The Legacy of Luna.* The relentless debate between loggers and environmentalists is epitomized in the valiant battle waged by Julia against the abuses of Pacific Lumber. Determined to help save the California redwoods from destruction Julia, in her early twenties, joined activists in 1997 to tree-sit on the property of Pacific Lumber where a mud slide, caused by clear cutting of giant trees on steep sloping land, had decimated the little town of Stafford, California. Clear cutting is a controversial practice of uniformly cutting down all trees in an area, thereby eliminating tree root systems that store water and conserve soil fertility. The owner of Pacific Lumber/Maxxam Corporation, Charles Hurwitz, had bought out the family-owned business in 1985 and proceeded to turn the sustainable forestry practices of his predecessor upside-down by clear cutting every old growth tree in sight for mega-profits. Julia learned to climb a 200-foot tall, 12-foot wide, 1000 year old redwood that activists had named Luna. She make a home in Luna's branches—a small platform sheltered with tarps tied to the top branches where she weathered wind storms that often made her fear for her life. Julia lived in the tree for over two years. Her perseverance paid off as she was able, in the end, to save Luna. Julia describes how the bond between her and the giant tree grew, giving her courage and insight as to how to withstand the taunts and threats of loggers; she turned the anger that their greed had initially aroused into love. This philosophy of love for all species, but especially for the ancient trees she felt destined to protect, is evident in her first visit to the primeval fog-wrapped forest. She writes:

> As I headed farther into the forest, I could no longer hear the sounds of cars or smell their fumes. I breathed in the pure, wonderful air. It tasted sweet on my tongue. Everywhere I turned, there was life . . . for the first time, I really felt what it was like to be alive, to feel the connection of all life and its inherent truth. . . . The energy hit me in a wave. Gripped by the spirit of the forest, I dropped to my knees and began to sob. I sank my fingers into the layer of duff, which smelled so sweet and so rich and so full of layers of life, then lay my face down and breathed it in. Surrounded by these huge, ancient giants, I felt the film covering my senses from the imbalance of our fast-paced, technologically dependent society melt away. I could feel my whole being bursting forth into new life in this majestic cathedral.[25]

ECOLOGICAL IMBALANCE AND SOCIAL COLLAPSE

When an environmental stress like severe drought combines with wrong choices such as razing forests that hold water in order to create arable land then the probability of ecological crisis is magnified. The inability to foresee the consequences of such choices reflects a human tendency to forget the lessons of the past. This error creates a karmic repetition that solidifies *The Great Forgetting*—a term originally used by Australian Aborigines to describe the attrition of their culture due to two hundred years of white domination and assimilation.[26] Beneath that forgetting is egoic mind that defends the status quo. This mind is partially the product of enculturation. We tend to think and behave according to the ethos or core value system of our culture, even when ecological imbalance indicates that a cultural change is necessary.

There have been notable historical examples of ecological devastation incited by ill-contrived human choices. Jared Diamond, geographer and author of *Collapse: How Societies Choose to Fail or Succeed*, investigates the relationship between human societies and their natural environment and proposes four main reasons why societies collapse. First, a society may fail to anticipate signposts of encroaching ecological imbalance. Memories fade so that when conditions arise that closely resemble a past crisis they may not be recognized in time. Second, the problem may have arrived yet it is not perceived. Soil infertility is not visible from the surface. The white caps of polluted and acidifying oceans sparkle in the sun without revealing the underlying poisoning of marine life. The hidden damage is not seen; out of sight out of mind. Diamond notes that the gradual shrinking of glaciers due to global warming is not perceived due to a creeping normalcy known as *landscape amnesia*.[27] Global warming itself has been occurring at a slow tempo, masked by erratic fluctuations. It has taken scientists a long time in fact to discern an average upward trend in global surface temperature of 0.07 degrees C. per decade. However, since 1970 this 'fever' has jumped to about 0.17 degrees C. per decade—twice as fast as the 0.07 degrees C. observed for the entire period from 1880–2015.[28] In his book *The Vanishing Face of Gaia* James Lovelock asserts that even climate scientists may underestimate the severity of climate change. There is a difference, he says, between actual observations that measure climate change and future forecast computer-generated models which do not factor in the most reliable measurement of heat absorbed by the Earth—sea-level rise. Lovelock argues that while the prediction by the IPCC shows a smooth, gradual rise in sea level from 1990 through 2007, on-site measurement shows a much more rapid, sharp hike which reflects vacillating fluctuations that real observations disclose.

The third reason for social collapse, and the most frequent, says Diamond, is the failure to even try to solve the problem once it has been recognized. This failure is due to selfishness on the part of powerful special interest groups who are motivated to reap short-term profits and ignore long-term projected catastrophes. A lust for power obscures responsibility to the whole system. Diamond's third reason for societal collapse describes the current resistance in America—and in the global economy—to a bold adoption of clean energy alternatives. Members of the corporate elite, aligned with government and the military, have a vested interest in maintaining the current mode of production using fossil fuels. They prefer to believe that global warming is either a hoax, part of a natural geological cycle of climate changes, or treatable at a later date—the Scarlet O'Hara syndrome.

Diamond contrasts the failure to correct a perceived problem, because it benefits an elite segment of the population, to an even more detrimental response in which irrational ideas and behavior cause a whole society to reject any plan to save itself. The greed of the powerful drives the powerless in society to make irrational choices out of desperation. Poor fishermen in tropical coral reef regions, for example, increasingly use dynamite and cyanide to kill fish living in coral reefs in order to feed their families, knowing full well that in destroying the coral reef environment they destroy their own and their children's livelihood.

The fourth and final reason that propels a society into collapse is the circumstance in which a grave problem may be beyond a society's ability to solve. The solution may be very expensive or the effort to reverse the situation too late. For example, a geoengineering scheme to treat global warming is like placing a band-aid on a deep wound that needs surgery. Dependence upon technology to ameliorate the human assault on Earth's vital signs shows blindness to the fact that human health is guaranteed not by technological wizardry but by guarding the health of the basic elements of air, fire, water, and earth on which our lives depend.

LESSONS FROM THE PAST

The rear-view mirror of history provides a number of pre-industrial examples of ecological devastation that show the interplay between a cultural system— its values and miscalculations—and dire changes in the physical ecosystem. Sometimes this dissonant duet is compounded by heightened social conflicts, producing a complex set of conditions that exceed a critical threshold of destabilization, sending the whole ecocultural system into a tailspin. Often deforestation and soil erosion, accompanied by some form of climate change like prolonged drought, are the major denominators that shift the ecocultural system from adaptive to maladaptive. Let us consider a few examples of ecocultural collapse.

Easter Island, situated in the Pacific Ocean, was a lush paradise, a tropical wonderland that sustained its human inhabitants for a thousand years. By 1400 AD all traces of human occupation vanish, leaving a barren landscape strewn with crumbling, toppled statues of gigantic size that once depicted ancestral deities. Archaeologists have pieced together the puzzle of the islanders' demise. It seems these voyagers had arrived at the island by canoe from Polynesia. They were sustained for centuries by fishing and farming. Two plentiful tree species—a palm and a woody variety—were used to build canoes and houses and provide fuel. Wood was also the material used for construction of the sacred statuary—an activity that became a competitive contest between rival chiefs. The archaeological record shows that over time forests were decimated, soil fertility declined, and local shellfish supplies shrank. The chickens that people raised provided the only remaining source of protein; but the non-native rats that had arrived with the early settlers, hidden in their canoes, competed with humans by eating the chicks as well as the seabirds and palm tree nuts. When the wood to build canoes ran out there was no way to obtain the major food source on the open sea: fish and sea mammals. Villages raided each other for food. Mass mortality ensued. The question remains: why didn't the people realize the potential danger of their actions? Each of these negative conditions developed over an extended time, yet they were not perceived or, if perceived, were not attended to. Was the human proclivity to procrastination and the idea 'this won't happen to me' part of the mix?

One of the enduring mysteries of ecocultural collapse is the disappearance of the Mayan civilization, considered one of the most intellectually and spiritually advanced cultures in the world. Located in Mesoamerica, and occupying a large swath of land that included the modern nations of Mexico, Belize, Guatemala and Honduras the Mayan civilization experienced its Classic period from 250 AD to about 800 AD. The Mayan collapse is a complex staggered affair that affected different populations at different times, particularly at populated hubs such as Tikal and Copan. According to Diamond, a web of variables produced stresses that contributed to the Mayan fall—an ominous reminder that even advanced societies can perish. These variables included deforestation, soil erosion, climate change (especially severe droughts), population fluctuations, and rivalries amongst regional kings who competed in the erection of pyramids. These rulers also spent a lot of time and attention waging war on each other which probably intensified when food supplies diminished due to environmental degradation.

Farming required deforestation and intensive human labor as there were no animal-powered plows. From the northern tip of the Yucatan Peninsula going south rainfall increases and soils are thicker and more arable for planting crops. These factors support a denser population. Diamond describes a situation that took place around 650 AD in the southern city of Copan (Honduras). The population had grown to an extent that not only the valleys but also the hillsides were divested of trees and used for agriculture. The Maya of Copan did not anticipate that without trees to hold the hillsides sediment would flow down into the valley. As a consequence of soil erosion and the leaching of nutrients hillside farming became untenable. People had to compete for food in the increasingly acidic bottomland. Throughout the Mayan heartland periodic drought and unpredictable variations in rainfall contributed to the tenuous, changing environmental conditions. A narrow range of crops dominated by corn, which gives little protein, had to feed a stratified society of non-farmers—nobles, priests, soldiers, and the king. Mayan peasants, which made up at least 70 percent of the society, could only produce twice the needs of their families. This supply was not enough to fulfill their duty of feeding the upper classes. There were no large, edible domestic animals; nor were there pack animals to transport food, especially to soldiers at war.

A 'perfect storm' brought the above confluence of forces together in the ninth century when a severe drought hit the Classic Lowland Maya. This added stress probably incited greater warfare and civil strife. Some populations may have migrated north in hopes of finding the necessities for survival. Others succumbed to famine and thirst. The drought that had hit this same area in the third century was no longer in the public memory by the ninth century—an example of the phenomenon of forgetting ecological lessons of the past and thereby not anticipating their reoccurrence.

There are several contemporary incidences of ecological collapse which serve as a sober reminder that human manipulation of complex ecosystems may exacerbate rather than correct imbalances. The first example is that of the deterioration of Macquarie Island which is situated between Australia and Antarctica. The story of Macquarie reads like a slapstick comedy except that it involved serious miscalculations that ignored the interconnectedness of players in the ecosystem. In the late nineteenth century seal hunters introduced rabbits and cats to the lush island. The cats ate the rabbits as well as the seabirds; the cat population flourished. When it was decided to remove most of the cats to remedy the situation the rabbit population soared. Rabbits nibbled down native plants until Macquarie was a denuded moonscape. In 1968 a deadly virus was introduced to kill the rabbits. This strategy worked but some remaining cats began eating seabirds again and the native vegetation, degraded by loss of chlorophyll, was overrun by an invasive plant species whose dense growth prevented native seabirds from nesting. In 1985 Australian scientists began a program to again eliminate the non-native cats who were preying on the native burrowing birds. In 2009, twenty-four years later, the ecological debacle became obvious. No one had ever asked the question 'if we remove or kill one species what will be the consequences for the whole ecosystem?'.

An illuminating micro-example of miscues in ecological planning was reported in the January 2008 issue of *Science*. While walking in the Kenyan bush an ecologist from the University of Florida, Todd Palmer, saw that the acacia trees which grew in an area which had been fenced off to protect the trees from being eaten by giraffes and leaf-eating elephants were inexplicably withering and dying. Why, he wondered, was this benign intervention having such devastating results? It was discovered that the acacia and a species of ant who nests in the tree's thorns live in a symbiotic relationship called mutualism. The ants sip on the tree's nectar and, in return, swarm out ready to bite an intruder when the tree is disturbed. Once the intrusive herbivores were removed from the area the trees sensed that no one was nibbling on their leaves and therefore reduced the amount of thorn and nectar production. The trees seemed to decide that ants were expendable and the unwanted ants felt no obligation to defend the trees. Wood-boring beetles then invaded the trees, causing them to sicken and die. The ant-acacia mutualism which had evolved over thousands of years and included a third player—the herbivores—was suspended due to one human action that inadvertently caused imbalance in the delicately woven web of life. Palmer and his colleagues are working to restore the old pattern by reintroducing giraffes and elephants into the acacia grove.

Finally, the deterioration of the nation state of Syria is a current example of a disastrous combination of environmental stress and negative cultural forces. Environmental stress due mainly to deforestation dates back to the Agricultural Revolution when the vast oak forests of the Levant were burned to the ground to make way for farming and the domestication of animals. It was the goats in particular who fed on remaining scrub and plant cover. A hot, arid climate, soil erosion in a hilly terrain, and loss of water through run-off completed the environmental degradation that continues to affect the region. Thomas Friedman, editorial writer for *The New York Times*, recently analyzed the ecological and cultural factors that are prominent in the Syrian rebellion against the dictatorial Assad regime. He examines a confluence of three factors that plague Syria: the worse drought in the nation's modern history, a rapidly growing population suffering from unemployment, and an oppressive, corrupt political regime. This explosive combination has unleashed extreme sectarian and religious fervor, fomented political revolution and facilitated the entrance of the Islamic State (ISIS) into the ravaged Syrian landscape. Friedman quotes the Syrian economist Samir Aita who explains:

'The drought did not cause Syria's civil war . . .but the failure of the government to respond to the drought played a huge role in fueling the uprising. . . . After Assad took over in 2000 he opened up the regulated agricultural sector in Syria for big farmers, many of them government cronies, to buy up land and drill as much water as they wanted, eventually severely diminishing the water table. This began driving small farmers off the land into towns, where they had to scrounge for work. Because of the population explosion . . . huge families came and settled in towns around cities like Aleppo. Some of those small towns swelled from 2,000 people to 400,000 in a decade or so. The government failed to provide proper schools, jobs or services for this youth bulge. . . . Young people and farmers starved for jobs—and land starved for water—were a prescription for revolution.'[29]

BEHOLD: THE ANTHROPOCENE

There is mounting evidence that a rapid disappearance of species is due to a combination of three factors: global warming, habitat loss and increased toxicity of water and food sources. This alarming incidence of species extinction suggests that the complex but local ecocultural collapses described above may now be occurring on a global scale. While climate change is a natural process that happens over millennia it usually occurs in slow time-frames that allow for species adaptation. Because the current warming trend is rapid, artificially forced by human action, many species are not able to adapt fast enough. The Center for Biological Diversity notes that the planet is now experiencing its sixth mass extinction of plants and animals, the worse since the loss of the dinosaurs sixty-five million years ago. But whereas that mass extinction, and others going back five hundred million years, were due to natural events, such as asteroid strikes or sudden climate shifts, the current extinction is engineered by human beings. In fact, Dutch chemist Paul Crutzen, co-discoverer of the cause of ozone depletion in Antarctica and winner of a Nobel Prize, believes that the name of the current geological epoch which started at the end of the last ice age 11,700 years ago—the *Holocene* (which means *wholly recent*)—should be changed to the *Anthropocene*. We humans, he states, are the makers and breakers of this epoch. We are responsible for the emissions that cause global warming. We decimate the forests, over-fish the oceans, devitalize the soil, divert major rivers, and overdevelop the Earth's land surface.

It is interesting that the second mass extinction, at the end of the Permian period 252 million years ago, was triggered by global warming—without our help, obviously. Apparently a massive amount of carbon was released into air and water (we don't know why), oxygen levels fell, temperatures rose (the seas warmed 18 degrees), oceans acidified and possibly became contaminated with a bacteria which produces a poisonous substance, hydrogen sulfide. Ninety percent of the mostly marine species were wiped out overnight (that is, in less than 200,000 years). Paleontologist David Raup describes this and other mass extinctions or 'crashes' as part of a pattern that features "'long periods of boredom interrupted occasionally by panic.'"[30] Raup's use of comic relief does not change the facts; and, as John Adams famously quipped, "facts are stubborn things."[31]

The Earth is now losing species at 1,000 to 10,000 times the normal background rate of one to five species per year.[32] The number of endangered species is also on the rise, despite both the Wilderness Act of 1964—which David Brower, first executive director of the Sierra Club, defined as an effort to protect the places "where the hand of man has not set foot"—and the Endangered Species Act.[33] The latter, signed into law in 1973, was a defense against economic development that ignored conservationist principles. Conservation scientists David Wilcove and Lawrence Master estimate, from the available data, that in the United States alone the number of imperiled species is at least ten times more than the number currently protected under the Endangered Species Act.[34] Just as cutting one's finger while slicing an apple registers in the whole body which is alerted to the crisis, the disappearance of even one species sends vibrations of alarm throughout the planetary ecosystem.

Biodiversity—defined as the number of species in a given area—is used to gauge the health of an ecosystem, whether the area is as small as one's backyard or as large as the planet. Most species have a climatic niche—an optimal temperature and precipitation level for survival. According to John J. Wiens, University of Arizona professor of ecology and evolutionary biology, species usually adapt to changing climatic conditions at a rate of only 1 degree Celsius per million years. If, as the IPCC predicts, temperatures rise by 4 degrees over the next 100 years then many species will not survive.[35] Terrestrial vertebrates in particular, such as amphibians, birds and reptiles do not evolve fast enough to adapt to a dramatically warmer climate, especially in tropical zones. If a species cannot move to a higher latitude, for example, or acclimate readily, then that species is doomed to extinction.

In the mountainous Costa Rican rainforest there once lived a proliferation of harlequin frogs whose bright yellow bodies with brown polka dots were striking to see amidst the lush greenery. Two-thirds of the 110 harlequin frog species disappeared during the 1980s and 1990s due to a double assault: global warming and a deadly disease, chytrid fungus. The fungus proliferated due to ideal temperature conditions (for fungi)—a constant 63 to 77 degrees—caused by global warming. Because amphibian skin is very thin frogs are sensitive to even minor changes in temperature; this sensitivity plus vulnerability to the deadly fungus is exacting their demise.

Frogs have been on the earth for about 400 million years, ever since they crawled out of water onto land. Their pioneering efforts preceded birds and mammals and even the dinosaurs whose extinction frogs survived. The frog's liminal status—needing water and moisture especially as a reproductive milieu, but also adapted to land—has allowed this life form to proliferate. Now frogs are endangered. How many frog species will yet join the list of their extinct kin, like the gastric-brooding frogs that carried frog-babies in their stomachs and delivered them through their mouths?

If our human legacy is that we achieved what no other species has achieved—self-awareness—but instead of leading the whole creation into a more conscious stage of evolution chose to allow the continued demise of other species it will be, as biologist E. O. Wilson puts it, "the ultimate irony of organic evolution" for we will have doomed ourselves as well.[36] Wilson estimates that "if the biodiversity crisis remains largely ignored and natural habitats continue to decline, we will lose at least one quarter of the earth's species."[37] This amounts to millions of species, vanished on our watch.

The right of a species to live, to avoid suffering if it can, and to reproduce is recognized not only by animal rights activists and ecologists but also by people who show up to save a beached whale or rescue a bird covered in oil from an oil spill. We may even resist killing an insect. Humanity carries an ancient memory of unity and the knowledge, buried though it might be, that the biological right to life has a spiritual dimension as well. For the Hindu, Buddhist and Jain this spiritual affinity and obligation is known as *ahimsa*, the practice of compassion and non-violence. Ahimsa begins in the mind with non-violent thoughts. Albert Schweitzer, Christian missionary and physician, echoes this sentiment when he writes:

> I cannot avoid compassion for everything that is called life. That is the begin-ning and foundation of morality. Once a man has experienced it and continues to do so—and he who has once experienced it will continue to do so—he is ethical. . . . It is our duty to share and maintain life. Reverence concerning all life is the greatest commandment in its most elementary form.[38]

The severe disturbance of the basic elements of life by human-induced climate change is producing a global ecocultural crisis that threatens all life. Signs of imminent collapse are visible. In order to recapture the ancient mem-ory of an interconnected world and construct a new cultural ethos in which human beings, as children of the Earth, take responsibility to protect the lives of all species, it is necessary to uncover the underlying mental framework of ideas and beliefs that have obscured this memory and precipitated errors in judgment that now portend grave results. Uncovering this mental framework, and then examining the practical effects of its implementation in society, will be the aim of the next three chapters which comprise Part Two: Departure. What is the psychology behind the choice that humanity has made to disre-gard the laws of interdependence and reciprocity which govern and protect all members of the web of life? Moreover, how has this choice led to the creation of a flawed socio-economic system in which the gifts of Mother Na-ture—clean water, soil and air—are polluted and depleted for material gain?

Part II

DEPARTURE

Chapter Four

The Psychology
of Leaving Home

There is nothing either good or bad but thinking makes it so.

—Hamlet, *Hamlet* II:2

By disconnecting the mind from the natural world humankind has given birth to an ecological crisis which extends into the far reaches of the globe. In the previous chapters facts were presented and discussed that make human-induced climate change and its dire effects undeniable. Now a penetration of the underlying psychological factors that precipitated the subtle but consequential dissociation from our planetary home is in order. Without a causal diagnosis the cure will be symptomatic at best.

What motivated us to leave the security of an intimate relationship with Mother Earth and what psychic wounds fester, in need of urgent therapeutic care? The development of an anthropocentric worldview indicative of species arrogance has been alluded to as a primary factor in the ecological deterioration of the planet. The perception and conception of the human species as both separate from and better than other species are entrenched in Western industrialized culture and have metastasized globally. The pre-industrial examples previously examined, showing the link between environmental damage and social collapse, were localized phenomena. Human-induced climate change is a global phenomenon which can only be resolved in the end by the global community, prodded into action by incessant local efforts at reform.

This chapter will probe possible origins of the illusion that ultimate power and control reside in the human species. From a psychological perspective it is clear that the motives of ego, unleashed from any restraint, can lead to a destructive narcissism that infects society. Myths and stories of a fall from grace due to hubris abide in many cultures. A review of Western cultural history will also show how the disappearance of a cultural acknowl-edgement of *anima mundi*—the world soul and embodiment of procreative female energy—and the emergence of a reductionist mindset aligned with scientific empiricism have upheld this illusion of power that now threatens planetary health.

THE PRIMAL MATRIX

In her insightful book *My Name is Chellis and I'm in Recovery From Western Civilization* psychologist Chellis Glendinning traces the malaise of modern society to a voluntary abandonment of our home, the natural world, which she calls the *Primal Matrix*. When we humans left the womb of the Primal Matrix to use, abuse and dominate Nature we experienced physical, mental, and spiritual anguish. By extension, the social, economic and political institu-tions that define our cultures became corrupted. Whether consciously felt or not, we continue to be traumatized.

By means of reflection upon her own biography of parental abuse Glendinning extrapolates from memories of personal trauma to collective evidence—gathered from individual and social histories—of psychological trauma imprinted in all our psyches as a result of wars, rapes, witch hunts and other atrocities that mark human history and continue to occur in a chronic, intergenerational cycle of abuse and victimization. Today, as we violate and damage the ecosystems of the Earth the psychic wounds within us fester and enlarge; the interplay of the personal and the planetary is acted out. Indeed, the original trauma to afflict humanity can be traced, says Glendinning, to a displacement from the land. This separation from the natural world occurred around 10,000 years ago with the advent of agriculture and the domestication of animals—seed forms of civilization—and solidified during the Industrial Revolution. Taming, managing and exploiting Nature as an inanimate object became the norm. Glendinning describes our society as a collection "of trau-matized individuals, and our culture has come into being through a univer-sally traumatizing process. The outcome—today's technological civilization with its massive psychopathologies and unending ecological disasters—is a collective reflection of the traumatized personality."[1]

By contrast, if we listen to nature-based cultures, says Glendinning, we can begin to heal because the history of native peoples shows a perception of humanity and the land as a joint identity. Individual selfhood is linked to tribal identity which is linked to the natural world as a continuum or matrix. Severance from the Primal Matrix breeds fear of the 'other' and an inability to converse with our relatives in the natural world. We forget who we are.

Becoming alienated from ourselves we act as aliens; our actions are prompted by fear, selfishness, and greed.

Glendinning defines the modern solution to traumatization as the technological utopia in which we occupy ourselves with technological gadgetry, drugs, and other addictive means of denial. This technological fix allows us to stay sick. "Techno-addictions" are, says Glendinning (quoting Lewis Mumford), the "'ultimate religion of our seemingly rational age—the Myth of the Machine! Bigger and bigger, more and more, farther and farther, faster and faster.'"[2]

In fact, there is no quick fix to mending the tear in the umbilical cord that attaches human beings to Mother Earth. Glendinning insists that the first step in the recovery process is to admit our inner brokenness, to recognize the self-inflicted wound in our collective psyche caused by a desire to be independent from the rest of Creation. Rumi illuminated this first step in healing when he said, centuries ago, "Don't turn your head. / Keep looking at the bandaged place. / That's where the light enters you."[3] In other words, we must face the wrong inflicted on the body of the Earth—just as we would need to face abuse of our own bodies, recollecting into a whole all parts of ourselves good and bad. The therapeutic act of seeing and admitting to actions of abuse is the gateway to healing and reclaiming our original wholeness.

Wholeness requires that we begin to experience Earth as home and the community of living beings as family. This requires a conscious awakening of the senses so that we feel at home in our own bodies and in the body of the Earth. Glendinning explains:

> . . . listening to one another, we begin the task of reuniting the body of the human community. Finally, we re-embody ourselves when we reconnect with the body of the Earth. . . . Only on the scale of the senses—the 'human' scale upon which our ancestors evolved—do we enter into revitalized communion with the Earth; only in embodied intimacy do we begin to see the natural world as our ultimate source of wholeness and, therefore, safety.[4]

In this journey back into the Primal Matrix the guidance of the spirit world is available through non-ordinary states of consciousness which become subtle bridges to health. Glendinning includes the following Anishinaabe/ Ojibway prayer as an example of invoking guidance from the spirit world:

> 'Grandfather,
> Look at our brokenness.
>
> We know that in all creation
> Only the human family
> Has strayed from the Sacred Way.

We know that we are the ones
Who are divided
And we are the ones
Who must come together
To walk in the Sacred Way.

Grandfather,
Sacred One
Teach us love, compassion and honor
That we may heal the earth and heal each other'.[5]

It is odd that even though our inner being as well as our moving body converse daily with the natural environment we are *not sufficiently aware* of this interaction, nor of the ways in which we as a species have inoculated ourselves against perceiving and responding to our own abusive acts against the Earth. Recall what Charles Tart offered as a reason for a lack of response. He identifies a *perceptual defense*, created by the conscious mind, which kicks in to reshape, rationalize and normalize a situation which may actually be precarious. This reactive defense mechanism replaces the instinct for self-preservation housed in the unconscious mind which should take effect automatically. Tart's reasoning coincides with Diamond's analysis of how societies collapse, especially the decision by a power elite to uphold the status quo, a move which may be temporarily adaptive, but in the long run is maladaptive because it endangers society's survival.

Glendinning argues that in order to relieve our homelessness and live in harmony with the Earth we must call upon the "internal witness who can provide a haven of safety, some would say a part of our psyches that is bigger than the problem and not identified with it . . . the observer-friend."[6] In spiritual teachings this 'observer-friend' is the Witness, the true *I* or authentic self—that which sees the truth or reality underneath the illusion. The life quest of a spiritual aspirant is to uncover this *I* by paring away, through the discriminating faculty of mind, all the limiting ideas and opinions that compose the *not I*. Central to this process of elimination is the practice of awareness or mindfulness which is the adaptive tool whereby health is restored, both to ourselves and to the planet.

Tibetan Buddhist teacher Chögyam Trungpa asserts that being aware is the weapon that the spiritual warrior uses to discover *drala*—"the magical quality of existence or natural wisdom."[7] *Dra* means *enemy* or *opponent* and *la* means *above*. To be 'above the enemy' means to perceive unity instead of duality; aggression is thereby dissolved and replaced by communion. Since, according to Buddhist teaching, all life forms are dependent and co-arising, the experience of being embodied in the one consciousness *is* magical: I am the world and I love the world as my incarnate self.

THE NARCISSISTIC SELF

In *The Sane Society*, first published in 1955, psychologist Erich Fromm differentiates the normal narcissism of the child from a later developmental narcissism in which the growing child fails to develop the capacity to love. Fromm states that this failure to relate meaningfully to the world is the "essence of all severe psychic pathology."[8] This unnatural narcissism is in fact a sign of insanity. By implication, the society created by narcissistic individuals is insane, or unhealthy (the word *sane* means *healthy*). Unlike tribal societies, in which solidarity with one's fellows is a given, modern capitalist society weakens social bonds, in effect creating individuals "estranged from each other but held together by selfish interests and by the necessity to make use of each other."[9] This selfishness, says Fromm, contravenes the natural social instinct in man, inhibiting his need to share his life and help his fellows.

The estrangement from one's immediate world has only deepened as the twenty-first century unfolds with the fragmentation of the family and the alienation from Nature. The modern addiction to a way of thinking and a way of life that chain the natural world to human desire is not freedom—unless we define freedom as the right to do as we please. We are witnessing the deterioration of the natural world caused by such 'free' acts. The inevitable diminishment in quality of life can only enslave us in due course. This is ego's deceptive definition of freedom. Real freedom involves character traits such as self-control, detachment from desire, and equanimity in the face of adversity. The Buddha, for example, describes an enlightened person as one who "has sovereignty over himself."[10]

Our first task, therefore, in overcoming an increasingly distorted worldview is to face the supremacy of ego as lead actor on the world stage. The ambition for power over others and over Earth's resources and the desire for monetary wealth with all the creature comforts it brings have built a political, economic and social hierarchy of players who ignore the needs of less powerful citizens and seize the resources of less developed nations.

Eckhart Tolle is a German-born spiritual teacher and author whose first book, *The Power of Now*, galvanized a spiritual awakening in many people. His teaching centers on the deceptively simple practice of presence—of learning to stay connected to the present moment instead of getting lost in daydreams, imaginings, and other random thoughts that preoccupy the mind.

Tolle credits his own awakening to a transformative experience that brought him out of chronic depression into a level of consciousness he defines as blissful. In *A New Earth: Awakening to Your Life's Purpose* Tolle explains how humanity is currently stuck in a stage of egoic mind that conflates being with having—the fiction of ownership. "I have, therefore I am. And the more I have, the more I am."[11] For ego, enough is never enough.

Egoic mind is conditioned by the past and feeds on past experiences, especially negative experiences, which have consolidated into a "pain-body" which is both individual and collective. This pain-body resembles the collected experiences of Glendinning's traumatized personality. We feel alienated; we are always trying to get home, but never feel at home, says Tolle. This is because the 'me' that feels separate and alienated is not the real me; it parades as me. This false or illusory self comes into existence by identification with a 'voice in the head' that constantly prattles its commentaries, judgments, opinions, and preconceptions. Ego adopts an allotment of ideas and beliefs to 'think about' and uses these files of habitual thinking, stored in memory, to defend its ideas and further its designs. How can such thinking be creative or free? We can learn from the past; but without the practice of presence we will act mechanically, unable to pick up what the present moment has to teach us. Take the example of meeting an old acquaintance. Whom do we see? Do we see the person afresh or do we see our ideas about the person, formed by past interactions? Perhaps he or she has changed. Will we recognize that change? Not if we view the world through filters to which ego has given its stamp of approval.

The collective pain-body of the human ego has cultivated a habitual pattern of conflict and conquest by which it inflicts harm on itself and the world. That harm now extends to the planet. However, according to Tolle, this stage of evolution cannot last because it is a dysfunctional display of madness, poised through science and technology to threaten the survival of life. He states: "To recognize one's own insanity is, of course, the arising of sanity, the beginning of healing and transcendence."[12] The human species is in transition as a new spirituality arises—one which is not built on traditional religious dogma and structure but on a deep awakening to one's true identity beyond ego. This is "the new heaven."[13] The new earth will be a planetary reflection of this awakening as more and more people realize that "humanity is now faced with a stark choice: Evolve or die."[14] During the transition social violence, says Tolle, will intensify because the collective pain-body will resist dissolution, but "the ego . . . and all its ossified structures, whether they be religious, or other institutions, corporations, or governments will disintegrate from within, no matter how deeply entrenched they appear to be."[15]

EDEN

Ironically, fairy tales and nursery rhymes meant for children hold wisdom well suited for adult reading. Consider the nursery rhyme about Humpty Dumpty: Humpty Dumpty sat on the wall / Humpty Dumpty had a great fall / All the king's horses and all the king's men / Couldn't put Humpty together again.

The origins of this nursery rhyme are obscure. A number of theories as to its meaning range from a reference to political events in English history to its use as a symbol for the Fall of Man in James Joyce's *Finnegan's Wake*. The latter may be instructive for the following argument. Humpty Dumpty is an animated, anthropomorphic egg; that is, he is given human traits. This tendency to anthropomorphize non-human entities is ancient and may point to an innate remembrance of the unity of all life forms. It is interesting that a common creation myth in diverse cultures is that of a cosmic egg from which the universe emerges, including primordial man. For example, the *Rig Veda*, one of the Hindu Vedic scriptures, describes in two myths the arising of the cosmos and man. In one myth, Hiranyagarbha, the world egg, produces the Creation. In the second myth, the world appears through the sacrifice of Purusha, a cosmic anthropomorphic being, who undergoes dismemberment. His body parts become the material universe. Purusha is defined as the eternal Self or Consciousness through which all created beings are connected.

The Dogon, an ancient tribal people who live in Mali, West Africa, also have a cosmic mythology that features an egg. This cosmic egg, *aduno tal*, releases seven vibrations in a spiral or helix pattern that creates the whole cosmos and every particular within it. Thus microcosm reflects macrocosm. The creative process originates in the center of the egg as a germinating seed. Primordial man is viewed as enclosed and prefigured in this egg of the world; an entwined man and cosmos develop together.

Various cultural myths and stories also tell of a *fall* caused by an error in judgment which dislocates man from his primordial home within the cosmos. Man's disobedience in the Garden of Eden, related in the Book of Genesis, is one such story. Returning to the nursery rhyme, we read that Humpty Dumpty has "a great fall." Humpty Dumpty's fate can be related to the creation myths outlined above: he is created but suffers a fall and "all the king's horses and all the king's men" symbolize worldly authority which is powerless to repair his fallen state. From our modern perspective, if this anthropomorphized egg is seen as the human species falling under the weight of a crisis which it has created, then the rhyme argues that the spiritual illness of hubris, the cardinal sin of pride, cannot be healed at a worldly level of authority. The cure must come from a higher level which effects a spiritual cleansing. According to indigenous peoples all sickness begins in the spiritual realm and must be treated by a shaman at that causal level. The ecological crisis which now confronts us has erupted from a spiritual illness which has infected our memory and made us forget our status as children of the Earth.

In his novel *Ishmael* Daniel Quinn uses a gorilla named Ishmael to teach an inquisitive, disenchanted human being about two types of people: takers and leavers. Leavers have been around for close to three million years, minding their own business and subsisting mainly through hunting/gathering and/ or horticulture. The takers are the conquerors of this world who eradicate or assimilate people and their cultures. They rule the world through their definition of who is right and good (they and people like them are right and good). This violent trajectory started some 10,000 years ago with the advent of agriculture; it will end, says Ishmael, the only way it can, in self-destruction because "the people of your culture [takers] said, 'We're as wise as the gods and can rule the world as well as they.' When they took *into their own hands* the power of life and death over the world, their doom was assured."[16] Leavers do not have this knowledge, nor therefore the desperation to impose their way of life on anyone. Their contentment with just being and letting be is their wisdom.

The Fall of Man, as recorded in the Book of Genesis, is rich in meaning. One way to interpret the story is the following. Our parents, Adam and Eve, are given a job to till the garden. The word for *tilling* in Hebrew is *leawod.* This word also connotes service. Adam and Eve are caretakers of paradise, sustained by the Tree of Life. When Adam and Eve eat the apple of temptation on the Tree of the Knowledge of Good and Evil in order to become masters instead of servants, they are expelled. This disobedience is the original sin. It is more accurate to say they left of their own free will by spurning the privilege of serving God by tending the Garden which was Earth in its perfected form. Each day that our kinship with the Earth is denied we are being expelled from the Garden by our own thoughts and actions. The memory of the Garden as home fades as our minds are distracted by a constant stream of addictive stimulants that deliver instant gratification and temporarily anaesthetize the pain-body we carry within us. These pain-killers include alcohol, drugs, sex, spectator sports, shopping, gambling, TV, smart phones, and a marketplace of ever-evolving technological gadgetry.

Thomas Merton views the Fall as the continual decision, even at a subliminal level, to leave our divine center. Whenever ego is in charge we are leaving the Garden of Eden. Merton describes how Adam put "the lusts and ambitions of a selfish and fleshly ego" between his true self and God and "mentally reconstructed the whole universe in his own image and likeness. That is the painful and useless labor which has been inherited by his descendants."[17] In order to return to the Garden the new Adam must "go back by the way he came. The path lies through the center of our own soul. . . . Before we can realize who we really are we must become conscious of the fact that the person we think we are is at best an impostor and a stranger."[18]

In *Up From Eden*, integral theorist Ken Wilber analyzes the Fall. His description resembles Merton's in notable ways. The Creation, says Wilber, is a process of *involution* downwards and outwards, a movement towards matter, away from unity towards differentiation, separation and dismemberment. The sense of a separate self, an ego, *is* the Fall itself. In other words, the Fall or Original Sin is not an action but a perception, an awareness of separation and loss, a forgetting of Unity. According to Wilber, this fall into egoic consciousness is a necessary stage in human development because it releases the human being from the "uroboric consciousness" or innocence of the Garden.[19] Being separate from the true self or *Atman* (Wilber uses the Hindu term) the human being invents "the Atman Project" which is the creation of a series of substitute gratifications that cannot satisfy because they are delusory.[20] Spiritual evolution reverses this dispersive process. The human species matures through a transmutation of ego energy into finer vibrations that stimulate a centripetal movement of successive unifications and integrations. This move towards wholeness resurrects the memory of one's true self and the Larger Self in which that self is embedded. Creation is part of the Fall but does not prevent a return to unity so long as man recognizes Creation as the face of Spirit.

The Earth is suffering because the boundaries that ego has set up to protect its turf prevent the human being from recognizing that all species have equal value in co-creating a stable and healthy environment. In a description reminiscent of the Confucian circles of relationships, Stalking Wolf, an Apache shaman, states:

Man is like an island, a circle within circles. Man is separated from these outer circles by his mind, his beliefs, and the limitations put upon him by a life away from the Earth. His isolation from the greater circles of self is suffocating and prevents him from seeing life clearly and purely. Beyond man's island of ego, his prison, lies the world of the spirit-that-moves-in-all-things, the force that is found in all things. It is a world that expands man's universe and helps him to fuse himself to the Earth.[21]

ANIMA MUNDI: HER RISE AND DEMISE

Intimations of a universal primal energy—often personified as a god or goddess—inspired the cosmologies of ancient civilizations such as the Chinese, Indian, Greek and Egyptian. These civilizations conceived of the universe as a whole, created and pervaded by an ineffable substance. The celestial, natural and human domains coalesced in a holistic synthesis. The task of the human mind was to comprehend this organic unity, of which it was a part, and live by its laws. Only thus could one know one's true self.

The early Greek philosophers such as Heraclitus and Plato espoused a living *kosmos* which held and nourished a network of life forms. Heraclitus describes a divine *Logos* or Supreme Thought that "'steers all things through all things.'"[22] Plato calls this Thought the *Good*. Eternal Ideas that manifest as material forms are contained within the Good. Thus the idea of *tree*, for example, manifests as oak, beech, and maple; and these differentiate further into specific types of oak, beech and maple. Life is infused into the kosmos through the agency of *anima mundi*, the world soul, which in turn is enlivened by the Great Architect. By means of anima mundi, writes Plato in the *Timaeus*, the Great Architect translates the Ideas into physical form with "the soul woven right through from the centre to the outermost heaven."[23]

Plotinus (204–270 AD), the mystical Neoplatonist philosopher of Egyptian descent, adds to this Platonic design the idea of a Cosmic Mind or *Nous* that emanates from the *One* (or the Good) and pervades the body of the One, which is the universe. To the scholastics of the High Middle Ages, such as Duns Scotus, this unity of life appeared as the *unus mundus*, or *one world*. The idea of a single Whole, from which all diversified individual organisms emerged and shared existence, and into which they ultimately merged was revived in the twentieth century by Carl Jung. The unus mundus is closely associated with the concept of anima mundi which, according to Jung, is one of the archetypes held in humanity's collective unconscious.

From the classical Greek era to the present time the cultural history of the West has shown slow but dramatic changes in worldview. By tracing these changes we discern a gradual but distinctive reductionist trend in how the mind is defined and used. History reveals an inventive yet hazardous detour by which humans condone an indiscriminate appropriation of natural resources. A holistic use of the full panoply of mental-emotional functions shrinks to a mechanized, aggressive use of the mind in service to the human goal of conquest. This self-serving use of mind coincides with the erosion of the influence of female energy embodied in the archetype of anima mundi. Anthropologist Loren Eiseley is unequivocal about the dark path that modern man has chosen. He writes: "Modern man, the world eater, respects no space and no thing green or furred as sacred. The march of the machines has entered his blood."[24] And his mind. The goals of quantification, efficiency, material comfort and expediency gradually dwarf higher faculties of reason and compassion. American transcendentalist philosopher Henry David Thoreau put the situation succinctly when he said: "Men have become the tools of their tools."[25] If an alignment with the cosmic order is the way of redemption for modern man then the way forward is to recognize and practice a mind free of ideas of self-aggrandizement.

When Greek culture was transplanted to Rome, and, after the collapse of the Roman Empire, bled into the medieval worldview the early vision of a single universal order illuminated by anima mundi was transmitted to Christian theology. Europe as a continent of nation-states was but a gleam in history's eye. Instead, from 1000 AD to about 1400 AD this landmass was synonymous with *Christendom*. For the medieval mind, God's design consisted of a well-defined feudal society, divinely ordained kings and, reigning over all, the Roman Catholic Church which wielded sacred and secular authority.

In the Christian adaptation of the Greco-Roman geocentric/Ptolemaic model of the universe a giant, perfectly formed organism of seven spheres or orders of being (comprising Heaven, Earth and Hell) included celestial beings, planets, and the animal, vegetable and mineral kingdoms. All spheres revolved around the Earth at the center and were permeated and connected by anima mundi who was powered by God's omnipresence and divine will. God ruled over all, surrounded by his angels. Christ was the new Apollo—the Sun/ Son of divine illumination. The faithful were enjoined by the Pope, clerics and their feudal counterparts in authority to worship the new *Logos* or Word of God by obeying the dictates of Mother Church. A vertical Great Chain of Being defined each creature's fixed place in the divine hierarchy.

Humans, being made in the image of God, were placed just below the angels. As Psalm 8 states: "For thou hast made him a little lower than the angels and has crowned him with glory and honour. Thou madest him to have dominion over the works of thy hands; thou hast put all things under his feet."[26] The Great Chain of Being reflected a mythic geography that was accepted as reality because the mythic imagination and vision, as in ancient cultures, still pervaded the medieval mind.

In his five-volume masterwork *Utriusque Cosmi*, seventeenth century English Anglican physician and occult philosopher Robert Fludd displays an interesting interpretation of medieval cosmology that suggests an androgynous blend of male and female powers. For example, in one of his engravings the female anima mundi, featured at the center, is conflated with both the male kabbalistic angel Metattron (world-soul and divine form of the Jewish Messiah) and with Jesus Christ.[27]

The Christian anima mundi continued to perform her ancient service as creative and nurturing intermediary between matter and spirit, between the natural order and the supernatural order. This elevation of the feminine as a fructifying energy recalls the indigenous animistic world of the Earth Mother and the fertility Goddess of early agrarian-based societies. However, in her Platonic role, anima mundi was less sensuous, more conceptual and ethereal.

Figure 4.1.   Great Chain of Being, 1579.
Drawing from *Rhetorica christiana* by Fray Diego de Valades.

It was Plato after all who believed that the soul or *anima* of an individual needed to escape the body and the world of Nature in order to be purified. Plato's vision of a disembodied anima mundi resonated with the early Church Fathers who called upon the faithful to transcend attachment to the temporal, impure material world and find immortality in heaven. Thus, although the medieval vision of an *ensouled universe*, reflecting a God-centered paradigm, continued to espouse anima mundi as a ruling symbol she, as corruptible Nature, became increasingly divested of power and identified with pagan idolatry and animistic folk religion. The loss of her exalted position was not unexpected; anima mundi was never fully embraced by the male-dominated

Church of Rome. By assimilating the female characteristics of anima mundi to the Virgin Mary the Church cleansed her of sexual connotation and, by assuming her maternal aspects, became mother and nurturer to the faithful.

Christian doctrine about the natural world is threaded with ambiguity. On the one hand nature mystics like St. Francis of Assisi promoted an inclusive view in which God was equally present in all creatures through the loving, maternal image of anima mundi as Nature. On the other hand, St. Thomas Aquinas reasoned that, according to the Great Chain of Being, plants and animals achieve their divine function and legitimacy by serving man, the most sublime of God's creatures. By placing the human species on a higher rung

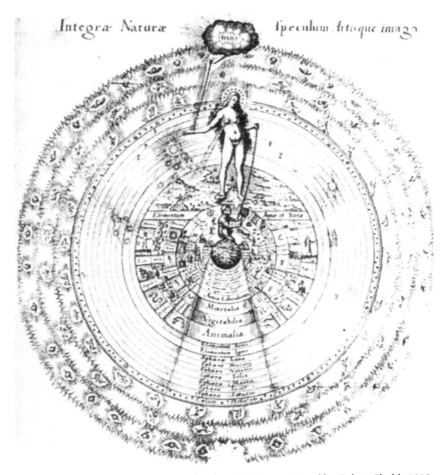

Figure 4.2. *Integra Naturae*, engraving from *Utriusque Cosmi* by Robert Fludd, 1618.
Courtesy of Wellcome Images.

than all other species in Nature conceptual seeds were sown that eventually rendered matter inanimate and vulnerable to abuse. As the Church moved towards concluding that the natural world was a desacralized domain, created by God but tainted with profane matter, it was inevitable that Nature (and anima mundi) would become the abode of the devil.

As the power of anima mundi waned, the way was paved for an identification of female energy with subversive activities, prompting accusations of heresy and witchcraft. The Late Middle Ages was a turbulent time of protracted wars, the Black Death (1347–1350) which decimated one-third of the population of Christendom, outbreaks of famine, and a schism in the Church which revealed both deep-seated corruption and a desperate grasp for power as the ties of sympathy between clergy and the faithful frayed. These calamities spurred a series of inquisitions beginning in the mid-1200s in France and lasting until the 1500s with the Spanish Inquisition. The major victims of these spurious trials were women. Accused of pagan nature-worship and witchcraft many of these women were burned at the stake. Catholic clergyman Heinrich Kramer helped his besieged Church find scapegoats by publishing the *Malleus Maleficarum* in 1487—a treatise on the diagnosis and extermination of witches.

It is instructive at this point in the story of anima mundi to discuss the prevailing worldview that justified—and to some extent continues to justify—the subordinate position of women. Since the time of Aristotle the cultural belief in woman's innate inferiority of soul and body was attended by folk superstitions that associated women with black magic and witchery. In folk belief women had the power to usurp male authority by depleting a man's life force through the sexual act. It was believed that the brain marrow was one and the same substance as semen, giving males a natural intelligence imperiled by women's wiles. Anthropologist Mary Douglas points to a cross-cultural perception of bodily emissions, such as menstrual blood, as polluting and therefore threatening. The ambiguous status of blood, being of the body but also exiting the body during menstruation, is magnified by the fact that blood itself is symbolic of the opposing powers of life and death. During the witchcraze midwives were often accused of witchcraft because their work put them in touch with defiling bodily fluids.

A long-standing identification of the female sex with Nature compounds this cross-cultural denigration of the female body. In a seminal essay called "Is Female to Male as Nature is to Culture?" (1974) anthropologist Sherry Ortner cites extensive research that shows a universal perception of women as closer to Nature than men who are seen as the creators of Culture. The equation of the female sex with Nature is understandable as a statement of the biological function of giving birth and nurturing the young, but in male-dominated cultures this association can translate as identification of the female with the wild (and therefore inferior) status of Nature whilst the male's role to remake and redeem Nature bestows superior status. The identification of Nature as female underlies the indiscriminate exploitation of natural resources by man's cultural achievement—industrialization. Culture is identified with reason, the province of man; Nature and the female are associated with emotion. Again, a similar hierarchy prevails: as Nature is beneath Culture so is emotion beneath reason.

As the witchcraze was subsiding in the Old World a more localized but equally irrational phenomenon—the Salem witch trials of 1692—caught fire in the Massachusetts Bay Colony of Puritan America. This strange eruption of paranoia can be traced to an ambivalent attitude about wilderness. The first colonists who stepped off the Mayflower in 1620 were overwhelmed by a vast wilderness—Nature in the raw. This vision aroused opposing reactions. William Bradford, for example, saw "'a hideous and desolate wilderness'"— chaotic and demonic. John Winthrop, on the other hand, saw the Garden of Eden as he breathed in the luscious aroma of wild strawberries that wafted onto the deck of the *Arabella*.[28] Each man knew, however, that it was his duty under God to subdue, tame and civilize the wilderness so that paradise would be revealed.

The civilized landscape of the New England village with its white church, village green and well-tended farms represented God's saving grace. Satan's realm was the dark, forested wilderness beyond the village. Wilderness was perceived as a danger—both the interior and the exterior wilderness. This subliminal anxiety was exacerbated by a repressive Calvinist dogma, especially in regards to sexual activity, preached by a male-dominated, theocratic governing body. The Salem witch trials were a culmination of fear and repression imprinted from the Old World. Women, perceived as bereft of reason and aligned with the dangers of untamed wilderness, made up the majority of the accused whereas the accusers were young girls who were trusted by the judges because of their premenstrual purity. In fact the girls were acting out their repressive Calvinist upbringing.

It is ironic that the first woman accused of witchery in the Massachusetts Bay Colony, Anne Hutchinson, was known for her impressive intellect. Although a devout Christian and mother of sixteen children, Hutchinson's activities as midwife and leader of women's meetings to discuss scripture were used by the autocratic Governor Winthrop to fabricate a case for witchery which led to her untimely death.

Returning to the story of anima mundi: as the sixteenth century arrived, a cultural florescence known as the Renaissance countered the regressive trends of the Late Middle Ages by temporarily resurrecting anima mundi.

Geographically centered in Florence, Italy the Renaissance revived an exalted anima mundi by identifying female energy with the beauty of Nature. Philosophers and artists experienced the natural world as a divine incarnation where all beings were present to each other in harmony, engendering in the beholder a cosmic love. An explosive enthusiasm and confidence in human intellectual and artistic capacities suggest a powerful merging of male and female energies that pointed to a new vision of the human self. Like a bird let out of its cage the human being no longer felt himself confined to the role of servant to God and Church but became conscious of innate god-like powers. Indeed, he was capable of wondrous deeds which were actualized in the arts, philosophy and science. And just as the body of Nature was restored to a place of honor, so the human body was no longer viewed as a hindrance to the soul's salvation but as a work of art to be celebrated—as exemplified in the sculptures of Michelangelo and the anatomical drawings of Leonardo de Vinci. In Botticelli's exquisite painting, *La Primavera* (1482), the rendering of the central figure of Venus demonstrates this new convergence of body and spirit. She looks both seductive and chaste, earthly and celestial. The sensuous energy of anima mundi combines with attributes of the Virgin Mary, as a cupid of romantic love hovers over Venus' head.

The Platonic Academy, established by philosopher Marsilio Ficino (1433–1499), renewed the study of Greek philosophy, especially the 'divine Plato.' Ficino taught that the maternal anima mundi transmits seeds from which all natural things are born; the artist's task is to transform Nature to an even finer perfection through mind's creative energy. Meanwhile, the Renaissance physician and alchemist Paracelsus was laying the early foundations of modern medicine and chemistry. Following the hermetic tradition he believed that healing was associated with discovering the hidden correspondences that harmonized man as microcosm with Nature as macrocosm. As an alchemist he was familiar with the high and vulgar forms of alchemy in the probing of Nature's secrets, held in the bosom of anima mundi. It was the vulgar form that would usher in the birth of science. Theodore Roszak, pioneer in the study of ecopsychology, comments on this pivotal historical juncture in his book *The Voice of the Earth*. He states:

> Their ways with the *anima mundi* were very different. Their hope was that by occult means, they might harness the forces of the universe. High and vulgar alchemy represent two divergent approaches to the natural world, one based on respectful communion, the other on brute force. Of the two, it was vulgar alchemy that was destined to inherit the future.[29]

The efforts of alchemists to magically manipulate natural forces—an activity shared by indigenous cultures—"is based on the assumption that there is a responsive mind on the 'other side' of nature whose sympathy we can elicit and whose secrets we can probe.'"[30] Today that magic which man increasingly uses to manipulate Nature is called technology but the belief in a responsive mind on the other side has vanished.

The sixteenth century advanced into the seventeenth century with a religious institution reeling from charges of corruption. Pope Alexander VI, for example, was accused of simony, nepotism and violation of his vow of chastity by fathering four children. The waning of ecclesiastical power was compounded by new cosmological evidence from the Polish astronomer Copernicus (1473–1543) published in 1543. His thesis, supported later by technological improvements to the telescope perfected by Galileo (1564–1642), pronounced the universe as heliocentric, not geocentric. Because the Copernican worldview invalidated the Great Chain of Being it was resisted by the Church as contrary to scripture. In 1615 the Roman Inquisition banned the heliocentric model; however, by that time there was no refuting the evidence.

The medieval worldview was being challenged and subverted from both religious and scientific angles while at the same time the social structure of feudalism that constituted everyday life was breaking down. The principal reformers of the Church and pioneers of the Protestant Reformation, Martin Luther (1483–1546) and John Calvin (1509–1564), did little to advance the cause of anima mundi as no intermediary between God and man was necessary when the individual could have direct contact with God as a member of the *priesthood of all believers*. Luther placed Nature on the "'left hand of God'" which associated her "'hostile energies'" with demonic powers.[31] This denigration of the natural world, however, was not embraced by every Protestant, particularly the mystics. One mystic, Thomas Traherne (1636–1674), an English Anglican poet and clergyman, describes in his *Centuries of Meditations* the rapturous experiences of communing with God in and through Nature. George Fox (1624–1691), founder of the Religious Society of Friends, known as the Quakers, insisted that the light of God's presence within the soul was just as accessible in the meadows and woods as in a house of prayer.

Calvin imagined God as a male authoritarian figure and the natural world as the arena whereby God's agents—the elect—were entitled to imitate God and glorify Him by wresting control of Nature's bounty. Out of this doctrine emerged the Protestant Ethic, a work ethic which applauded individual enterprise as a means of praising God. A profitable business was a sign of God's favor, an assurance of personal salvation. As the Western capitalist mode of production developed, however, the purist doctrine of the Protestant Ethic would twist into license to accumulate wealth for ego's pleasure and power.

The Protestant reformist platform of individual agency and industriousness, with the natural world as a God-given but spiritually flawed material

comparing them to feminine wiles. Just as the female sex is wild by nature and needs to be tamed by the male in an aggressive manner so the scientist has a duty, said Bacon, to bind and constrain Nature in order to penetrate her secrets. He must not feel any guilt about the "'inquisition of nature'" because only the human species is given a soul by God; the non-human world, though created by God, is soulless, without self-will or purpose and moved by mechanical laws.[34] Baconian misogyny contributed to the cultural formation of the patriarchal model that legitimized gender inequality in Western society. Carolyn Merchant, environmental historian of science, incorporates Bacon's own words in a summation of his view when she writes that "Nature must be 'bound into service' and made a 'slave'. . . . As a woman's womb had symbolically yielded to the forceps, so nature's womb harbored secrets that through technology could be wrested from her grasp for use in the improvement of the human condition."[35]

Ethical concerns were dismissed. In fact, Christianity was used by Bacon, Descartes and later Enlightenment thinkers to bolster an anthropocentric design. Biblical scripture—Genesis 1:28 in particular—provided a handy justification for desacralizing the natural landscape and legitimizing man's plunder of Nature. The verse reads: "Be fruitful and multiply, and fill the earth and subdue it; and have dominion over the fish of the sea and over the birds of the air and over every living thing that moves upon the earth."[36] By interpreting the word *dominion* to mean *domination* instead of *stewardship*, man could simply enact his God-given status as ruler of the world.

Rene Descartes was a mathematician, philosopher and scientist who had a strong influence on Western cultural history. He saw himself in a dual role as man of science and son of the Roman Catholic Church. Yet his passion to promulgate a new 'faith'—that man could know about God and self directly through the divine gift of reason—was in actuality a veiled critique of ecclesiastical power.[37] Consumed with existential questions such as 'how do I know I exist?' and 'how do I know God exists?' Descartes endeavors to answer these questions by applying logic. The Greek *Logos* is reduced to logic which becomes the premier methodology of science. Descartes deduces that man's mind is the evidence of the existence of both man and God. It is logical, says Descartes, in his *Meditations*, that because I can think I therefore exist, and "the fact that I exist and have an idea in me of a perfect entity—that is, God—conclusively entails that God does in fact exist."[38] By hinging God's existence upon man's existence Descartes' argument, while logical, lacks the discriminating force of intellect. Moreover, by elevating human reason to the infallible position once held by ecclesiastical authority Descartes, in Richard Tarnas' words, "unintentionally began a theological Copernican revolution, for his mode of reasoning suggested that God's existence was established by human reason and not vice versa."[39] When Descartes asserts that thinking precedes being he is also inverting the mystical experience at the heart of all religions which posits that the true *I* is not ego but Spirit: '*I* am, therefore I (as ego) think and act.'

For Descartes only the human species has mind and soul. Animal species exist only as bodies, which are machines. All bodies, including the human body, are *automata* or machines. Thus mind is not only superior to and separate from body—the famous Cartesian split—but a more ominous dichotomy is set up that separates the human being from Nature which is denuded of all animate, intelligent and spiritual qualities. This dichotomy would be consequential because it denies human participation in Nature and legitimizes the plundering of the world.[40]

Looking back to the beginning of this timeline in the 5th c. BCE Greece, we see that the image of anima mundi has undergone a progressive reduction from animate and sacred, to inanimate and profane, to a point where She is irrelevant—except as an object (Nature) to exploit. By the end of the seventeenth century the embodiment of a female, nurturing energy had gone underground. Her counter-cultural voice spoke through a few philosophers such as William Gilbert and Blaise Pascal, through peasants (especially women) and, as colonial explorers would discover, through indigenous peoples who revered Mother Earth. Heart—associated with female energy and anima mundi—bowed before head which was identified with male energy, science, and, as the next chapter will reveal, an industrial economy. The organic mind-heart unity had ruptured, causing a deep internal psychological rift between intellect and emotion and an equally deep external tension between humanity and Nature. Memory of a Primal Matrix had retreated into the dim shadowland of the mind.

Chapter Five

Capitalism and the Rule of Technological Mind

Suit the action to the word, the word to the action, with this special observance, that you o'erstep not the modesty of nature; for anything so overdone is from the purpose of playing, whose end . . . is to hold, as 'twere, the mirror up to nature. . . .

—Hamlet, *Hamlet* III:2.

The word *economics* contains the same root as *ecology*: *eco* which means *house*, from the Greek *oikos*. The study of the physical and biological laws of the house of the universe, and in particular this planet Earth, known as ecology, is mirrored in economics as the study of the *nomos* or laws and customs of the house in regards to the production, distribution and consumption of goods and services. When the Industrial Revolution began in the late eighteenth century the term *political economy* was used interchangeably with *economics*. Indeed, the close relationship between economic and political systems revealed that the parliamentary system of England, where industrialization began, and the American democracy where it traveled and flourished provided a fertile political environment based in laws that protected the freedom of individuals and groups (which later formed as companies, then corporations) to pursue business endeavors unencumbered.

Industrialization accentuated the mechanistic paradigm elucidated by Bacon and Descartes in which Nature is seen as dead matter to be exploited for human use. In this chapter an investigation into the origin and development of capitalism will reveal the ways in which a fixation on material gain contributed to a growing imbalance in the capitalist system. An analysis of Alexis de Tocqueville's early impressions of the American blend of democracy and capitalism suggests that when profit outweighs service a nation's health is endangered. The emergence of a corporate capitalist ideology, susceptible to greed, and a narrow use of mental faculties called *technological mind*, have produced inequities in the distribution of wealth, created a society of consumers alienated from each other and the natural world, and led to the unregulated use of natural resources. The ecological crises we now face are products of the Industrial Revolution which placed the capstone on the achievements of the Scientific Revolution even as it revealed an underlying menace: *wétiko*.

Wétiko is a Native American word that means *cannibal*. In *The Last Hours of Ancient Sunlight* Thom Hartmann uses the word to describe the modern Western worldview which condones the enslavement of both people and Nature. This worldview legitimizes the brutal consumption of human lives: "we 'eat' (consume) other humans by destroying them," says Hartmann, "by destroying their lands, and consuming their life-force by enslaving them either physically or economically."[1] Slavery of any sort, says Hartmann, is "another way of taking the sunlight stored in somebody else's body and 'harnessing' it for the benefit of the exploiter."[2]

Colonialism exemplifies *wétiko*. The colonial conquest of native peoples of the Americas and Africa, which dates back to the sixteenth century, is linked in the nineteenth century to Social Darwinism—the justification of slavery through a culturally condoned idea of superior and inferior races based on natural selection and the *survival of the fittest*.[3] The colonial worldview dovetailed with the early factory abuses in Europe's first industrial nation—England—and continues to influence today's economic behavior in the form of neocolonialism. David Korten, former professor at Harvard Business School and critic of the globalized corporate ideology, calls the efforts by multinational corporations to take over resources in third world countries *imperial consciousness*.[4] The predictable results of this injustice are environmental deterioration and the impoverishment and displacement of native peoples. Neocolonialism is also evident in the abuse of migrant farm workers and sweatshop laborers who become the collateral damage of a corrupted form of free enterprise. Underlying these abuses is the abuse of the Earth herself: the ultimate *wétiko*.

THE BIRTH OF CAPITALISM

The Industrial Revolution strengthened the paradigm that science had introduced—a man-centered universe whose ruling symbol was the machine—and expanded it into the world of economics. A vigorous economy bolstered the idea of European cultural supremacy and reshaped the Judeo-Christian belief in the ultimate fulfillment of the chosen people, giving it a secular packaging. The capacity to harness and use the forces of Nature to make a new world was fulfilled through industrialization.

Perception of the natural world as an encyclopedia of facts and figures to be quantified and analyzed neglects the existence of nonphysical facts which, as British economist E. F. Schumacher says, "remain unnoticed unless the work of the senses is controlled and completed by certain 'higher' faculties of mind."[5] These higher powers are accessed through self-awareness which "is the power that makes man human and also capable of transcending his humanity."[6] For Bacon and Descartes, however, the purview of science was physical facts alone and the purpose of science was the manipulation of Nature for man's benefit. As Schumacher notes, "'science for manipulation' tends almost inevitably to advance from the manipulation of nature to that of people."[7]

The economic system which emerged from 'science for manipulation' was capitalism. Through capitalism the conquest of Nature—known as Progress—was fast-tracked. It was believed that in its pure form capitalism followed the market law of supply and demand which corresponded to the laws of Nature. This pure form is known as *laizzez-faire* capitalism. The laws of Nature, which are based in competition *and* cooperation, continually repair and sustain equilibrium in the web of life through the principles of interconnectedness and reciprocity. These same principles were thought to apply to an economic system when the web of trade is operating in a balanced way. However, as in any system, corruption can occur. The balance from which Nature never veers is susceptible in human affairs to manipulation so that imbalance allows the forces of competition to overshadow cooperation. Mahatma Gandhi stated the case succinctly when he said: "There is a sufficiency in the world for man's need but not for man's greed."[8] When trust, integrity and sacrifice—qualities which nourish the economic web—fade, greed takes over.

In a web, whether it be an ecosystem or an economic system, the laws of interconnectedness and reciprocity are in effect *whether the system is healthy or not*. A loss of equilibrium affects every member of the web so that, for example, reciprocity, rather than advantaging each party, as in a bartering transaction, is skewed to favor one and harm the other. In the current political-economic climate in the United States it could be argued that political power and economic wealth are held by a small percentage of the population (the one-percenters) who own or are associated with multinational corporations and financial institutions who abide by no national boundary or loyalty. These corporate entities play the system to their advantage, putting the powerless at a disadvantage.

With the dramatic shift in cosmological perspective, from a geocentric to a heliocentric universe, man's perception of himself shrank to a speck in a desacralized universe. Now, with the birth of capitalism, man was about to exchange that puny role for an equally inferior one—that of cog in a machine. Wendell Berry deftly describes the effusive but illusive hope that the Scientific and Industrial Revolutions engendered:

> 'We became less and less capable of seeing ourselves as small within the creation, partly because we thought we could comprehend it statistically, but also because we were becoming creators ourselves, of a mechanical creation by which we felt ourselves greatly magnified. . . . Why, after all, should one get excited about a mountain when one can see almost as far from the top of a building, much farther from an airplane, farther still from a space capsule?'[9]

England was fertile ground for the genesis of a capitalist industrial economy. It was a nation rich in coal, which was mined for fuel, and iron ore which was used to make machines. Factories sprouted up to accompany inventions such as the spinning jenny, the power loom, the cotton gin, and the Watt steam engine. These innovations, in entering the marketplace, accelerated production. Land previously held in common for the grazing of sheep disappeared as landowners expanded their properties through enclosures—a process which historians call the *tragedy of the commons*. Craftsmen who weaved their own cloth and carved their own furniture and tailors whose suits were custom-made to fit customers they knew were replaced by factory workers and machines. There were rebellions, such as that of the Luddites who broke into factories and destroyed machinery, but the momentum of factory production through the use of fossil fuels was unstoppable. Sanitary factory conditions, decent wages, reasonable hours, and child labor laws had to await acts of Parliament. The smog and health issues of modern civilization were literally inaugurated in Britain's factories. Poet William Blake's castigation of "dark Satanic Mills" besmirching "England's green and pleasant Land" was a futile plea for reason to intervene.[10]

The rise of the market economy in England and the emergence of the modern nation-state produced a synthesis which Hungarian political economist Karl Polanyi calls a *market society* because market incentives and values dominate social relations. Polanyi, a socialist, predicted that the laboring many would become subservient to market forces—to those few with capital who own the means of production which includes property.

In his poem "God's Grandeur," Gerard Manley Hopkins (1844–1889), an English Roman Catholic priest, laments the dark visage of industrialization in 'the black West' but professes faith in the ability of Nature to regain health guided by God's spirit. He writes:

The world is charged with the grandeur of God,
It will flame out, like shining from shook foil . . .
Generations have trod, have trod, have trod;
And all is seared with trade; bleared, smeared with toil;
And wears man's smudge and shares man's smell: the soil
Is bare now, nor can foot feel, being shod.

And for all this, nature is never spent;
There lives the dearest freshness deep down things;
And though the last lights off the black West went
Oh, morning, at the brown brink eastward, springs—
Because the Holy Ghost over the bent
World broods with warm breast and with ah! bright wings.[11]

In the first great treatise on capitalism, *The Wealth of Nations* (1776),
author Adam Smith asserted that the market self-regulates through an *Invisible Hand* that guarantees fair exchange and distribution. The religious connotation is obvious; the book title itself is taken from Isaiah 60 in which the
prophet speaks of the great wealth and power that will be generated by the
Gentiles and given to the future messiah. However, history has shown that
the desire for self-aggrandizement, not the Invisible Hand, is the fuel of the
ever-expanding productivity of the market 'machine' as well as the progenitor of economic inequities. As the machines of industry turn the machine of
the market, and man manipulates that market to satisfy desire, he in turn
begins to behave like a machine. In *A New Earth* Eckhart Tolle weighs in on
ego's professed need to accrue material goods in order to mollify an inner
insecurity. He writes:

> The physical needs for food, water, shelter, clothing, and basic comforts could
> be easily met for all humans on the planet, were it not for the imbalance of resources created by the insane and rapacious need for more, the greed of the ego.
> It finds collective expression in the economic structures of this world, such as
> the huge corporations, which are egoic entities that compete with each other for
> more. Their only blind aim is profit. They pursue that aim with absolute ruthlessness. Nature, animals, people, even their own employees, are no more than
> digits on a balance sheet, lifeless objects to be used, then discarded.[12]

When work is no longer valued for its own sake but becomes a means,
often unpleasant and monotonous, to get a pay check then the egoic self—
which forms the assumed identity of most people—must pad itself with
material objects to ease the pain of an inner void. Deep down we know that
this insular self is an imposter. We also know that the goal of non-stop material gratification is delusional because we observe that it doesn't give lasting

satisfaction. Yet we keep accumulating, and we are depressed and bored until we get the next fix from Amazon. The situation is like Aesop's fable of the frog in the pond who, in wanting to be bigger than any other frog, keeps eating until he is so bloated that he finally explodes.

In "Choruses from 'The Rock'" (1934), T. S. Eliot reflects upon the poverty of the modern industrial age. The poet writes:

> O weariness of men who turn from God
> To the grandeur of your mind and the glory of your action,
> To arts and inventions and daring enterprises,
> To schemes of human greatness thoroughly discredited,
> Binding the earth and the water to your service,
> Exploiting the seas and developing the mountains,
> Dividing the stars into common and preferred,
> Engaged in devising the perfect refrigerator,
> Engaged in working out a rational morality,
> Engaged in printing as many books as possible,
> Plotting of happiness and flinging empty bottles,
> Turning from your vacancy to fevered enthusiasm
> For nation or race or what you call humanity;
> Though you forget the way to the Temple
> There is one who remembers the way to your door:
> Life you may evade, but Death you shall not.
> You shall not deny the Stranger.[13]

THE AMERICAN DREAM

When French political philosopher and historian Alexis de Tocqueville visited America in 1831 and subsequently chronicled his observations of the fledgling capitalist democracy in his two-volume work, *Democracy in America* (1835/1840), he gave an insightful judgment regarding the future outcome of this newly established nation. Industry was rudimentary, yet De Tocqueville observed and praised the industriousness and religiosity of its citizens, qualities which were guiding a vibrant trade and commerce. At the same time de Tocqueville warned that if the welfare of the whole community was sacrificed to the profit-making of a few businessmen a fall into tyranny would be imminent. He argued that the much-valued American individualism would then lead to isolation of citizens from each other and an increase in avaricious behavior. De Tocqueville concluded that the fervent religiosity he observed was acting as a restraint on this predatory human instinct, particularly through the Protestant Ethic of hard work, fairness and desire for personal salvation.

De Tocqueville describes the balance of individual pursuit of success in the marketplace and community awareness as "self-interest well understood."[14] Self-interest that is furthered through competition, he said, can be a healthy motivation so long as cooperative action that answers the needs of one's countrymen is equally valued. Indeed, this principle of maintaining an economic equilibrium that balances competition with cooperation for the benefit of all citizens does mimic nature by reflecting the two laws of ecology: interdependence and reciprocity. De Tocqueville remarks that the awareness of community—which turns the energy of greed into generosity—is not just an altruistic impulse; it also preserves individual free enterprise by preventing demagoguery. If and when the words *well understood* are lopped off in the mind of society then greed intensifies and economic inequality deepens, tipping the ship of state into perilously rough waters. The current disparity in America between the wealthy, who retain power both politically and economically, and the rest of the population, which includes a shrinking middle class and an increasing number of people who live at or below the poverty line, are indicators of a weakening in the democratic design of self-interest well understood.

De Tocqueville explains this weakening process. He states that, contrary to an aristocracy, a democratic form of government gives more people the opportunity to rise in economic status—a healthy effect. However, this leveling process also tends to extinguish more lofty ambitions that could serve the greater society and it enervates and softens the expression of those human attributes of freedom of will and discernment that sustain a healthy democracy. As people become obsessed with material gratification so their acknowledgment of the common bond that forms their democracy fades. De Tocqueville explains:

> When the taste for material enjoyments develops in one of these [democratic] peoples more rapidly than enlightenment and the habits of freedom, there comes a moment when men are swept away and almost beside themselves at the sight of the new goods that they are ready to grasp. Preoccupied with the sole care of making a fortune, they no longer perceive the tight bond that unites the particular fortune of each of them to the prosperity of all. There is no need to tear from such citizens the rights they possess; they themselves willingly allow them to escape.[15]

De Tocqueville's explanation hits a contemporary cultural nerve ending. In present day America might his argument be translated as an erosion in elected government officials and business CEOs of the practice of unselfish service to their respective constituents and consumers? And, in the case of constituents and consumers, is there a slackening of the discrimination necessary to hold the 'servants' of government and business accountable due to a sense of powerlessness in the face of powerful bureaucratic institutions, complacency (which encourages an uninformed public) and a preoccupation with economic gain and material comfort?

The fixation on material gain makes Americans restive, says de Tocqueville, always on the move to attain their uppermost goal: material wellbeing. "Men who live in democratic times have many passions," he writes, "but most of their passions end in love of wealth or issue from it. That comes from the fact not that their souls are smaller, but the importance of money really is greater."[16]

Whether one agrees with this trenchant verdict or not, it calls out for a national exercise in self-examination because in tying the cupidity which de Tocqueville perceived in the American people to their political system, he is warning of a future in which the very democracy which permits the accumulation of wealth is imperiled because it invites what he calls the *tyranny of the majority*. The lowering of awareness and discernment that distinguishes this debilitating condition further deteriorates into a "mild despotism" in which individuals are willing to sacrifice their freedom and political sovereignty to attain a modicum of material comfort.[17] They become tamed, reduced to a "herd of timid and industrious animals" of which the government is the shepherd."[18] De Tocqueville's scenario hearkens back to Plato who argued in *The Republic* that the next stage below a failed democracy is tyranny.

By way of comparison it is interesting that amongst tribal peoples—whose economic system of exchange demands strict adherence to the law of reciprocity by which each individual's worth and health depend upon the solidarity and health of the whole community—the Kabana of New Britain, Papua New Guinea educate their children to value a concept similar to de Tocqueville's self-interest well understood. For the Kabana self-interest is not only permissible but laudatory—with this caveat: one's actions must not impinge upon the self-interest of anyone else. Acquisitiveness is kept in check through the fear of sorcery. If someone's freedom to act in a self-aggrandizing manner is disturbed, particularly if the victim gets sick, it is believed that the perpetrator used sorcery. A complex procedure ensues to discover the identity of the sorcerer. Stamping out such anti-social behavior involves the whole community. The sorcery of modern culture is unscrupulous business behavior; its practitioners, who dispossess others for their own gain (like those who indulge in insider trading), are our contemporary sorcerers. How to keep the avaricious motive in check—this is the problem.

THE COST OF MATERIAL ACQUISITIVENESS

In prophetic tone Henry David Thoreau foresaw how the adulation of money accompanies a devaluation of work and the worker. He states:

'The aim of the laborer should be, not to get his living, to get 'a good job', but to perform well a certain work; and even in a pecuniary sense . . . to pay laborers so well that they would not feel that they were working for low ends. . . . Do not hire a man who does your work for money, but him who does it for love of it. . . . Even if we grant that the American has freed himself from a political tyrant, he is still the slave of an economical and moral tyrant.'[19]

Nineteenth century Russian novelist, Leo Tolstoy, shows an equal disdain for the pecuniary motive. He had no great love for the technology of his time either. For Tolstoy, railways, the telegraph, and electricity were signs of a materially-based civilization that "'spoil the whole world'" by distracting people from the true purpose of life—enlightenment.[20] One of Tolstoy's stories called "How Much Land Does a Man Need?" shows the fatal effect of greed. The cost is high when man forgets that needs are simple and that true satisfaction comes from an inner contentment.

The story revolves around Pahom, a peasant who is part of an agricultural commune system. Although his wife is perfectly content with her life Pahom is discontented because he wants land of his own. He begins to buy and accumulate land. Each purchase starts out with pleasure and ends with the pain of wanting more. One day he hears about a rich landowner in a distant land who is selling, at a cheap price, as much land as a man can walk in a day. Pahom travels in mid-summer to meet this man. Sitting high on the knoll of a hill overlooking vast pastures and forests, dressed in a fancy robe amid an impressive entourage, is the chief of the Bashkirs. With an engaging smile the chief instructs Pahom as to the rules: everywhere you walk, it shall be yours for only 1000 rubles a day but you must be back here by sunset or else you lose everything. Pahom agrees and sets out with great anticipation. He is enamored with many sites. As noon approaches he sees that he must turn in order to mark off the land he desires and be back by sunset. About 3 pm he can see the chief and his entourage like tiny specks in the distance. He hurries his steps. He is tiring. But just then he passes a particularly beautiful pasture that he feels he must have, so he makes a detour to include this area. It is larger than he thought but he walks quickly. He sees the sun in the west beginning its descent. He hadn't realized how far he still had to go. Sweating from the heat and fatigued, he sees that he must now run in order to get back to the starting point before sunset. He begins running and increases his speed as the hill approaches at the top of which sits the chief, laughing and urging him on with a wave of his hand. Pahom, breathing heavily now, staggers to the top just as the sun is setting. He stands there a moment, then collapses— dead. Tolstoy ends the story by reminding the reader that Pahom only needed enough land—a six-foot plot in fact—wherein to be buried. . . .

When land is conceived as property to be owned, and when its wealth in resources is grasped indiscriminately, then a deleterious effect on Earth's eco-systems is inevitable. This claim on land and its resources concerned nineteenth century political economist Henry George (1839–1897). With the Industrial Revolution in full swing, this was the era of the infamous *robber barons* who bought up and profited from land related to the railroad boom. George observed the rising value of land associated with the construction of railroads in Califor-nia and realized that the appropriation by wealthy men of land to build on or rent out in order to make more personal wealth was largely responsible for the economic inequality and poverty that beset an otherwise thriving economy. He foresaw that if natural resources like water, air and earth were not protected as a public trust, and if land itself deemed valuable by the community or nation was not taxed to provide revenue for public works, then the gap in wealth would deepen. He advised a land valuation tax which would be levied not on an own-er's improvements to personal property but on the unearned wealth of the land itself. George's reasonable solution has yet to materialize in the United States.[21]

THE ALIENATED SOCIETY

As the industrial economy deepened its roots in Western culture during the nineteenth century, and into the twentieth, the religious imperative of the Protestant Ethic bowed to the profit motive. Working hard to be spiritually redeemed was replaced by working hard to make money. For the dispos-sessed and exploited, work became forced labor with little reward to mol-lify a growing sense of isolation and meaninglessness. Sociologist Émile Durkheim (1858–1917) describes this condition, which he calls *anomie*, as a dysfunctional loss of meaningful social structures that provide the sense of connectedness that tribal cultures display. Instead, individuals follow a "'rest-less movement, a planless self-development, an aim of living which has no criterion of value and in which happiness lies always in the future, and never in any present achievement.'"[22] Released from social bonds, says Durkheim, the lone individual faces a frightening "'futility of endless pursuit.'"[23]

Karl Marx (1818–1883) also observed a growing malaise which he associ-ated with industrialization: the alienation of the worker from the work. He decried the growing gap in wealth between company owners and the work-ers—the proletariat. A further alienation would develop—the alienation of the human being from the world. According to Hannah Arendt, the deleteri-ous effect of capitalism on modern culture was not self-alienation, as Marx thought, but world alienation. The use of the world as a thing to further the self is now causing the ecological deterioration we observe and experience.

In *The Sane Society* (1955) psychologist Erich Fromm examines modern capitalist society and finds it to be an alienated society. People are alienated from themselves, their fellow human beings, and the natural world. This affliction invites a question which Fromm proceeds to consider: is such a society sane? Even as capitalism has facilitated upward social mobility and encouraged individual opportunity, Fromm counters that the dignity of personhood which exists in tribal cultures has increasingly eroded. The alienated personality "experiences himself as a thing to be employed successfully on the market . . . his body, his mind and his soul are his capital . . . [but] *things* have no self and men who have become things can have no self."[24] People, he says, are reduced to animate machines whose relationships are based on use of one another. These non-persons become so involved in the routine and commodities of a man-made, artificial world that they lose touch with the natural world, the place where the raw material of every pursuit originates.

Fromm highlights the power of conformity, and, echoing the insight of de Tocqueville, states that a person voluntarily submits to "giving up oneself, becoming part and parcel of the herd, and liking it."[25] This adoption of a lower level of mental performance by citizens, and their political leaders, is facilitated by media advertising. The gullibility of citizens to accept commercial advertising of products is aligned to the "manufacturing of the popular will" in regards to social and political issues.[26] Fromm exposes the "trick of producing opinion by reiterated assertion . . . that avoids rational argument and the danger of awakening the critical faculties of the people."[27]

The observations and conclusions that Fromm offered more than sixty years ago have only increased in relevance, particularly in regard to the compulsive, witless urge to consume the goods of the Earth which a capitalism that has forgotten self-interest well understood fosters. A market that seduces people from all walks of life to buy and collect—a non-stop activity that squanders the life force of all people—produces a new type of enslavement. Fromm writes powerfully of this mesmerizing routine of consumerism:

> . . . the aim is to receive, to 'drink in', to have something new all the time, to live with a continuously open mouth, as it were . . . the passive and alienated consumer. He 'consumes' ball games, moving pictures, newspapers, magazines, books, lectures, natural scenery, social gatherings, in the same alienated and abstractified way in which he consumes the commodities he has bought. He does not participate actively, he wants to 'take in' all there is to be had, and to have as much as possible of pleasure . . . actually, he is not free to enjoy 'his' leisure; his leisure-time consumption is determined by industry, as are the commodities he buys; his taste is manipulated, he wants to see and to hear what he is conditioned to want to see and to hear.[28]

Fromm could not have envisioned the extreme alienation from Nature that now threatens all species. His analysis of the deterioration of the faculty of reason foreshadows Huxley's *Brave New World* in which the passivity of the non-person renders self-awareness and conscious choice dormant. The inner tools to repair our world become inoperable. To use a simple analogy, a runaway train is difficult to control, much less stop—especially if the engineer is incapacitated.

The wars and conflicts to which capitalist greed contribute intensify the fear and sense of helplessness that ordinary people experience. In describing the excessive division of labor and bureaucratization that industrial society mandates, in which no one person can see the whole, Fromm argues that "the more powerful and gigantic the forces are which he unleashes, the more powerless he feels himself as a human being. He confronts himself with his own forces embodied in things he has created, alienated from himself."[29]

THE MODEL T

The first half of the twentieth century witnessed two world wars and a severe economic depression. Atrocities such as the Holocaust sank the hopes of many in a just and equitable world and created an existential wound in the human psyche, exacerbating the psychological experience of alienation. Meanwhile, the human face of work was hidden behind the machine. As the capitalist system spread across the world, American corporations capitalized on rights gained by the Supreme Court decision of 1888 which defined corporate entities as people. The drive to produce and consume more commodities began to resemble the pathology of an obsessive-compulsive disorder. In his classic work *The Acquisitive Society* (1920) British socialist R. H. Tawney summed up the major flaw in capitalist society as obsessive consumption. He describes this drive as "'a poison which inflames every wound and turns each trivial scratch into a malignant ulcer.'"[30] The only remedy, he said, is to assign an industrial economy its "'proper place as the servant, not a master, of society.'"[31] Tawny's advice has so far not stopped the industrial economy from overstepping the laws of nature by the unmeasured use of fossil fuels to provide energy for the homes, businesses and vehicles of a growing world population.

The invention of the car remains an iconic industrial symbol of both technological progress and alienation. Enclosed inside metal, windows shut to the world with heat and air-conditioning readily available, the individual is master of a machine that is fueled with 'ancient sunlight' and expels clouds of carbon that pollute the air. Cars satisfy the professed need for speed and power, but from their inception cars were particularly emblematic of freedom, a national virtue. Cars provided mobility. In the early 1900s Henry

Ford wanted to make a car that the common man could afford. In this regard his intention was noble. He wanted to help the city dweller find respite, by excursions into the countryside, and aid the farmer in bringing his goods to the city market. He even built an optional sidecar on the Model T so that the farmer could transport livestock.

Figure 5.1.   Model T on the way to market.

From "We'll Race You, Henry: A Story about Henry Ford" by Barbara Mitchell, illustrated by Kathy Haubrich, used with permission of Millbrook Press, a division of Lerner Publishing Group, Inc. Illustration copyright © 1986 by Lerner Publishing Group, Inc.

Even the gem of Ford's genius, the assembly line, was designed to make work more efficient, enabling the worker to concentrate on one process—a refinement of the division of labor. But the power of mechanization also made man part of the machinery that made the cars and household appliances rather than an active agent of the work. The age of computers was foreshadowed even then; as Fromm astutely puts it: "instead of the machine being the substitute for human energy, man has become a substitute for the machine. *His work can be defined as the performance of acts which cannot yet be performed by machines.*"[32] Computers have reduced the *"performance of acts"* required by the human being, making him or her ancillary to the machine. Frederick Taylor's principles of scientific management, outlined in full in 1911 in the *Taylor System*, reflected a philosophy that is still the buttress of industry, the military, and education. That philosophy defines the main goal of human labor and thought as efficiency.

A searing satire and critique of this worldview and the effects of industrialization appear in Charlie Chaplin's 1905 silent film *Modern Times*. Charlie Chaplin plays an ordinary workman who faithfully performs his monotonous job in the big factory, tightening bolts on an assembly line. His lunch break is made shorter and more efficient by a machine that the factory owner wishes to experiment with; it is designed to feed the worker and thus free him to return to work faster. The machine breaks down and starts making berserk movements, splashing soup and pudding in Chaplin's face. He ends up swallowing some bolts that are thrown into his mouth by the machine's arm. As the afternoon progresses Chaplin gets more and more agitated and begins to hallucinate. He falls into the assembly line track and we see his body traveling into the 'intestines' of the machine until he is retrieved. By this time Chaplin has gone mad, dancing around the factory floor, moving in jerky motions that mimic the mechanistic movements that his work requires and pulling levers that finally make the big machines explode. The situation is comical; we laugh, but the dehumanization which is depicted is as believable and frightening now as it was in 1905. As Marx astutely put it: "'All our inventions and progress seem to result in endowing material things with intellectual life and stultifying human life into a material force.'"[33] Below, the modernist portrait of man by artist Max Ernst presents a confusing image that makes the viewer ask, has man become a machine; does he see himself as a machine?

In his encyclical letter of 1981, *On Human Work*, Pope John Paul II called for a return to the dignity of work as the means by which man expresses his inherent worth. Work has an ethical meaning, he says, because "through work man not only transforms nature, adapting it to his own needs, but he also achieves fulfillment as a human being."[34] While work can be made into a means for exploiting man the natural virtue of industriousness elevates man

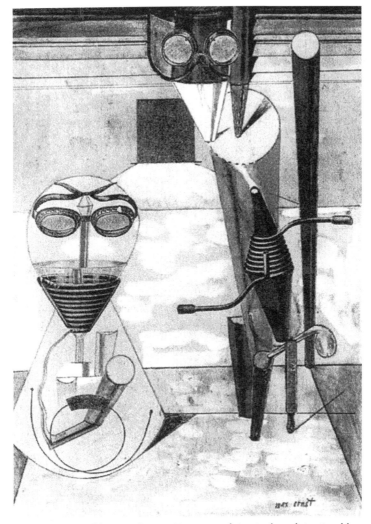

Figure 5.2. Ambiguous Figures (1 copper plate, 1 zinc plate, 1 rubber cloth, 2 calipers, 1 drainpipe telescope, 1 piping man) by Max Ernst, 1919. Courtesy of Max Ernst.

above the matter he works with and molds. In criticizing modern capitalism Pope John Paul argues that this system does not reflect the primacy of work over capital and property. The "exclusive right to private ownership of the means of production" is indefensible, says the Pope, because capital "as the whole of the means of production, is at the same time the product of the work of generations. . . . All these means of production can be seen as a great workbench at which the present generation of workers is working day after day."[35] Furthermore, each perfected technological 'instrument' is the result of work. Technology itself remains subordinate to work and the subject of that work, man. Thus "the whole collection of instruments, no matter how perfect they may be in themselves, are only a mere instrument, subordinate to human labor."[36]

In *The Human Condition* Hannah Arendt describes the modern age of industrial capitalism as a reversal of two worldviews about life. There is the *vita activa*, or active life, and the *vita contemplativa*, contemplative life. The latter ruled the Middle Ages and the Renaissance. In the building of the Gothic cathedrals, for example, introspective contemplation was viewed as a necessary precursor to active work. The idea was formulated first; it then infused creative endeavor. Arendt argues that with the advent of science the experiment—and then later, with the Industrial Revolution, the production process—became tantamount. The idea was fused in the doing, in the experiment, in the invented product. Doing was everything. *Homo faber* (*man the maker*) and *vita activa* reigned—and still do.

The fall into obscurity of *vita contemplativa* can be traced even today in the advertising of a major sports clothing company, Nike. *Just do it*, accompanied by the large check mark logo, suggests speed; do it quickly and get on to the next activity. All around us speed rules: fast food, fast driving, fast (and verbose) talking—to fill up space. There is no need to think, no time to think: just do it. There is no acknowledgement of the fact that the energy to do comes from the universe. The energy is not initiated by us; it is bestowed.

It could be argued that industrialized society, as a progressive improvement on nonindustrial societies, has evolved—but mainly in reference to technology. No one would want to part with her refrigerator, vacuum cleaner, telephone, car, or indoor plumbing for that matter. However, the evolutionary status of a culture deserves a broader scope of definition. A people may choose from a variety of objectives—technology being one—that in time weave the fabric of their culture, giving it a veneer of enlightenment. For example, an advanced culture may be defined by its robust governance under laws that insure equal rights and equal job opportunities for its citizens. It may encourage proficiency in the arts, literature, and philosophy; or it may deliver to the world a vibrant spirituality. The outstanding accomplishment of the Renaissance was the mental capacity of its star-studded cast to develop and illuminate a kaleidoscope of the above objectives.

Furthermore, economic wealth is not the only measure of prosperity in a society or nation. According to anthropologist Marshall Sahlins, the "original affluent society" was not the industrialized model but the 'primitive' tribal culture.[37] A tribe's typical day consisted of morning work in which men hunted animals and women gathered whatever fruits, greens and other eatables the natural world provided. A small vegetable garden might also be cultivated. The afternoons were devoted to creative leisure activities like arts and crafts, communal religious rituals, and visiting and ministering to the sick. It could be argued that such 'leisure activities' that build community are better metrics for gauging the prosperity of a society than economic prowess through industrialization. The latter is particularly questionable when new data unveiled in an Oxfam report in January 2016 shows that, whereas in 2010 the wealth of 388 of the world's richest people equaled that of a combined 3.5 billion people who occupy the bottom half of the world's income scale, that number in 2015 had shrunk from 388 to 62.[38] When inequities become this severe it may be time to re-examine the evolutionary status of the capitalist cultural model that de Tocqueville once praised as self-interest well understood.

THE RULE OF TECHNOLOGICAL MIND

Technological mind is an influential modality of thinking that characterizes modern society. It is a mindset that grew out of a narrowing use of mental capacities that accompanied the historical shifts in the Western worldview traced in the last chapter. Through enculturation people learned to focus their thinking on the attainment of materialistic goals like monetary wealth and accumulation of creature comforts, continually upgraded by advances in technology. Understanding the dominance of technological mind is key to understanding why and how human beings psychologically lost their foothold in the Earth's loamy soil and learned to condone actions that violate natural laws—particularly the ecological laws of interdependence and reciprocity.

The rise of technological mind can be traced to the advent of science in the seventeenth century. Its hold on Western culture was then strengthened by the Industrial Revolution. In many ways technological breakthroughs have benefited mankind, beginning with the first fire lit by a bow drill made of dry wood. Today, magnetic resonance imaging (MRI) for the diagnosis and treatment of debilitating diseases, for example, can improve and even extend human life. The cell phone and computer allow for instant global communication. And who would want to exchange the 'horseless' carriage for the horse? But to treat every problem as a technical one when it may be a systemic one with grave implications—like human-induced climate change that reflects a distorted worldview—is short-sighted and dismissive of a more rounded use of human mental capacity. To use a common adage, it is not seeing the forest for the trees and then reducing the trees to marketable wood.

Technology is neutral; it is the cultural mindset that determines how technology is used. The anthropocentric view that it is man's prerogative to exploit Nature's resources has encouraged the preference for technological mind. In education today the STEM disciplines (science, technology, engineering and math) are emphasized. They have greater clout in the marketplace than the humanities—subjects such as history, philosophy, literature and the arts—even though it could be said that the latter are invaluable gateways to understanding the complexities of human nature and to dealing with conflicts in a rapidly globalized world.

In the first quarter of the twenty-first century we are awash in technological gadgetry—much of which we enjoy and benefit from. But questions arise at the same time, such as what is the long term effect of our preoccupation with iPhones, iPods and other electronic devices? Will our connection to each other and to the natural world be affected? Enhanced or diminished? Does the preoccupation with the digital world erode mental faculties such as discrimination, judgment and empathy which differentiate human beings from machines? Is our attention so absorbed in this human-machine tête-à-tête that the human brain, whose plasticity has been noted by neuroscientists, is registering this new addiction in its neural networks?

Technological mind implements the capitalist economic system. In *Conjectures of a Guilty Bystander,* published in 1967, Thomas Merton provides a prophetic critique of the association between technological mind, science and capitalism in modern society. He writes: "The central problem of the modern world is the complete emancipation and autonomy of the technological mind at a time when unlimited possibilities lie open to it and all the resources seem to be at hand." For modern man the unforgiveable sin is to lose faith in science, for science, says Merton, "can do everything . . . must be permitted to do everything it likes. . . . The consequence of this is that technology and science are now responsible to no power and submit to no control other than their own. . . . What *can* be done efficiently must be done.[39]

The dedication of technological mind to the proliferation of vehicles, industrial machines, electronics and weapons of mass destruction that run on fossil fuels is, Merton reminds us, based not in reason and traditional morality but purely in utilitarian practicality. Because "technology represents the rule of *quantity*, not the rule of reason (quality) . . . man the person, the subject of qualified and perfectible freedom, becomes *quantified*, that is, becomes part of a mass—mass man—whose only function is to enter anonymously into the process of production and consumption.[40]

Merton concludes that the end of this "totally emancipated technology is the regression of man to a climate of moral infancy, in total dependence not on 'mother nature' . . . but on the pseudonature of technology."[41] If Merton's prognosis is correct and science's mantra remains "what *can* be done efficiently must be done" then the technological know-how to extricate more fossil fuels from the earth will continue and climate change will be the ultimate weapon of mass destruction.

Merton's *mass man* is the *one-dimensional man* described in Herbert Marcuse's classic *One Dimensional Man* (1964). Empirical science and technology, says Marcuse, are based on the reductionist philosophy of positivism which asserts that facts, ascertained through the application of logic and mathematics on observable sensory experience, are the only valid means of knowledge and meaning. One-dimensional thought subsumes all ambiguity and contradiction into a radicalized rationality joined to consumerism, repressing higher dimensions of thought that characterize cultural creativity, social critique, philosophical inquiry, and religious mysticism. "Thinking," says Marcuse, "is pressed into the straightjacket of common usage."[42] Thought is reduced to instrumentality—technological mind. Discourse becomes stale, robotic and reflective of the influence of the media, a process that recalls Fromm's reference to the media as an instrument that can be used to entice gullible citizens whose discrimination has eroded. Because an historical perspective is renounced, states Marcuse, "cultural alternatives" are not examined; instead, society is trapped in a "Happy Consciousness" (fed by McDonald's 'happy meals'?) that obscures the totalitarian nature of advanced productivity in capitalist society.[43] One hears de Tocqueville's voice in Marcuse's critique of capitalist democracy. One also hears Diamond who proposes that when a society forgets past lessons and inoculates itself against cultural alternatives that society is headed for collapse. A phrase attributed to Thomas Jefferson—'honesty is the best policy'—once defined truthfulness as an important American value. One trusted another person's words as springing from fact because, as Jefferson also said, 'a man's word is his bond.' But in the current cultural climate in America not only is the value of ascertaining and speaking the truth fading, but the manipulation of 'reality' foments confusion in the public as news stories are debated as to their factual basis and politicians use the media to state their own 'truths' while labeling the words of the opposition 'lies.'

The flattening of thought (and thus of the human being) into Marcuse's shallow one-dimensional level is the *flatland* that Ken Wilber assigns to the modern era. When Descartes and his Enlightenment successors lifted human consciousness to a new level of empowerment they inadvertently got stuck in *flatland*—an amputated reality that disposed of the vertical transcendental exploration of Spirit dear to the medieval mind. In place of the latter they substituted a horizontal world of material surfaces known through empirical analysis. The human mind deduced that "if something can't be simply located in physical space, then it isn't 'really real'"—a mental error that Alfred North Whitehead calls the *fallacy of simple location*. [44]

Wilber connects this development to a new type of mentality "altogether productive and technical and instrumental" wherein the "it-domain" is selected for.[45] If everything and everyone is an *it* then *it*—land, resources, people—can be taken and used for personal gain with impunity and in perpetuity (since *it* is not organic and does not suffer death). This it-world becomes the face of a perverted capitalism. All problems once considered and solved by people (by *I* and *We*), are converted into technical problems to be solved by the it-domain of science.

In his 1992 book *Technopoly*, Neil Postman offers a persuasive reason as to why American culture has not been able to spearhead a paradigm shift that would generate a global roadmap to a sustainable economy and lifestyle. If a nation, says Postman, is stuck in a worldview that promotes technology as the cure for problems that were created by technology then there is no way out of this circular reasoning. A nation that practices this worldview is a *technopoly*. Technocrats, who believe that technological expertise is superior to human judgment, run government and business. These 'experts' who benefit from the existing industrial paradigm do not want to change the technological mindset even if it is self-destructive. Postman attributes the transformation of American culture into a technopoly to certain American character traits, such as the appeal of innovative enterprises and the importance of progress. The latter fosters a distrust of constraints and an implicit competition to outdo the Old World. These traits are bolstered by an addiction to commodities and the genius of certain capitalist entrepreneurs who know how to exploit the economic possibilities of new technologies—men like Henry Ford in the 1900s or Steve Jobs in this century.

Central to the development of a technopoly, says Postman, is *scientific management* (ie. the Taylor System) which relieves workers of having to think. Postman uses the fictitious but prescient image of a future society of automatons in Aldous Huxley's *Brave New World* to describe the dangers that a technopoly poses. Huxley in fact differentiates between BF (before Ford) and AF (after Ford) to pinpoint the momentous cultural change in America inaugurated by the invention of the car and assembly line.

In an article called "The Capitalist Manifesto: Greed is Good (To a Point)" which made the cover of *Newsweek* in June 2009, political pundit Fareed Zakaria wrote that after the 2008 recession American capitalism was rebounding with some chastening from the government directed at the big banks. However, says Zakaria, stability is not inherent in the capitalist system, nor is morality; as corporations resume 'business as usual' a replay is likely. A lasting solution to the volatile market's inability to police itself is the adoption of an ethical standard at the top. No economic system, says Zakaria, can operate healthfully without a moral compass. With the Protestant Ethic tucked away as an obscure footnote in the history books it is unlikely that a business conscience will take shape, particularly as a global phenomenon, unless our thinking is overhauled. The machine of production-consumption is too well oiled with greed.

A particularly egregious form of modern capitalism, which reveals the face of *wétiko* and the rule of technological mind, is what journalist Naomi Klein has called *disaster capitalism*. In her book *The Shock Doctrine: the Rise of Disaster Capitalism* (2007) Klein describes a 'pure' deregulated capitalism as the product of neoliberalism, an ideology formulated primarily by Milton Friedman of the University of Chicago's School of Economics to deal with economic crises, for which he received a Nobel Prize in 1976.[46] The neoliberal economic formula, by which a poor developing country experiencing internal instability can get outside help, is based on three changes which that country must implement: first, privatization of industries; second, market deregulation, and finally, deep cuts in government spending on social benefits—particularly healthcare and education. This devastating triumvirate of rules, which Klein calls *economic shock therapy*, in fact impoverished everyone in the participating Latin American and African countries except native elites, multinational corporations, and the World Bank and IMF to whom the beneficiary countries were indebted. Klein uses a sentence from Orwell's *1984* to describe the mindset of this invasive economic policy: "'We shall squeeze you empty, and then we shall fill you with ourselves.'"[47] This mindset was exemplified, says Klein, in the aid which American economic advisors gave to the dictator Pinochet. When neoliberal policies were implemented in Chile in 1973 inflation shot up to 375 percent. Unemployment hit 30 percent by 1982 and by 1988 45 percent of Chileans lived below the poverty line.[48] This type of economic overhaul, argues Klein, does not produce a 'liberated' market but a *corporatist* one (the collusion of government with corporations). The word *corporatism* originally referred to Mussolini's model of a police state. Klein warns that the next stage of disaster capitalism is the deliberate destabilization by powerful nations of third-world countries, often by military intervention, in order to extract raw materials such as oil, gas, lumber, and even water through privatization. This imperial corporatism reformulates the colonial enterprise of *wétiko*. It is noteworthy that capitalism as a war machine was envisioned in President Eisenhower's farewell speech in April 1953 when he warned of a *military-industrial complex* that steals from the poor and needy while filling the pockets of the rich.

CAPITALISM AND CLIMATE CHANGE

A prerequisite to technology's existence and effectiveness is the health of the basic physical elements that it uses. Technology can be instrumental, for example, in harnessing water through the construction of a hydroelectric dam. But it cannot create clean water. It cannot produce rainfall. Technology cannot sustainably cool the planet, unless one accepts an expensive strategy of market logic that advises spraying sulfur dioxide (a pollutant) into the stratosphere to dim the sun. Such a solution may be clever but it is not reasonable, says Klein in *This Changes Everything*, a sequel to her first book. Klein identifies such geoengineering ideas as technological applications of *the shock doctrine*.

The neoliberal philosophy that legitimizes 'pure' capitalism feeds into the current climate crisis by legitimizing an unregulated extraction of fossil fuels by multinational entities like Exxon Mobil and Royal Dutch Shell. The gap between overconsumption by first world nations and underconsumption by third world nations renders the global capitalist system dysfunctional. Meanwhile, people of all income brackets sicken from pollutants and the Earth sickens from the *shock therapy* of incessant human interference. The moral compass referred to by Zakaria that could regulate and rebalance capitalist enterprise, giving Earth respite to regain equilibrium, is lacking. Klein describes the link between corrupt capitalism and climate change. Because neoliberal policies have released multinational corporations from constraints that might reduce greenhouse gas emissions "the liberation of world markets, a process powered by the liberation of unprecedented amounts of fossil fuels from the earth, has dramatically sped up the same process that is liberating Arctic ice from existence."[49]

The timing, says Klein, could not be worse in this first quarter of the twenty-first century as the *market fundamentalism* of unregulated capitalism collides with climate change. Indeed, Klein reports that global carbon dioxide emissions were tracked in 2013 as 61 percent percent higher than in 1990. She concludes that "our economic system and our planetary system are now at war. Or, more accurately, our economy is at war with many forms of life on earth, including human life. What the climate needs to avoid collapse is a contraction in humanity's use of resources; what our economic model demands to avoid collapse is unfettered expansion."[50]

From its inception, the capitalist industrial system was perceived as a means by which the eighteenth century Enlightenment ideal of progress could come to fruition as the natural route of human evolution. When combined with a democratic political system, such as de Tocqueville witnessed in the new republic of America, such an economy, managed by self-made, free *men* (noticeably absent in this idyllic picture is the notion of gender and racial equality) would tend to be healthy and stable. The possibility that each person regardless of class could make a decent living based on hard work elevated individual worth and stimulated ambition. The promise of this new system, however, has slowly faded. With the birth of science, nationhood, colonial conquest and industrialization the capitalist worldview increasingly favors those few who can corner the almighty Market. Technology based in fossil fuels is fused with a philosophy of manipulation that favors an elite minority. The "great gift economy" of Nature—the ultimate source of the market that gives freely to all—is forgotten.[51] Forgotten also is the idea that the profit motive needs to be balanced with integrity and service to others. In his book *Small is Beautiful* E. F. Schumacher writes that an unsustainable economy that does not serve everyone's needs, including the Earth's, is doomed because "a way of life that bases itself on materialism, i.e. on permanent, limitless expansionism in a finite environment, cannot last long."[52]

The rise of capitalism in its predatory aspect, sustained by technological mind, accentuates a growing rift between humanity and Nature. Is the capitalist system redeemable? Can de Tocqueville's standard of self-interest well understood be restored? Or is capitalism inherently unjust and in need of replacement—and, if so, by what?

These questions await consideration in a later chapter, but what has been revealed in this study so far is the fact that an industrialized capitalist economy in its present form encourages narcissism, particularly the compulsive drive to accumulate material possessions for me and mine, which in turn leads to inequities in the social and economic fabric of society. This self-absorption and growing dependence upon technological mind—the mindset that says technology is the answer to all our desires and our problems—prevent us from appreciating how alienated we have become from each other and from the Earth. We have turned the planet into a marketplace where natural resources, as commodities, are bought and sold. This marketplace is accessed and consumed through two major engines of modern capitalism: the fossil fuel industry and agribusiness. The next chapter zooms in on these two formidable gears of the capitalist machine.

Chapter Six

A Double-Barreled Shotgun

O! My offense is rank, it smells to heaven

—Claudius, *Hamlet* III:3

Each invention of human enterprise that has defined the meaning of progress includes a downside as well as an upside. Or, as the Chinese proverb puts it, 'every front has a back.' The fossil fuel industry and agribusiness are two powerful converging forces that threaten the health of the biosphere, even as they deliver material benefits. Like a double-barreled shotgun fired at close range these two forces impact the Earth's entire ecosystem—which includes humans—in a potentially lethal assault.

Fossil fuels—progeny of the Industrial Revolution—provide abundant energy to fuel our cars, heat our houses and office buildings, and run our machines. But fossil fuels also pollute the air with excessive carbon emissions from coal-fired power plants and gasoline powered vehicles, causing a daily uptick in global warming. The U.S. Energy Information Administration (EIA) reports that in 2016 coal-fired power plants released 1,241 million metric tons of carbon dioxide into the atmosphere.[1] Car emissions come in a strong second with about 20 lbs. of carbon dioxide spewing forth from the tailpipe of just one car per gallon of gas.[2] As of 2014 the United States produced 12 percent of the world's oil and used 25 percent of the global supply.[3] According to Jeffrey Sachs, Director of the Earth Institute at Columbia University, we have the technological know-how to transform the world economy into a low-carbon energy system but the oil industry has "lobbied Washington to a state of paralysis, and as is so often true, greed is at the root of the crisis, with the politicians getting in line to feed at the oil trough. The climate deniers are not the real problem."[4] Fossil fuels also pollute water systems, mainly through spills of coal ash and oil as well as potential methane leaks during hydraulic fracturing operations.

The health of all species is impacted by the baneful effects of fossil fuels. For example, a sharp drop in breeding among California raptors has been blamed on the state's prolonged drought, associated with global warming. Lack of water kills the insects and small rodents on which the birds feed. A report by the National Audubon Society released in September 2014 predicts that about half of the approximately 650 species of birds in North America will lose their range of climate and habitat due to global warming over the next sixty-five years. Some may find safe haven by migrating north, like the Baltimore oriole; others like the trumpeter swan could become extinct.[5]

The other barrel of the double-barreled shotgun—intensive farming and its corporate arm, agribusiness—multiplies our food crops to feed a growing global population. The intent is good but the methods are counterproductive because they are unsustainable. Intensive farming degrades and exhausts the soil through the use of chemical fertilizers and the application of herbicides and pesticides that coat our food crops with poison which sickens all species, including birds, bees, fish, livestock, and people. Water is also contaminated by run-off of chemical fertilizers, herbicides and pesticides from agricultural fields, affecting fish and other marine life. Storage ponds on pig farms that hold fecal waste tend to rupture sending *e coli* and other bacteria into streams and rivers to further degrade water quality.

One species that is being adversely affected by intensive farming is the honeybee. A very resilient species, the honeybee has flourished for forty million years. Since 2006, however, a steady decline in bee populations has alarmed scientists. In fact 2014 was the first year that summer deaths of bees exceeded winter deaths. A condition named colony collapse disorder or CCD causes adult bees to leave their hives and die off. Biologists see a network of causal factors at play, including infestation by the varroa mite (a deadly parasite), the disappearance of nesting sites and wild foraging areas that once provided diverse nutritional sources of nectar and pollen, and the use of pesticides on crops. The latter two phenomena are due to intensive farming methods. Studies now point to pesticides as the main culprit of CCD. A typical honeybee colony reveals a residue of more than 120 pesticides—a toxic synergistic brew that can reduce bees' immune systems. A new class of insecticides on the market called neonicotinoids is being singled out for its potency. For example, a July 2015 study published in the *Journal of Environmental Chemistry* cites analysis of pollen and honey samples from sixty-two hives in ten Massachusetts counties showing significant levels of neonicotinoids.[6] A further study published in the Proceedings of the Royal Society B in July 2016 found that two chemicals from the neonicotinoid family decrease the sperm count in drones (male honeybees) by nearly 40 percent, interfering with successful reproduction.[7] The European Commission has banned the use of three varieties of this pesticide on all flowering plants. The EPA in the United States is considering regulatory action. As a response to the increase in bee deaths Ortho announced in April 2016 that it is phasing out neonicotinoid chemicals in eight of its pesticide products by 2021. However, neonicotinoid manufacturers like Bayer Crop-Science are disputing the need for a ban and Syngenta, a Swiss agribusiness competitor of Monsanto, wants to increase the amount of neonicotinoid pesticide to treat crops such as corn, barley, wheat and alfalfa. According to the US Department of Agriculture one-third of the human diet comes from plants pollinated by insects, 80 percent of which are pollinated by honeybees.[8] California's almond trees depend entirely on honeybee pollination at bloom time.

In the pages that follow the double-barreled shotgun will be examined in detail. An exploration of the discovery of coal, oil and natural gas will reveal their source in the vegetable world—hence the name 'fossil' fuels. This harmless origin contrasts with the toxic effects of their use in industry. A comparison of intensive farming and traditional agriculture (and its modern descendant, organic farming) will expose the harmful impact of agribusiness on the health of the soil, crops, and all species of plants and animals.

THE FOSSIL FUEL INDUSTRY

Frank Morris, a member of the Board of Directors of Sierra Club, uses the name *King Kong* to refer to the three fossil fuels.[9] In order of dirtiness these energy sources are coal (K), oil (O), and natural gas (NG). The great ape of the film is an apt image. These three sources of energy now threaten to change the Earth's ecosystems through their emission of pollutants that contribute to global warming.

The story of extraction and burning of fossil fuels begins in the Carboniferous Period, 410 to 360 million years ago, when microbes of cyanobacteria in the oceans developed the ability to make multi-celled algae, fungi and plants. Scientists have found that the DNA in chloroplasts—chlorophyll-pigmented organelles in plant cells which conduct photosynthesis by capturing sunlight—is very similar to the DNA of these ancient bacteria. Plants eventually expanded their habitat by colonizing the dry land. The Earth's atmosphere was very high in carbon dioxide which made temperatures much higher than they are today. The warm, humid conditions and copious carbon in the atmosphere allowed plant life to flourish on Earth's landmass which was concentrated in one huge continent called Pangaea.

Figure 6.1.   Pangaea map with continents.
Courtesy of Pangaea continents.png; image made by en:User:Kieff.

As air proportions mutated from the dominant carbon dioxide to a mixture of nitrogen (78%), oxygen (20.15%), and argon (.93%) herbivores and then carnivores evolved. A co-evolution was afoot: as life forms changed the atmosphere to fit their needs they also evolved to adapt to the environment they helped create.

Over the millennia giant ferns and leafy plants formed thickening layers of decaying vegetation that accumulated and metamorphosed through the action of bacteria creating peat bogs and lagoons. This carbon-filled material became coal in its various forms. The harder bituminous coal burns readily and is used as fuel in industries and as a source of heat; as a result, coal-fired power plants remain a major worldwide generator of electricity. The fact that coal is 'fossilized' vegetation is confirmed by the existence of carbon fibers, stems, leaves and seeds visible to the human eye in softer varieties of coal, detected with a microscope in harder types of coal.

In the surrounding oceans this same process of plant decomposition was happening but it involved simpler plants such as algae, cyanobacteria, and even mollusks, seaweed and peat. This plant matter fell to the ocean floor and over millennia compressed into a biologic sludge we call petroleum or oil which is refined to produce gasoline. At the end of the Paleozoic geological epoch, about 250 million years ago, a massive disaster—perhaps a collision with a comet or asteroid—caused violent tectonic movement under the Earth's crust, breaking up Pangaea into landmasses that resemble today's continents. The dense mats of vegetation spread, consolidated, and sank underground. The vegetation continued to cook into fossil fuels in the hot belly of the Earth.

In *The Last Hours of Ancient Sunlight* Thom Hartmann examines the problem of ecological deterioration and points to the fossil fuel industry, and the cultural forces which sustain it, as causal factors. In an intriguing take on the problem of global warming Hartmann begins his argument by describing coal and oil as ancient sunlight: indeed, these substances are the products of the natural process of photosynthesis. He uses a monetary metaphor, calling ancient sunlight our capital or savings which is stored in the Earth as in a bank. We are all made out of this ancient sunlight as it moves through the food chain. What follows is a brief history of the emergence and use of fossil fuels as Hartmann relays it.

In 1100 AD coal was discovered in Europe and Asia; our ancestors began to mine and burn this ancient sunlight and use it for heat and fuel. Since trees, the 'current sunlight,' were no longer needed for fuel they could be cut down to make room for crops that needed the current sunlight to grow. As more food was available the population grew; as the population grew more deforestation was necessary in order to plant more crops. By 1800 the population had multiplied from about 500 million people to one billion.

Oil was discovered as early as the 5th century BCE when Herodotus described its properties. It was recognized as a visible scum on the surface of ponds and streams and was scooped up for use. The modern petroleum industry began in 1859 when E. L. Drake drilled into an oil field in Pennsylvania in a town called Titusville. This event started an oil well-drilling frenzy. Kerosene was the main finished product; lamps lit by kerosene soon replaced whale-oil lamps. The great advantage of oil was its use as an efficient energy source to fuel tractors that replaced farm animals like horses and oxen whose energy depended on current sunlight absorbed by the grasses which they ate. It was discovered that oil could be converted into resins, plastics, and fabrics like nylon and polyester which meant that land devoted to sheep-grazing for wool and cotton fields could be converted to agricultural use to feed a growing population. By converting oil into chemical fertilizers and pesticides more food could be produced. As the number of cars increased so the need for gasoline skyrocketed. It takes 90 tons of ancient plants to create 4 liters of gasoline.[10] The population by 1930 hit two billion.

In *The Story of B* Daniel Quinn explores the feedback between population growth and food supply which work in tandem as one of Nature's self-regulating systems. Up until the Agricultural Revolution 10,000 years ago populations grew very slowly, doubling every 19,000 years. But with the explosion of agriculture that ratio drastically changed. In fact, as of 2000, the world population is doubling in less than forty years due to intensive farming.[11] The solution to overpopulation is not an acceleration of intensive food production which requires an increase in fossil fuels even as it degrades the environment. On the contrary, increasing the food supply promotes population growth and prolongs an unsustainable cycle.

Coal

Although all three fossil fuels contribute to global warming coal is the most carbon intensive and therefore the 'dirtiest' of the fossil fuels. In the United States about 63 percent of electricity is currently produced by coal and natural gas.[12] Surface coal mining—strip mines and mountain top removal—accounts for 65 percent of the coal supply.[13] In strip mining explosives are used to take out the earth, called *overburden*, so that coal seams or strips are exposed. In the mountainous areas of Appalachia, the coal capital of the nation, tops of mountains are deforested, then blown up. More than one million acres of forested mountains in Central and Southern Appalachia have been turned into moonscapes.[14] As coal is prepared for burning toxic chemicals are used to wash the coal. Coal contains toxic substances and heavy metals such as cadmium, boron, beryllium, arsenic, lead, mercury, cobalt, sulfur, thallium, and cancer-causing chromium. When coal is burned the coal-fired power plants emit these toxic substances into the atmosphere along with greenhouse gases including sulfur oxide. When conditions are propitious sulfur oxide transmutes into sulfuric acid which combines with water molecules in the air to produce acid rain that sickens trees.

The toxic waste from emissions is called *coal ash*, of which there are two types. Fly ash, a fine silica powder, is somewhat minimized through scrubbers in the power plant chimney but the bottom ash accumulates at the base of the furnace where it drops into a storage area and is mixed with water, forming a slurry. The slurry is retained in waste ponds which are vulnerable to rupture. This vulnerability became evident on December 22, 2008 when a coal ash containment site at the Kingston Power Station near Harriman, Tennessee, operated by the Tennessee Valley Authority, ruptured, spilling 5.4 million cubic yards of coal ash slurry into the Emory and Clinch Rivers.[15] Residential areas bordering the rivers—a total of 300 acres—were affected. Drinking water became polluted. Starting in 2009 lawsuits began to be filed against the TVA attesting to cases of toxic poisoning in people who had contact with the polluted material in soil or water. The latest lawsuit, filed in March 2018—almost ten years after the spill—claims that 180 workers who were hired to clean up the site of the spill became sick, and some died, from toxic fly ash exposure.[16] A list of forty-four coal ash pond sites that pose a significant hazard to human life was made public by the EPA at the urging of environmental groups in response to the Kingston Power Station coal ash disaster.

In February of 2014 a coal ash spill near Eden, NC at a containment site operated by Duke Energy, the nation's largest utility in generating electricity from coal, released 39,000 tons of coal ash into the Dan River, coating the river bottom for 70 miles downstream, endangering aquatic life and drinking water.[17] The Duke Energy spill is the third-largest coal ash spill on record. It was linked to the state's environmental politics led by the then Republican governor, Pat McCrory, and his conservative Republican legislature. McCrory worked at Duke Energy for twenty-eight years. Once in office as governor he led a pugilistic campaign to intimidate and weaken the powers of the state's Department of Environment and Natural Resources, once one of the most aggressive watchdog agencies in the Southeast. The department was told to abandon its regulatory role in favor of giving environmental permits to businesses. Duke Energy was subpoenaed and a federal investigation launched, to the embarrassment of the governor. It was determined that leaky, unlined waste ponds near sources of drinking water were the cause of the spill. The company, in collusion with the watchdog agency who dutifully looked the other way, had neglected to make the necessary repairs. In March 2016 the state fined Duke Energy 6.6 million for the Dan River spill. Duke was already paying out 102 million in fines and restitution for unlawful leaks in its coal ash ponds at five other North Carolina plants.[18]

James Hansen calls coal plants "factories of death."[19] A variety of respiratory illnesses such as Black Lung recall the early days of coal mining in the 1930s. Men, many of whom were immigrants from Eastern Europe without knowledge of the English language, worked in the underground mine shafts of western Pennsylvania for a dollar a day, in constant fear of mine shaft collapse. In states like West Virginia and Tennessee, where jobs have depended on coal mining for decades, lives have been disfigured by coal as miners became the collateral damage of the fossil fuel industry's corporate beneficiaries.

Personal stories abound that speak to the misery caused by coal mining—from asthma attacks, cancer, and kidney failure to emotional breakdowns. Donna Branham grew up in a coal camp in Scarlet, West Virginia with a large extended family. Coal dust, noise and pollution were facts of life. Her dad worked thirty-nine years in the mine. When he retired the mine was shut down, but then the same company returned to strip-mine the area. It was not long before the blasting sounds tore the house's foundation apart and caused leaks in the roof. Several days later, when a blast at 7 PM in the evening shook the house like a fierce earthquake, her father had a heart attack. The Branham family relocated but the sorrow in leaving home weakened Donna's mother who died a year later. In May of 2012 Donna joined more than a dozen women and a few men to stand in protest on the steps of the West Virginia State Capitol. They had shaved their heads in solidarity against mountain top removal mining. Donna states:

'They always talk about the cost of coal. I can tell you the *true* cost of that lump of coal. It cost my family. The only people that get rich are the people that own the coal mines. When I felt those first streaks of the razor in my hair today, I felt empowered. I felt liberated. . . . I want the world to know how much it hurts my people. . . . My hair will grow back, but the mountains will not.'[20]

Mercury is a potent nerve poison. About 70 percent of the mercury to which humans are exposed comes from the burning of coal.[21] Rich Gelfond, CEO of the film-technology company IMAX, recounts a harrowing experience in which he became sick as a result of adjusting his diet to include a disproportionate amount of seafood to boost his health. He was unaware that the two fish he favored—tuna and swordfish—are high in mercury. Rich began to show neurological symptoms like tremors and difficulty walking. At first doctors feared a brain tumor, but it turned out that the 'healthy' diet of fish was to blame. When mercury is released in emissions from coal-fired power plants it settles into lakes, waterways and oceans. While inorganic mercury cannot be easily assimilated into the human body, when it enters a water environment bacteria convert it into an organic form—methylmercury—which is easily assimilated and builds up in the living tissue of fish. In a 2006 study published in the *American Journal of Industrial Medicine* Dr. Leonardo Trasande, from Mt. Sinai Medical Center, calculated that between 316,000 and 647,000 American babies are born yearly with mercury levels high enough to cause brain damage.[22]

For decades the coal industry has had the support of the American Legislative Exchange Council or ALEC. This obstructionist agency matches fossil fuel magnates like Koch Industries with compliant legislators who work on their behalf to combat the passage of environmental regulations on carbon emissions. Even so, as the toxicity of coal production becomes indisputable, a counter move to adopt renewable sources of energy is gaining traction via market forces and city and state initiatives bulwarked by the inspirational signing of the Paris Agreement on climate change in 2016. In Western states like California, Kansas and Wyoming wind turbines hug the desert floor, spinning their sleek white arms over the parched earth. Even as coal miners are losing their jobs, in the nation's premier coal-producing state—Wyoming—a flat terrain favors the transition to wind power. Both investors and conservative politicians are seeing an economic opportunity in wind farms that promise to make Wyoming the wind capital of the world.

Oil

Oil runs our cars, buses, trains and airplanes. It heats buildings and produces electricity. Drilling for oil on land and water takes place all over the world. As of January 2018 there were 175 active rigs in the Gulf of Mexico.[23] Risks accompany drilling in the ocean environment. Among these risks are explosions, fires and toxic spills that can contaminate the water for miles beyond the oilrig site. The Deepwater Horizon BP spill exemplifies these risks.

Efforts to regulate the oil industry are overshadowed by the rapid development of a 167,000 mile network of oil pipelines across the United States with the attendant possibility of spills. Accidents involving leakage of land-based pipelines have increased almost 60 percent since 2009 with two-thirds of these leaks due to corroded or damaged pipes.[24] In July 2010 an Enbridge Energy pipeline spill sent 840,000 gallons of heavy crude into the Kalamazoo River near Marshall, Michigan. The cleanup cost $500 million. Then, in the summer of 2011, an Exxon Mobil pipeline burst in Montana sending 42,000 gallons of crude into the Yellowstone River. Another Exxon Mobil pipeline running from Patoka, Illinois, to Nederland, Texas ruptured in central Arkansas in April of 2013, dumping about 400,000 gallons of crude into the streets of the small town of Mayflower, causing evacuation of twenty-two homes. Only a month earlier a Chevron pipeline leaked 25,000 gallons of diesel fuel into a wetlands area in Utah, endangering wildlife. The northern tip of this pipeline is set to connect to the existing TransCanada Keystone pipeline that draws a particularly gritty mixture of crude oil from the Canadian tar sands, requiring an addition of chemicals to ease its flow through the pipes. Sediment tested from lakes surrounding the vast tar sands mines is already showing elevated levels of cancer-causing compounds.

Regulatory monitoring by the Pipeline and Hazardous Materials Safety Administration, under the auspices of the US Department of Transportation, is handcuffed by meager funding. Chronic inspector shortage, weak penalties on companies who hedge on repairing pipelines, and a dependence on companies to self-regulate are warnings, say environmentalists and concerned citizens, that the big project which was waiting in the wings—the Keystone

XL—should be rejected. This giant pipeline would bisect the nation from Alberta, Canada to the Gulf of Mexico.

On November 6, 2015, heeding pressure from environmental groups, First Nations in Canada, and farmers and ranchers along the proposed Keystone XL route, President Obama rejected the Presidential permit to approve the pipeline. One of the states through which the pipeline would have traversed is Nebraska. In a unique coalition of forces Nebraskans had for months been fiercely speaking out against the pipeline. The voices of ranchers, farmers, landowners, Republicans and Democrats, urbanites, Native Americans, students and senior citizens including the Apple Pie Brigade of grandmothers who began visiting the governor's office every Monday bearing gifts and letters from citizens—all came together to create a symphony of opposition. The route would have crossed the Sand Hills and entered the ancient Ogallala Aquifer which is the Great Plains oasis for agriculture and raising beef cattle, especially when rainfall is inadequate. In response to current drought conditions Nebraskans were unified in opposing any action that would jeopardize this water source. As one rancher put it: "'there is no red water or blue water, there is clean water or dirty water.'"[25] Mary Pipher, psychologist and author, writes with passion about saving the state where she and her ancestors were born:

> Whatever our politics, we all believe in the sanctity of home. . . . Our coalition allowed us to . . . become agents of our fates . . . and joined together in what the Rev. Dr. Martin Luther King Jr. called 'a beloved community.' We became a state of ordinary heroes who decided that money couldn't buy everything and that some things were sacred.[26]

Despite this valiant struggle the Keystone XL project has been revived due to President Trump's reversal of Obama's decision. Nebraskans will need to reenergize their protests.

Over the late summer and fall of 2016 a four-month confrontation between the Standing Rock Sioux and governmental authorities became front page news. Joined by more than 300 members of other tribes, the Standing Rock Sioux staged a non-violent protest against the plan approved by the state of North Dakota and the US Army Corp of Engineers to build a nearly 1,200 mile long pipeline adjacent to what the tribe attests are sacred ancestral sites. The Dakota Access Pipeline, as it is called, is the property of a Texas oil company. With construction underway the Sioux and fellow protestors stood their ground at the confluence of the Cannonball and Missouri Rivers, through freezing temperatures and pushback from authorities who used fire hoses and rubber bullets to disperse the growing crowds. The designated route of the pipeline originates in the Bakken oil fields in north-western North Dakota and slithers southwest into Illinois, with a section running underneath the Missouri River. This route was chosen by the engineers to avoid the populous city of Bismarck. Perceived by Native Americans as a reenactment of colonial prejudice and outright theft of native lands the construction, according to the Sioux, would not only infringe on sacred sites but also threaten a precious resource: water. The protestors call themselves 'water-protectors' and their protest *Mni Wiconi* or *Water is Life*. An Ojibwe supporter calls this protest "a new Thanksgiving gift" for *all* Americans.[27] Although President Obama ordered a halt to construction of the pipeline, pending a new review, President Trump has given the go-ahead to resume construction of the Dakota Access Pipeline.

Even as the current administration pursues goals that eviscerate regulatory environmental laws there is pushback. Both cities and states are stepping forward to combat climate change. Renewables, once on the fringe of the market, are making headway as competitors with the oil industry. In May of 2007, for example, Greenberg, Kansas suffered a one and one-half mile wide tornado that destroyed the city. Residents began to rebuild using wind farms along with oil as sources of energy. This 'greening' of Greenberg confronts a two billion dollar oil industry owned by the Koch Brothers who are natives of Kansas. A Renewable Portfolio Standard was passed in the state legislature that compels the state to reach 20 percent of its energy needs through wind energy by 2020. Ranchers and farmers across Kansas applaud this action. The Koch Brothers are trying to repeal the law to protect their oil interests.

Another development that challenges the fossil fuel industry is the divestment movement which began in 2011 on certain college campuses and has now spread worldwide. In a stunning announcement timed to precede the opening of the United Nations Climate Change Summit in September 2014 Steven Rockefeller, Valerie Rockefeller Wayne (chairwoman of the Rockefeller Brothers Fund) and Stephen Heintz, the fund's president, said that the $860 million dollar philanthropic organization was withdrawing investments in oil. The irony that John D. Rockefeller amassed his fortune in oil, specifically Standard Oil, is not lost on these three executives. In fact they believe that the first Rockefeller would approve this action as a political, financial and, most importantly, an ethical statement. The fund has already eliminated investments related to coal and tar sands.

Investors in the business and institutional worlds are dropping fossil fuel stocks from their portfolios at a remarkable rate. In June of 2015, for example, Norway's Parliament voted to order the 890 billion dollar government pension fund, considered the largest in the world, to sell off many of its investments in the coal industry.[28] Norway is a major producer of fossil fuels; the fund itself was built on revenues from North Sea oil. As of December 2017 Norway is poised to divest from oil as well. A recent decision by another big player, the World Bank, is worthy of note. In solidarity with the Paris Agreement, the World Bank says it will withdraw financial support not only from coal mining (a previous decision) but also from oil and gas exploration by 2019.[29]

Natural Gas

Natural gas has been touted as an alternative to coal and oil, a panacea that comes close to 'clean energy' because it emits less carbon dioxide than coal and degrades faster in the atmosphere. Scientists in this camp believe that methane—the base substance of natural gas—is more controllable than carbon dioxide emissions from coal and that an aggressive plan to minimize methane leaks from hydraulic fracturing is the most feasible and immediate way to reduce global warming. Anthony Ingraffea, a longtime oil and gas engineer who helped develop hydraulic (or hydro) fracturing for the Energy Department, disagrees. He writes in a *New York Times* editorial in July 2013:

> This gas is not 'clean' . . . and is not a 'bridge' to a renewable energy future—it's a gangplank to more warming and away from clean energy investments. . . . Methane is a far more powerful greenhouse gas than carbon dioxide, though it doesn't last nearly as long in the atmosphere. Still, over a 20-year period, one pound of it traps as much heat as at least 72 pounds of carbon dioxide. Its potency declines, but even after a century, it is at least 25 times as powerful as carbon dioxide. When burned, natural gas emits half the carbon dioxide of coal, but methane leakage eviscerates this advantage because of its heat-trapping power.[30]

The concentration of methane (CH_4) in the atmosphere has more than doubled since preindustrial times. In 1950 methane concentrations were at 1000 ppb. Since then a steady increase has been recorded. A sharp hike that surprises scientists occurred over the past decade, with a dramatic increase of 20 ppb between 2014 and 2015. Today the total methane concentration is 1,830 ppb.[31] While intensive farming is a factor in the release of methane, leakage from hydrofracturing operations can also contribute. Hydrofracturing has become the main method for extracting natural gas, providing two-thirds of America's natural gas supply.[32]

Methane is a natural product of vegetative decay; its odor is evident in swamps and landfills. It serves life by assisting the process of dissolution and death. Methane is also buried deep in tundra areas of the globe where it is poised to escape into the atmosphere as the tundra melts due to global warming. The new technique of hydrofracturing, commonly known as fracking, while efficient at reaching deep levels of shale, involves pressurized pumping of enormous amounts of fluid underground—a mix of water, sand and chemicals—to crack the shale and drive the released gas to the surface. According to the U.S. Energy Information Administration global resources of shale oil and gas are abundant.

In regions that are economically depressed big oil companies are promoting fracking as a job-creator. In South Africa, for example, where unemployment is over 26 percent, Shell is trying to set up fracking operations. Many South Africans fear that Shell's possible use of the aquifer to supply water, and the threat of methane leakage from pipelines which distribute the natural gas, will create devastating effects. They argue that the development of solar and wind is more suitable to a landscape of sun-drenched flatlands.

Safety measures for fracking operations are often put aside for later consideration, especially in the developing world where the lure of quick energy and money for investors is driving the natural gas incentive. The Indonesian government, for example, is considering allowing shale drilling in a section of Java where, in 2006, drilling led to the eruption of a mud volcano which killed at least thirteen people and left many homeless.

Fracking poses two risks to water systems. First, the operation requires vast quantities of water. The depletion of water sources is particularly problematic in drought-prone regions. Second, contamination of water can occur from methane leakage in cracked pipelines and from *flowback*—the used water that holds the natural gas which drilling regurgitates to the surface. Flowback is laced with as many as 632 chemicals including acetaldehyde, ammonium chloride, arsenic, benzene, formaldehyde, lead, mercury, and radioactive radium. 25 percent of these chemicals are linked to cancer; 37 percent impact hormones; 40 percent to 50 percent affect the nervous, immune and cardiovascular systems and the kidneys; and 75 percent affect sensory organs and gastrointestinal and respiratory systems.[33]

Fracking on farmland is particularly hazardous to the food supply and livestock who graze near toxic wastewater which is stored in open pits or ponds before being trucked away. Thirty to seventy percent of spent fracking fluid is not removed and remains to pollute subsoil and possibly water systems for years to come.[34] As shown by filmmaker and activist Josh Fox, in his 2010 documentary *Gasland*, leakage of methane and chemicals into ground water has affected the tap water in a number of communities. One scene in the film shows a resident of Dimmick, PA turning on the kitchen faucet only to witness a burst of flames.

Fracking companies are also luring residents to sell their land for drilling rights. Monetary compensation is a tempting incentive and some landowners have buckled, becoming *shaleionaires* overnight. But not all. Some homeowners, like Walter Jaworski of Northfield, Massachusetts, are speaking out. Jaworski is a retired veterinarian whose new hobby is cattle ranching on his

200 acres of forest and pasture. In 2014 Kinder Morgan, an energy company giant, submitted a proposal to build a 188-mile natural gas pipeline across the state of Massachusetts, at a cost of two to three billion dollars. The pipeline would slice right through Jaworski's property. Kinder Morgan at first received compliance from Jaworski to do the survey, but when he found out that core drilling was a part of the survey he sent the company a letter revoking its right to survey. He and other homeowners who opposed the pipeline started a resistance strategy, holding protest marches and persuading senators and congressmen to help them stop the pipeline. In April of 2016 Kinder Morgan withdrew its pipeline proposal.

Advances in computer processing are allowing geologists to now see evidence of gas and oil fields in the oceans' depths, way below what has been explored and drilled. In fact, scientists now think that only about 10 percent of the world's deepwater reserves have been tapped. New mining and drilling technologies using very strong alloys would allow drill bits to go into hot, high-pressure fields deep in the Gulf of Mexico, off the coasts of Brazil, Australia and India, and along the west coast of Africa. The Arctic remains an enticing area for exploration. Will the world's leaders in government and business listen to the IPCC's 2014 recommendation that deep deposits of fossil fuels remain untouched? Or will they flaunt this warning and take the plunge into deepwater reserves, leaving the adoption of renewable energies for another day? Will concerned citizens like Walter Jaworski gather in grass-roots organizations and make their voices heard in the halls of government and the offices of powerful corporations? The Berkshire Environmental Action Team (BEAT), for example, actively opposes further pipeline projects and, as a broader mission, amasses support to obstruct the fossil fuel industry in the Northeast and promote clean energy alternatives.

AGRIBUSINESS

Between 1987 and 1993 Heather Apple was president of the Heritage Seed Program, a branch of the Canadian Organic Growers association. She catapulted this program into public awareness by taking to the airwaves of radio and film to inspire fellow gardeners to come together and establish a seed bank. Her mission was to preserve seeds used by our ancestors for future generations. Heather recognized the growing disconnect between farming and culture, between the field (L. *ager*) and a community's work in cultivating the field. She was witnessing the descent of agri*culture* into agri*business*. Heather established a grass-roots program that invited people to donate seeds, many of which had a family story attached. The seeds would then be distributed to groups of gardeners and small farmers who would agree to plant and care for the seeds. Specimens of each seed would also be safeguarded in a central seed bank. Today, under a new name—Seeds of Diversity Canada—the bond between the soil, seeds, and communities continues.

All food comes from seed. In response to the threat of climate change a global seed bank was erected in 2008 beneath the permafrost on an island north of mainland Norway in the Arctic Ocean. This year Norway is spending $13 million to upgrade the facility. Referred to as the 'doomsday vault' because it was built to be impervious even to the ravages of nuclear war this repository, the Svalbard Global Seed Vault, stores over 800,000 seed samples from 4.5 million crop varieties as well as their wild kinfolk.[35] These seeds hold in their genes the history of the Agricultural Revolution. Svalbard serves as a hub for a global network of seed banks that regularly send backup seed samples to be stored in the vault for future generations.

Agri*culture* is all about cultivating good food. It is about farmers and farming communities growing crops on a small scale, raising livestock, and using local distribution to sell their produce. Agri*business* is about using food to make money. The corporate worldview defines soil, plants and animals as inanimate resources for human use and consumption. The catchwords of corporate policy are speed and volume. Efficiency and productivity are achieved through fossil fuel-powered machinery, monoculture—the massive planting of one crop such as corn or soybeans—and inputs such as chemical fertilizers, pesticides and herbicides.

Corporate farms have supplanted the small-scale traditional farming operation. Hundreds of acres of land are set aside for monoculture using the latest in tractors and harvesters. Without crop diversity, which would protect plants from pest infestation, pesticides become a necessary evil. Nature would replenish the exhausted soil over time, but this process is too slow for agribusiness so chemical fertilizers are applied to accelerate growth. By the time the finished product—food—arrives at your supermarket (by means of fossil fuels) it has been nutritionally degraded and tainted with poison. The very word *product* to define food connotes an object rather than a living organism. Meanwhile, packaged varieties of 'food' are doctored through processing with additives and preservatives inserted to imitate the natural taste and extend shelf life. In *Fast Food Nation* Eric Schlosser discusses how the artificial flavor industry is busy making real food obsolete at profitable revenues of about $1.4 billion annually. For example, the artificial strawberry milkshake sold by Burger King mimics the real thing. Just the smell of a strawberry engages at least 350 different natural chemicals in infinitesimal amounts, so the industry figures out how to replicate Nature by concocting a stew of chemical compounds which, along with a dash of color additive, conjures up the strawberry milkshake.

Intensive farming methods deliver the similitude of perfect, nutritious food. Peeling back the cornhusk reveals rows of plump, perfect corn kernels bulging with sweet juices (genetically modified corn may now be even more perfect). The apple in the supermarket is a shiny red, without blemish. Its skin contains a pesticide but it looks good and that is what counts. One is reminded of the fairytale in which the wicked queen, disguised as an old crone, visits Snow White at the cottage of the seven dwarfs and offers a most delectable apple, one bite of which will put Snow White into a deadly sleep.

In the October 9, 2016 issue of *The New York Times Magazine* journalist and activist Michael Pollan writes about agribusiness' Big Food pyramid. At its base is Big Ag, the powerhouse of the Farm Belt's soybean-corn industry along with growers of other major crops as well as companies like Monsanto that supply these mega growers with seeds, pesticides and herbicides. Big Ag also supplies raw ingredients (e.g., corn) for the packaged food sector to process (e.g., high fructose corn syrup), plus feed grain for Big Meat which occupies the second level of the pyramid. Here reside the select mega companies that manage and process the flesh of all the animals we eat (e.g., cows, pigs, chickens). At the pyramid's zenith sit retail supermarkets and fast food chains that sell the so-called food.

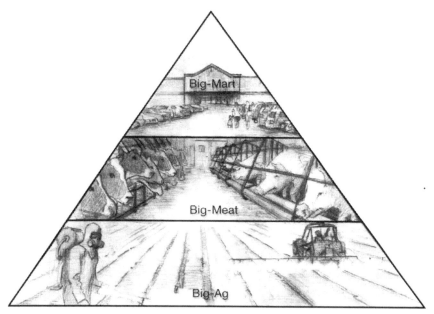

Figure 6.2.   Big Food Pyramid by Dominique Medici.
Used with the permission of Dominique Medici.

Let us for a moment take a closer look at the second level of the pyramid—Big Meat. Here, for example, are cows, crowded into unsanitary pens where they stand in their own feces. They are fattened on grain, which is poorly digested by their double stomachs, and then butchered. Body parts are washed in ammonia to kill *e coli* from feces smeared on the carcasses; then the flesh is ground up, made into patties, packaged and shipped to fast-food destinations and supermarkets for human consumption. If any of us were to witness this assembly line process up close, with its smells and mechanized treatment of life, we might never eat another hamburger.

Traditional farmers (and their modern equivalent, organic farmers) understand the rhythms of the land and can anticipate the vagaries of weather by storing up for times of scarcity or by leaving the land fallow for a season to rest. Their instinctive respect for the web of life leads them to use natural ways to preserve the integrity of that web. They remember that Nature is their teacher. By acquainting themselves with her methods they mimic her successes. Crop diversity, crop rotation, and applying natural fertilizers such as manure, peat humus, and compost have been practiced for centuries all over the world, with success. Moving the broccoli to another location next spring is known to fool certain bugs; and planting some pungent marigolds next to the tomatoes discourages those nasty tomato hornworms. Herbs for medicinal purposes and perennial favorites like asparagus are part of an overall design. Cover crops such as grasses of timothy, alfalfa, clover, oats and hops are planted for grazing and for winter soil enrichment, particularly the legumes such as clover and alfalfa whose root systems harbor the symbiotic bacteria that draw nitrogen into the soil. If corn is planted one year in a certain plot of land then the next year alfalfa grass will be substituted to restore soil fertility.

Grass is the foundation of an intricate food chain of symbiotic relationships that make up the agricultural ecosystem. Walt Whitman reminds us of the beauty and worth of this simple verdant substance we call grass. He writes:

> A child said *What is the grass?* Fetching it to me with full hands;
> How could I answer the child? I do not know what it
>   is any more than he.
> I guess it must be the flag of my disposition, out of
>   hopeful green stuff woven.
> Or I guess it is the handkerchief of the Lord,
> A scented gift and remembrancer designedly dropt,
> Bearing the owner's name someway in the corners,
>   that we may see and remark, and say *Whose?*[36]

Joel Salatin is an organic farmer and founder of a small-scale sustainable livestock farm called Polyface Farm in Virginia. Salatin promotes the practices of traditional farming. He speaks of a relationship between grasses, cows, pigs and chickens. Beef cattle graze on grass, their natural diet, in two plant-ings. Cleanup is accomplished by the hens (Salatin calls them his "'sanitation crew'") who are set loose in the pasture to eat fly larvae and grubs out of the cow patties.[37] This activity keeps parasitical bacteria in check so that cows don't have to be injected with antibiotics. A great diversity of grasses, legumes, wildflowers and insects enrich the pasture which also stays lush and green from the waste of both cows and hens. Each grazing area is allowed to sit fallow until the second grazing area has been used. Pigs are allowed to forage, as is their pleasure, aerating the soil as they go until time for slaughter which is done humanely, unlike the brutality of the killing floors in factory farms.

But there is even something more basic than grass, and that is the soil. Beneath and supporting all grasses and plants is the Earth herself. Good soil is alive with all kinds of little beings working as a community of interest to turn the soil into healthy, food-bearing loam. The Hebrew word for *earth* or *soil* is *adama*. The Hebrew word for *living* is *hava*—or *eve*. So our ancestors Adam and Eve were born from and manifested the *living earth*—*hava adama*. The garden which they tended was themselves.

The womb of life, the soil, is a moist mix that contains a plethora of mi-croorganisms such as fungi, protozoa, nematodes and bacteria. Salatin calls the soil the "'earth's stomach.'"[38] One teaspoon of rich soil or humus can contain one billion bacteria comprising 40,000 species, plus 20,000 species of fungi![39] The decay of plants and animals softened by rain and snow, digested and excreted in this microscopic factory, becomes the compost that replen-ishes the soil. It is of concern to scientists to recently discover that microbial organisms in the soil of the southwest desert of the United States, who protect against topsoil erosion and fertilize the soil, are showing signs of stress in response to the warming temperatures of the earth's crust.

The soil is in our bodies through the food we eat—be it rich in wholesome, vital nutrients or laced with pesticides. A home gardener knows that when soil quality deteriorates plants lose nutritional value and are prone to pests and disease, just as pathogens invade our bodies when stress reduces the body's resistance. As human beings remove themselves mentally and spiritu-ally from the Earth the soil is no longer appreciated as Earth's body. While most of us would not relish returning to a pre-mechanized age it is important to recognize the difference between walking behind an ox, as the wooden plow turns up the moist earth that smells of springtime, and sitting in the cocoon-like cab of a spanking new, air-conditioned seven foot tall harvester that allows the farmer to never touch the earth with his foot nor smell its loamy freshness. In such an enclosure who cannot but lose awareness of the subtle connection between the human body and the breathing earth?

Wendell Berry is a farmer turned ecologist, philosopher and poet. He worries that the removal of the human being from a hands-on connection to his work by mechanical conveniences may also atrophy his mental faculties. In his book *Home Economics* Berry relates the *lesser or human economy* to the *Great Economy* of Nature. When the former breaks off from and disobeys the laws of the *Great Economy* upon which it depends—when, for example, farming conglomerates allow top soil erosion for quick profits or companies make inferior products—then not only is the quality of work and product degraded but so too is the mind of the person that did the inferior work.[40] Berry suggests an even deeper corruption, a deprivation of heart and spirit that is tied to a lack of responsibility and care for the thing made.

Inputs

The word *intensive* in intensive farming refers to the intensification of food productivity through monocropping and the application of three major inputs: chemical fertilizers, pesticides, and herbicides. When these inputs are 'put into' the soil and onto plants the soil suffers nutrient depletion, pollution and exhaustion. The living earth—*hava adama*—becomes the dying earth. According to population biologist David Pimental, "'over the past 40 years it is estimated that 30 percent of the world's cropland has been rendered unproductive.'"[41]

How exactly do these three types of input harm the soil and the crops that grow in that soil? Inorganic chemical fertilizers contain a high nitrogen count (N) with negligible phosphorus (P) and potassium (K). They are not the same as organic, decayed plant matter known as humus which contains, in addition to those three major ingredients, micronutrients such as trace minerals. These minerals enhance a plant's ability to produce polyphenols which are antioxidants that protect plants from pests. Without natural protection plants attract pests—thus the need for pesticides. In the 1920s chemical fertilizers were synthesized using energy from natural gas (methane) to transform atmospheric nitrogen into gaseous ammonia (NH_3) which, when combined with nitric acid (HNO_3), becomes ammonium nitrate. This chemical compound has explosive properties and was used in the munitions industry in World War II. After the war ammonium nitrate became a quick-fix agricultural fertilizer because its high nitrogen content promoted high crop yields. However, several dangers surfaced including nitrogen burn, mineral depletion, and toxic soil acidification. The latter increases the amount of aluminum and other toxic metals like uranium in the soil. When this soil leaches into ground water and contaminates it, that water, if consumed, can cause high blood pressure, kidney damage and cancer.

Moreover, nitrogen-rich fertilizer run-off from croplands is contaminating water in lakes and seas, causing dead zones to develop. In the Gulf of Mexico the runoff from farmlands abutting the Mississippi River has created a hypoxic zone, killing fish and threatening the nation's commercial and recreational marine resources.

From an insect's point of view the farmer's crop is food for the taking. To solve the perennial battle between man and insect the agrochemical industry invented a powerful weapon: pesticides. The problem with this miracle product is that its toxicity not only impairs the designated insect; it sickens the human being, and can harm beneficial insects. Every time the pest mutates out of harm's way the agrochemical company has to come up with a more toxic pesticide. Sevin joins a number of virulent pesticides that contain carbaryl, a wide-spectrum insecticide which has a moderate to very toxic effect on humans through skin contact with sprayed crops, inhalation of the spray, or ingestion of sprayed crops. Carbaryl has been shown to have mutagenic effects in rats, affecting cell mitosis and chromosomes, and, when combined with nitrite, produces carcinogenic effects.

A series of chemicals called endocrine disruptors are also used prominently in pesticides. Atrazine, for example, behaves like weak estrogen and can seep into the water supply causing strange deformities in amphibians and fish, especially in their sexual organs. Male frogs, for example, are showing female characteristics such as producing eggs.[42] Sexual abnormalities are being matched among humans, particularly among newborn boys where the incidence of undescended testicles is increasing.[43]

Herbicides, the third input, were invented to kill unwanted plants or weeds. The first herbicide to be developed, 2,4-D, is an ingredient in Agent Orange, the Vietnam War defoliant that caused health problems in returning soldiers. 2,4-D was commercialized by the Sherwin-Williams Paint company in the late 1940s. It is still used today because it is easy and inexpensive to manufacture. Some herbicides are known to have mutagenic and carcinogenic effects. Research now shows that the herbicide paraquat, which is exported to the United States from Britain but is banned in Britain and the European Union, poses a risk of Parkinson's disease.

The most famous and popular herbicide, glyphosate, is a tiny molecule, an analog of glycine that joins 19 other amino acids as the building blocks of proteins in all living organisms. Invented by the Stauffer Chemical Co. in the 1950s as a descaling agent to clean mineral deposits off industrial machines, glyphosate was bought out and patented in 1969 by Monsanto to use as an herbicide under the brand name Roundup. It had been discovered that glyphosate's ability to bind and deactivate mineral deposits came with another talent: the capacity of the chemical to disrupt the biochemical pathway that all bacteria and plants have in creating their own proteins by removing an essential enzyme from the process of synthesizing all twenty amino acids. When applied to the plant (aka weed) it promptly dies. Until about ten years ago it was believed by scientists that the protein-producing pathway was not present in animals, making Roundup a safe herbicide.

With Roundup heralded as the safest herbicide by scientists and government regulatory agencies Monsanto proceeded to create the first herbicide-tolerant crop through biotechnology. By genetically engineering a corn seed to be resistant to Roundup Monsanto became the premier agrochemical company in the world. Seeds of Roundup Ready corn could be planted and the herbicide applied on weeds without harming the corn stalks. The company won a Supreme Court ruling in 1982 that reversed a long-standing decision that living things could not be patented allowing the company to patent its new genetically modified corn seed. This victory, which opened the door for Monsanto to become a seed monopoly, has fomented controversy particularly amongst farmers whose custom of saving, reusing and even developing seed varieties is now challenged by Monsanto's legal team. Furthermore, about ten years ago scientists were alarmed to discover that the protein-producing pathway is not exclusive to bacteria and plants but exists in animal physiology as well, specifically in the 100 trillion bacterial cells that live in the intestines of animals and stimulate health in all organs. Therefore, when we human beings eat Roundup Ready crops we ingest glyphosate. As this substance slowly degrades in our vital organs, it acts as an antibiotic, killing the bacteria necessary to bodily health. We are also ingesting Roundup's inactive ingredients such as *adjuvants* which have been found to kill human embryonic, placental and umbilical cells in vitro even at low dosages. It is Roundup, also, which when sprayed on milkweed, kills the larva of the endangered monarch butterfly whose exclusive breeding ground is the milkweed pod.

The Dust Bowl

In the United States, the Dust Bowl remains an instructive example of an eco-cultural disaster involving misuse of the soil combined with severe drought. During the Depression of the 1930s a series of severe dust storms hit the plains states of Texas, Oklahoma, and Kansas. Deep plowing and intensive planting of wheat (a non-drought resistant crop) by farmers who had migrated in droves to the area had depleted the virgin topsoil, turning it into dust. A look at the geography and weather patterns of the area might have warned the enthusiastic settlers that the only thing holding and nurturing the soil was the prairie grass. This landmass is semi-arid with years of extended drought alternating with years of unusual wetness that support agriculture. The region is

Figure 6.3.   Dust Storm in Spearman Texas.
Courtesy of National Oceanic and Atmospheric Administration (NOAA).

also susceptible to winds higher than any other location except coastal areas. The pendulum swing to a confluence of drought and heavy winds marked the 1930s which became known as the *dirty thirties.*

On April 14, 1935, known as Black Sunday, twenty mammoth dust storms caused great damage to lands and houses. Day was turned to night and roosters, thinking it was night, went to sleep. Families were displaced. Many of the 500,000 people who were left homeless traveled to California in search of work. During his first 100 days in office President Franklin Delano Roosevelt implemented governmental programs to restore ecological balance. One agency, the Soil Erosion Service, remains active under its new name, the Natural Resources Conservation Service (NRCS). Roosevelt set up a grand plan for reforestation knowing full well the critical role that trees play in holding and nurturing the soil. He offered a sober prediction, warning that "the nation that destroys its soil destroys itself."[44] Topsoil is becoming an endangered species. According to a 2006 study by David Pimental the United States is losing its topsoil through erosion ten times faster than it takes for soil to naturally replenish itself—a process which entails 500 years to produce one inch of topsoil—while China and India are losing soil at an even faster rate.[45]

Since the Agricultural Revolution 10,000 years ago we have been subsisting on food that comes mostly from grasses that produce edible seeds. These cereals in turn depend upon the soil for their nutritional quality. Wes Jackson, founder of the Land Institute in Salina, Kansas, views soil as a casualty of industrial agriculture, stating that "'soil is more important than oil and just as nonrenewable.'"[46] Jackson is on a mission to change annual monoculture by switching to a sustainable prairie-like system of perennial polyculture. He believes prairies are models for fields containing varieties of complementary species that can pollinate each other, mutually ward off pests and diseases and thereby flourish without chemical fertilizers and pesticides. His first successful product, cultivated at the Land Institute, is a domesticated wild perennial grain called Kernza from which a chewy, delectable bread can be made.

Gmos

Gmo means *genetically modified organism*. Genetic engineering or biotechnology has been controversial from the start. Those in favor of genetically manipulating staple crops point to their potential as a means to abate global hunger. For example, Golden Rice, developed in the Philippines, is a unique blend containing a corn gene and a bacterium gene, making it the only variety of rice to produce beta-carotene, an important source of Vitamin A. In August of 2013 protestors smashed down high fences surrounding a Golden Rice field and uprooted the plants in the Bricol region of the Philippines. These activists, as well as other critics, cited the possible risk of genetically engineered crops to human health and accused the big agrochemical companies of profiteering at the expense of poor farmers and consumers.

Today about 90 percent of soybeans and 70 percent of corn and cotton are herbicide-resistant through Roundup or rival brands that feature genetic modification. But it is not clear that these crops are fulfilling their promised bounty or facilitating a decline in herbicide and pesticide use. In the Southern United States, for example, a tenacious plant, *Palmer amaranth* (pigweed), repels herbicides and is overrunning cotton fields. Critics argue that weeds will win the warfare by mutating and that more sustainable methods to contain them, like cover crops or crop rotation, are needed. A coalition of fruit and vegetable farmers and canners who call themselves Save Our Crops Coalition are petitioning the US government to intervene in the twenty genetically engineered herbicide-resistant crops awaiting approval. United Nations data released in October 2016 shows that, contrary to expectations, yield gains in genetically modified crops in the United States remain comparable to conventional crops grown in France and Germany where genetic modification is outlawed. Moreover, there is no evidence of a decrease in pesticide use, and the application of herbicides (which were touted as unnecessary) is on the rise.

A telling example of the questionable benefits of a Gmo product was the shift to genetically-modified, high-yielding rice, wheat and corn varieties as part of the Green Revolution in India. Because the goal was to feed a growing population quantity was the criterion. The 'improved' variety of rice had short roots and stems so that plant energy could go directly into grain. The dwarfing also enabled heavy seed heads swollen by chemical fertilizers and irrigation to be supported. Artificially bolstered by pesticides crop yields were impressive and the Green Revolution was praised, until evidence of meager nutritional value was discovered. People were being fed but undernourished.

Traditional farmers in India have long cultivated local *landraces* of rice that are dryland, non-irrigated crops. They do not yield the quantity that 'improved varieties' do but they taste better. It turns out that taste is not a superfluous trait in determining nutritional value. Evolution has wired human beings to seek out the neurochemical rewards of food highly packed with healthful ingredients by making it taste good. And it turns out that taste has to do with deep roots, which the landraces have. A rice plant cannot be bred to have both a short stem and long roots because both traits are controlled by the same gene. So a decision must be made as to the aim of rice production: is the aim quantity or quality? Long roots mean that the plant is more drought-tolerant, resilient, and nutritious because the roots can reach deeper for water and penetrate the highly mineralized subsoil. It is this array of minerals that manifests as taste and color in food as well as offering complete nutrition vital to brain function and over-all health. These scientific facts agree with the ancient Chhāndôgya Upanishad that states: "The finest quality of the food we swallow rises up as mind."[47]

Vandana Shiva, quantum physicist and environmental activist, is an advocate for traditional methods of farming in India, her home country. As founder of the Research Foundation for Science, Technology and Ecology and the Navdanya organic seed network she speaks out against the corporate take-over of agriculture, the shrinking of biological diversity, and the destruction of the world's ecosystems. In the 1970's Shiva joined the Chipko movement (*chipko* is Hindi for *hug*) in which women gathered around trees to prevent their being felled during the Green Revolution. In 1993 when Cargill filed for patents to control traditional Indian seeds Shiva and local farmers set fire to company files and led a mass demonstration in Delhi. Cargill backed down.

Shiva views biotechnology and patenting of life forms as *resourcism*—a utilitarian mindset that sees the world as a thing to be used and controlled: a new slave trade, but this time in genetic materials. Shiva's philosophy reflects the traditional Indian worldview of the natural world as sacred. There is, she says, an Earth family in which all beings, large and small, participate in the web of life equally. Each being has an obligation to uphold the natural balance.

The informed activism of Vandana Shiva shows us that it is possible for each of us to find ways to articulate and fight for a new ethical standard of socioeconomic policy and practice, one that values all life and rejects the current corporate control of economic and social policy which has become corrupted to favor those with wealth and status. It is evident that the two engines of modern capitalism—the fossil fuel industry and agribusiness—play a primary role in causing environmental deterioration. They must be replaced with life-affirming, sustainable energy alternatives and agricultural practices. Much of the technology for this shift in cultural practice is already in place. What lags behind is the robust shift in worldview that will energize people, from local communities to nations, to demand and execute cultural change. Speaking of a change in mindset it was Franklin Roosevelt who said: "Men are not prisoners of fate, but only prisoners of their own minds."[48]

The arc of *Homesick* turns now to the return journey—the return to our home in Mother Earth, the return to sanity. We begin by reestablishing a connection to the worldview of indigenous peoples whose dedication to sustaining the web of life and preserving the Earth as sacred space are cultural values that we, their descendants, have forgotten. A reengagement with the thinking and lifestyle of our earliest ancestors prepares us to expand the mind's horizon and broaden the heart's affections.

Indigenous peoples live the ecocentric paradigm that we in the modern world need once again to profess and translate into practice. The ruling symbol of this paradigm is a web—the web of life—which represents the reality of interconnectedness. By reconnecting to this web, in mind and heart, the illusion of separateness is pierced. The genius of the human species is directed away from what Jewish mystic Abraham Heschel calls "the arrogance that guides the traffic in our mind" and is guided towards a felt appreciation of life in all its myriad forms. [49] This ancient understanding, lying dormant within us, awaits resuscitation. It will lead us home.

Part III

RETURN

Chapter Seven

The Web of Life

There are more things in heaven and earth, Horatio,
Than are dreamt of in your philosophy

—*Hamlet*, Hamlet I:5

The ruby-throated hummingbird (*Archilochus colubris*) who graces our gardens with his sleek green and red body and superfast movements is perhaps the most well-known species of the Family *Trochilidae*. His brothers and sisters belong to two subfamilies: *Phaethornithinae* which has only 6 genera and *Trochilinae* (to which the ruby-throated belongs) which has 101 genera.

Our little friend is 3 to 5 inches long and has a wing flap of about 50 times per second (in some cases up to 200 flaps per second!)—the highest metabolism of any warm-blooded animal. This tiny gymnast also has the ability to fly very fast, above 34 mph. His aerodynamic skill includes backwards and upside-down motions. You may have seen him hovering in midair while drinking from the straw of his bill the sweet nectar of a red zinnia before zooming off into space. The hummingbird has even adapted to times of food scarcity by suspending animation—a hibernation-like skill—to lower his metabolism.

Scientists have studied the co-evolution of the hummingbird, a specialized nectarivore, with bird-pollinated flowers. In this symbiotic relationship the hummingbird's preference for flowers of red, orange and bright pink hues has been duly acknowledged by the flowers who through this narrow color spectrum help to reduce competition by insects and reserve their nectar for the hummingbird. The particular flowers that attract the hummingbird also produce nectar with more sucrose which is delectable to their winged friends. Insect-pollinated flowers, on the other hand, have a stronger nectar that contains more fructose and glucose which insects crave. In the northern Andes

Figure 7.1. Ruby-throated hummingbird (Archilochus colubris) at the flower gardens of the Biltmore Estate in Asheville, North Carolina.
Courtesy of Dick Daniels.

the co-evolution between hummingbird and flower is particularly striking. Here the sword-billed hummingbird, genus *Ensifera ensifera* (only one species), has devised a spectacular adaptation to his favorite flower, the pink tubular passion flower—*Passiflora mixta*, itself one of forty-seven species. This hummingbird's bill and tongue are long—longer than his body. In fact these unusual dimensions make grooming awkward; toilette must be done with the feet. But this inconvenience is outweighed by the precision with which the bill spears the inner chamber of the corolla, nestles in the delectable juices, and deftly extracts the nectar of his lover. It appears that the name Passionflower is a good fit.

Another ingenious example of symbiosis occurs in the legume family which includes peas, vetch, alfalfa, peanuts and clover. These plants grow in

Figure 7.2. Pea plant with nodules on roots by Dominique Medici.
Used with the permission of Dominique Medici.

their soil laboratory by means of an important lab assistant, rhizobia bacteria, who live in the nodules of the legume root system. Rhizobia are a type of cyanobacteria, ancient marine microorganisms which may be the first living organisms on the planet and perhaps the ancestral factory for photosynthesis.[1] The rhizobia are able to fix nitrogen in the soil by absorbing and converting inert atmospheric nitrogen (N2) into ammonium (NH4) and other nitrogen compounds important to plant growth. This transmutation also enables the fixed nitrogen to be released to enrich the soil when the plant dies, providing successor plants with the 'green manure' in which to grow.

The relationship of bird to flower and rhizobia bacteria to legume roots are but two in a myriad of examples of the ecological laws of interdependence and reciprocity at work in the world of Nature. Indeed, from the galaxies to the spider web in your backyard all life forms are members of an inclusive club called the *web of life.*

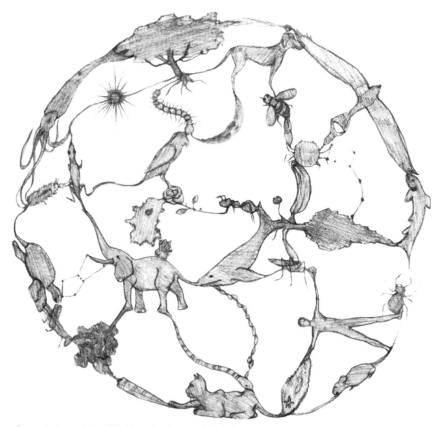

Figure 7.3. Web of life by Dominique Medici.
Used with the permission of Dominique Medici.

In *The Universe Story* Thomas Berry and co-author physicist Brian Swimme speak of three evolutionary principles to which life forms adhere: *differentiation*, or the diversification of species; *interiority* or *autopoiesis*, the ingenious uniqueness of each species as an expression of evolutionary diversity; and *communion*, the interdependence of all species in biological ecosystems. For Berry this communion is also a spiritual law between all created beings as part of an interconnected, sacred network. In *The Great Work* he states that the task of this age is "to realize in thought and action that the universe is a communion of subjects, not a collection of objects."[2] This realization requires a shift in human consciousness, away from the idea of exploitation of the world as object to the understanding of *cosmogenesis:* the emergence of this world as a planetary community, a web of organisms who share equally of the Earth's bounty. Berry argues that this shift depends upon the restoration in the human psyche of the female energy, the nurturing impulse, which is akin to Nature herself.

Sometimes when one is simply present to a natural setting—a sunset, a mountain view, a forest teeming with sounds and smells of the green earth—there is a sudden realization that one's interior consciousness is recognizing its outward form as the beloved. This is a glimpse of the ancient hermetic metaphor: *as above, so below; as without, so within.* In her book, *World as Lover, World as Self,* Joanna Macy brings Buddhist compassion and environmental activism together to remind us that this unified vision of lover and beloved happens in those moments when we see any and all inhabitants of the natural world as myself in another form. Love arises and this love inspires us to work to restore health to the world, and thus to ourselves.

Lame Deer, Lakota Sioux shaman, explains this heightened experience of unity in diversity as the effect of recognizing that every life form is *wakan—* holy. "Nothing is so small and unimportant," he writes, "but it has a spirit given to it by Wakan Tanka . . . splitting itself up into stones, trees, tiny insects even, making them all wakan by his ever-presence. And in turn all these myriad of things which make up the universe flowing back to their source, united in the one Grandfather Spirit."[3]

This comprehension of a sacred web of life appears in many cultures and philosophies. Marcus Aurelius, Roman emperor and Stoic philosopher, remarks in his *Meditations*:

Always think of the universe as one living organism, with a single substance and a single soul; and observe how all things are submitted to the single perceptivity of this one whole, all are moved by its single impulse, and all play their part in the causation of every event that happens. Remark the intricacy of the skein, the complexity of the web.[4]

While most of us in our daily routine live the illusion of a separate existence, in fact the reality is 180 degrees in the opposite direction. We are members of a web of life and we owe our existence to its healthy operation. When this web is examined closely—which is the intent of this chapter—it reveals three dimensions that co-exist: biological, social or cultural, and spiritual. These levels interweave, contracting and expanding in an accordion-like manner, depending upon the eye of the observer.

Beneath the biological web of ecosystems is the dance of the subatomic world. Physically the web of life starts here, in this microscopic terrain.

DANCING IN THE SUBATOMIC WEB

Discoveries in modern physics elucidate the complexity of the web of life in its microscopic form at the subatomic level. These discoveries offer a surprising and aesthetically pleasing metaphor for the web's magnificent design: the dance. Let us trace the main scientific developments that brought about this revelatory perspective.

When physicist Max Planck discovered that heat radiation delivers its energy in packets and not in a continuous stream he was recognizing a bizarre property of light and matter to appear as both energy particle and wave. Whether the manifestation at any moment is particle or wave depends upon environmental factors. This changeability makes sense when we factor in the existence of an intricate subatomic web in constant motion. Observation by physicists of the particle-wave paradox led to the formulation of quantum theory in which Einstein named these fundamental but strangely amoebic energy capsules *quanta*. Einstein theorized that light and every other type of electromagnetic radiation can manifest not only as electromagnetic waves but also as these quanta which, in the form of light, are called photons.

Einstein had begun to dislodge the linear Newtonian paradigm of a mechanical universe made of discrete, separate objects attracted to one another through the force of gravity and ruled by cause and effect. Newton's discoveries were not discredited. The weight of a ripe apple hanging from a branch does cause it to eventually be released and fall to the ground. But Einstein proved mathematically that at a subtle, underlying level, which we cannot see with the naked eye, matter is actually equivalent to energy—and energy is contiguous. Therefore, the chair that I sit on while working at the computer may appear solid and separate from my body which is, through gravity, able to stay seated; but in fact the entire scene involves millions of rapidly moving, interacting energy particle-waves.

The combination of Einstein's relativity theory and quantum theory revolutionized human thought about the natural world and the universe. In this new worldview relationships are seen as preceding, underlying and informing the mechanical operations of Nature. An underlying fluidity of substance, sometimes referred to as consciousness, suggests that interconnectedness, not separation, describes the 'real' reality. What used to be conceived as elementary particles, separate and independent, no longer holds true. As physicist Henry Stapp says of such pseudo-entities: "'An elementary particle is . . . in essence, a set of relationships that reach outward to other things.'"[5] Breathing is a simple example. Do we ordinarily think of our bodies as intimately linked at each breath with other breathing organisms? And yet here we are, breathing, totally dependent on the gift of oxygen from trees and plants.

When forms are believed to be separate from each other the anthropocentric urge to classify and rank them in linear fashion ensues. Thus the food chain with humans at the top obscures the reality that without the lowly protozoa there is no human being. If everything is the cause of everything else in the fluid environment of a web, then any effort to classify and control will not only fail but will probably cause harm to living forms. This is in fact what is happening in the human treatment of the natural world, as we hang on to the old paradigm of separation and control. Moreover, the focus on competition and survival of the fittest joins Newtonian atomism to infect the social sphere by defining and separating human relations through class and ethnic hierarchies which solidify ethnocentric and xenophobic attitudes.

Danish physicist Niels Bohr, in reassessing the superficially discrete boundaries of matter, watched them dissolve progressively at atomic and subatomic levels into a deeper reality that revealed a fundamental indivisibility. At these levels apparent parts coalesce into a whole, connected interdependently through an intricate, non-linear energy matrix of complex, changing relationships in which energy particle-waves sketch dance-like patterns of exchange. Common distinctions, like animate and inanimate matter, become fuzzy. When one's perception expands to the whole scene distinctions recede, even at the visible level, exposing a dance of interconnections. One is momentarily freed from the restricted, habitual view of the world as a stage set of separate, static objects in space. For example, a stream flowing down from a mountain source is home to myriad droplets of water that perpetually form and reform, interacting with each other and with the soil, pebbles and rocks in the water's path. Falling leaves, falling raindrops, filaments of sunlight join in the dance, as well as frogs and fish and any number of microscopic organisms. Each moment presents a new configuration of interdependent entities that play off each other so that, truly, as Heraclitus put it "'you cannot step into the same river twice.'"[6] For such phenomena, as physicist F. David Peat explains, ". . . it is more natural to think in terms of events unfolding out of a continuous background rather than built up in a piecewise fashion out of distinct elements. In addition, when things are no longer distinguished and flow one into the other, chains of causality are no longer appropriate."[7]

In fact, another physicist, Werner Heisenberg, discovered that the witness of any scene is also not separate from the scene. So if I am watching the stream as it flows I am part of the event too. While conducting an experiment Heisenberg realized that his role as observer and his intervention in the subatomic world of quanta had to be taken into account. There is no such thing as a purely objective witness because the living web encloses all actors in the play of Creation as they converse and dance in the exchange of energy. The human role within the natural world can be inferred from Heisenberg's discovery: we cannot escape our participation in the web. When we disturb that web life forms suffer. Wise participation in the web—the nurturing of its natural balance—requires the awakening of what deep ecologist Arne Naess calls *the ecological self.*

The image of the dance comes to fruition with the work of physicist Wolfgang Pauli. Pauli, a precocious but disturbed patient of Carl Jung, was working with the master doctor to explore the inner workings of his own mind. As Pauli gained a sense of inner symmetry the two men began to look outward to find more evidence of symmetry—Jung in the study of psychic patterns that ripen and manifest meaningfully in the outer world and Pauli in the subatomic world of physics. They also discovered a force of energy that guides the manifestation of both psychic patterns and subatomic activity: synchronicity. First explained by Jung, synchronicity refers to the existence of non-linear connections between phenomena—whether they are electrons, living creatures in the web of life, or synchronous events that happen which suggest a relationship beyond coincidence. Synchronicity complements but also broadens Newtonian causality by absorbing the Einsteinian perspective that describes the real world as a network of moving energy particle-waves. This energy network undergirds the visible pattern of cause and effect. In the subatomic world, for example, electrons distant from one another can nevertheless influence each other's behavior—a phenomenon called non-locality. In his study of African natives Jung discovered that they thought in this non-rational way. Unlike modern man who is convinced that the world is a rational place which he can control, indigenous man knows he has limited control over Nature. He also sees non-causal relationships between events that belie coincidence and he trusts in dreams and visions for guidance in an uncertain world.

Pauli used mathematics to express what is more easily understood as an image—the dance. At the quantum level, said Pauli, all participants—elementary particles and quanta of energy—engage in a dance. What is striking is that having a dance partner does not remove the integrity of each particle because partners with the same energy always keep some distance from each other. Individuality and community are simultaneous, orchestrated by an underlying holistic design. Imagine a couple dancing the twist, or the more recent phenomenon of hip-hop dance which includes more dancers in a loose but connected network. The connections or synchronicity exhibited in the dance of particle-waves is called the Pauli Exclusion Principle. "Synchronicity," Peat explains, ". . . arises out of the underlying patterns of the universe rather than through a causality of pushes and pulls that we normally associate with events in nature . . . Hence the underlying pattern of the whole dance has a profound effect on the behavior of each individual particle."[8]

Furthering this idea of the dance as the determining feature of systems is the consideration of the *variation principle* which states that motion and change in objects arise out of the universe as a whole. An impressive framework for the discovery of the variation principle is the Hamilton-Jacobi theory of dynamics which shows that all movements in nature and the patterns created are emerging from an underlying unity. This *law of the whole* may be responsible for the instinct in flocking birds to all move in unison. Alighting into the sky the birds synchronize their movements, turning and swooping gracefully as if, on cue, they are performing a rehearsed dance.[9] The Rockettes of Radio City Music Hall fame are the human equivalent of this avian symmetry. Perhaps the whole world is moving in a synchronous manner and we are simply not aware of it.

T. S. Eliot hints at this law of the whole as the inspiration for the dance when he writes: ". . . at the still point, there the dance is . . . / Where past and future are gathered. / Neither movement from, nor towards, / Neither ascent nor decline. Except for the point, the still point, / There would be no dance, and there is only the dance."[10]

The image of the dance reoccurs in physicist Fritjof Capra's description of the universe as a "dynamic web of inseparable energy patterns."[11] Capra compares this continuous dance of cosmic regeneration to the mystic dance of Shiva, the Hindu god of creation and destruction.

The fire of creative life encircles Shiva's dancing form. As the god dances the letters of the Sanskrit alphabet fall off his feet. According to Hindu Vedanta these letters combine to form the names and shapes of all life forms in the created world—or Maya. Maya displays in visible form the invisible ground of Consciousness itself. Life flows as a dance, an illusory magic show, with forms emerging from this ground, dying into it, and re-emerging in new permutations, new transmutations: to use the language of shamanism, a continual play of shapeshifting. We do not habitually see life in this fluid

Figure 7.4.   Shiva dancing.
Courtesy of Lyla Yastion.

way. Nor do we usually see the interplay of forces in life's daily routine. For example, there is a level of artistic expression at which an artist concedes that the final product, and even the artistic process itself, is to a large extent attributable to unknown forces. In a letter to an admirer who asked Mozart how he could write such intricate, beautiful music the composer replied that musical compositions in their entirety came to him unannounced when he was in a quiet state. From whence they came, and how they could be retained whole in his mind, he could not say.

Physicist David Bohm describes the cyclical emerging and retreating of forms as a perpetually reoccurring two-step rhythm. An unfolding of energy particle-waves out of the quantum field into manifestation as matter is followed by an enfolding of physical forms back into unmanifest, undifferentiated energy. Bohm calls the subtle energy field or ground which gives rise to the unfolding and enfolding process the *implicate order*. The ordinary world of apparent solid bodies created and located in space in an apparent linear time frame is the *explicate order*. The explicate order corresponds to the Newtonian vision of Nature—and to Maya—where bodies interact through local forces of cause and effect.

Consciousness itself, as the energy of mind or awareness, corresponds to the implicate order. As William James intimated in his description of consciousness, thoughts form in awareness; they arise from and fall back into this ground. Thoughts flow in and out of each other, as in a dance—a process that appears chaotic because it is not a causal succession of ideas lining up like railroad cars. Creativity is born out of this pregnant awareness.

THE EARTH COMMUNITY

In Sermon Four thirteenth century German mystic, Meister Eckhart, states: "God is in all things; the more he is in things, the more he is outside them . . . God created the whole world perfectly and entirely in the Now."[12] Each moment renews the creative process in which "all creatures are the utterance of God . . . all creatures wish to echo God in all their works. . . ."[13]

These pronouncements are reiterated in the following statement by Thomas Berry:

> In reality there is a single integral community of the Earth that includes all its component members whether human or other than human. In this community every being has its own role to fulfill, its own dignity, its inner spontaneity. Every being has its own voice. Every being declares itself to the entire universe. Every being enters into communion with other beings . . . So too every being has rights to be recognized and revered.[14]

The Earth community is equal in all its parts; that is, an egalitarian ethos prevails. The profusion of beauty, precision and mystery in all life forms, from ant to majestic whale, enlist our admiration and awe whenever we are present to the natural world.

One way in which the South American bush katydid declares itself, and communes with its environment, is through ears less than a millimeter long located on each leg.

Katydid's Ears

Figure 7.5.   South American bush katydid by Dominque Medici.
Used with the permission of Dominique Medici.

The katydid's ears are finely tuned to pick up subtle differences in frequency so that a friendly katydid sound is distinguished from a hunting bat. A tiny pressurized fluid-filled cavity called the acoustic vesicle picks up and analyzes sound just like the mammalian cochlea. Scientists are using this information to develop better hearing aids and make advances in ultrasonic engineering technology.

The common fruit fly is a staple specimen in the study of human genetics and neuroscience; but it declares itself as anything but common. Scientist Michael Dickinson marvels at its unique abilities, for fruit flies possess compound eyes, an advanced musculature, taste cells on their wings, "and, they can fly!"[15]

As we move from the insect world to that of flowering plants—or angiosperms—another wonder awaits us: a profusion of 422,000 species, some of whom may reside in your garden. What prompted this vast and diverse explosion of life? Fossilized records show that during the Cretaceous period, some 130 million years ago, in the shadow of ferns and non-flowering gymnosperms such as conifers and gingko, a shrub called Amborella was producing small, simple yellow flowers. A high level of CO2 in the atmosphere encouraged plant growth and, apparently, an impulse for diversity. Recent studies of plant DNA show that over millions of years genes for flower-building developed through genetic mutation causing petals to form out of leaves in some plants. This discovery proves Goethe's early assertion in a 1790 study on plant morphology that all plants are essentially leaves.

Ecuador has become the first nation to grant the amazing world of plants basic rights as living beings. Its new constitutional laws protect the essential role of plants in the web of life—their ability to harness the sun's energy to produce food and oxygen necessary to animal life. The laws go further by granting protection to all of Nature's ecosystems, including the lowly bacteria and algae, because *Pachamama* (the indigenous name for *Mother Earth*) must be shielded from further ecological deterioration. Even with these laws on the books, however, Ecuador now faces a stand-off between a large segment of the Ecuadorian population who want to leave abundant reserves of oil under the rich soil of the pristine rainforest of the Yasuni National Park—which serves as both a critical carbon sink and a refuge for displaced species due to the effects of climate change—and oil companies who want to drill in this preserve, the most biologically diverse area of the Amazon.

At the microscopic level life forms can defy our common definition of what *living* means and force us to rethink the conventional divide between life and non-life. In his book *The Lives of a Cell* biologist Lewis Thomas contemplates the biological unity of all life forms and questions the accepted dichotomy of living and non-living matter. In this regard he reflects the indigenous belief that all matter is alive. Thomas asks: since carbon is the chemical substance from which protoplasm evolves, and thus all life depends on carbon (which even exists in metals that show fatigue when overused), how is it that carbon is classified as non-living? Where is the line drawn between chemistry and biology, between non-life and life? He writes:

> The uniformity of the earth's life, more astonishing than its diversity, is accountable by the high probability that we derived, originally, from some single cell, fertilized in a bolt of lightning as the earth cooled . . . we still share genes around, and the resemblance of the enzymes of grasses to those of whales is a family resemblance.[16]

"We are shared, rented, occupied," says Thomas, by descendants of ancient bacteria called mitochondria that were engulfed by ancestors of our eukaryotic cells (cells having nuclei) more than a billion years ago.[17] Mitochondria leave an imprint through their independent DNA which is not in the nucleus but exists in cell organelles.

Most of a cell's energy—ATP adenosine triphosphate—is generated by mitochondria. Mitochondria also regulate and monitor the cell cycle—how each cell grows, divides through mitosis, returns to a quiescent phase and at some point dies a natural and programmed death (about 50 to 70 billion cells die each day in the adult body).[18] This regulatory control is crucial to a cell's survival because the mitochondria also detect and repair damaged genes at certain 'checkpoints' in the cell cycle and can help prevent uncontrolled (cancerous) cell division. It is noteworthy that mitochondrial dysfunction, caused in part by mutations both inherited and acquired, can be induced by certain drugs and environmental stresses such as pesticide exposure. Because mitochondria are so essential to proper cell functioning disorders can target any and all parts of the body including eyes, ears, muscles, and nervous, digestive, respiratory and circulatory systems. Studies show a relationship between mitochondrial dysfunction and dementia, bipolar disorder and autism.[19] If human-induced climate change continues unabated it is important to ask whether this environmental stress will destroy the capacity of the mitochondria to do their essential work in safeguarding bodily health.

And what about the mysterious, microscopic diatoms—borderline cases that tease our conceived notions of living and non-living? These 'living crystals' bridge the mineral, plant and animal kingdoms which puts them near the origin of the ancient evolutionary tree of life. Diatoms are microalgae. As uni-celled, eukaryotic organisms they string themselves together in colonies which assume the shape of ribbons, stars and fans. As algae they produce food, thus showing their plant identity. The cell walls, made of a siliceous material, reveal the mineral part of their bodies. Animal characteristics are displayed in their excretion of waste—urea—which is a converted, less toxic form of ammonia. Part of the urea cycle is facilitated by mitochondria. Thousands of diatoms can be gathered together and not occupy more than the head of a pin!

Even at the most elementary level of geometrical structure studied in antiquity by Pythagoras and Plato, a proportional symmetry is shared in the natural world. For example, a predominance of pentagonal forms reflect the golden section—a ratio that relates parts to the whole. Many marine animals like starfish, as well as most flowers, have this 5-fold form. Even elementary substances such as methane (CH_4), ammonia (NH_3), and water (H_2O) have internal pentagonal angles. According to esoteric numerology the number 5, represented by the pentagram and pentagon, stands for the life principle. The number 5 signifies potentiality, creativity, and harmonious relationships based in love—a fitting description of the web of life and the Earth community.

THE BIOLOGICAL WEB

Philosopher-scientist Arthur Koestler suggests that each part of a system—be it a human being in society, a nation in the world, or a species in an ecosystem—has a dual aspect and function. As an individual part it seeks survival and fulfillment; as a member of the greater whole it integrates its desires into the whole system by doing work that keeps that system viable. Koestler calls the part a *holon*. The congregation of holons is termed a *holarchy*. A holarchy is the opposite of a hierarchy. In a holarchy the horizontal dimension reveals partnership in contrast to the vertical ranking of ruler and ruled. A holarchy also corresponds to Pauli's metaphor of the dance at the subatomic level and to the biological web of life.

The biological web manifests as *ecosystems*. These ecosystems such as lake, mountain, meadow, and forest, consist of interdependent organisms within the greater ecosystem of planet Earth. Interdependence connotes an egalitarian status for each member of the whole. The human body is a remarkable ecosystem; the brain, for example, composes 85 billion cells that work together in harmony through neural channels and synapses to keep us alive, alert, thinking, and acting. However, scientists are finding that the brain is not the sole locus of intelligence. Rather, intelligence pervades the whole body. In *The Self-Aware Universe* Amit Goswami argues that there are two levels of the *brain-mind*—classical and quantum. The quantum level of mind is unitive consciousness in which the perception of 'other' disappears through a heightened consciousness of the whole. Mystical experiences coalesce with discoveries in quantum physics to reveal this level as the true reality. The perception of a world divided into separate objects (*maya*) observed by a subject (*ego*) occurs at the lower, classical level of mind.

When the members of an ecosystem play their parts correctly by following Nature's script of homeostasis then the ecosystem is healthy. At the present time human beings are not obeying the script. Through a cultivation of sensory awareness, however, it is possible to remember our inclusion in the web of life and act responsibly. David Abram gives a lucid description of the human immersion in this web. He writes:

> As breathing involves a continual oscillation between exhaling and inhaling, offering ourselves to the world at one moment and drawing the world into ourselves at the next, so sensory perception entails a like reciprocity, exploring the moss with our fingers while feeling the moss touch us back. . . . If I'm able to smell the zinging scent of the piñons and the strong fermentation of the compost, it is only because I too am a part of the olfactory field—because I have my own musk and effluvium, my own chemical emanations that any mosquito can pick up and follow back to my skin. . . .[20]

Both competition and cooperation sustain the biological web of life. Although competition as a Darwinian struggle for existence is endemic to life it could be argued that at a higher level the outcome of the life struggle is a form of cooperation. In the moment of combat one party yields and, in a sense, permits itself to be defeated. Every organism in some way consents to eat and/or be eaten. In Taoist terms, the yin force by its surrender propels life into the next moment. Contemporary American poet Gary Snyder sees this energy exchange as a spiritual process, a sacrament in which "all of nature is a gift-exchange, a potluck banquet, and there is no death that is not somebody's food, no life that is not somebody's death."[21] Therefore we can view ourselves at death as "an offering to the continuation of life."[22]

An example of this life-death cycle is the food web. Producers (green plants) feed primary consumers (herbivores) who feed secondary consumers (carnivores) and omnivores like us. All fall prey to bacterial decomposers (microconsumers) to re-fertilize the soil—" for dust thou art, and to dust shalt thou return"—at which point the cycle reignites.[23] The sun provides heat for plant photosynthesis; heat continues to be generated throughout the whole process. If you have a compost heap at home in the throes of decay and you stick your hand into its loamy factory you will feel the heat of new life quickening in the Earth.

In the *Taittireeya Upanishad* there is a stunning description of food as the omnipresent link between all living beings and Spirit. The scripture reads:

> Out of Spirit came air, out of air, wind; out of wind, fire; out of fire, water; out of water, earth; out of earth, vegetation; out of vegetation, food; out of food man. . . . From food are born all creatures; they live upon food, they are dissolved in food. Food is the chief of all things, the universal medicine. They who think of food as Spirit shall never lack. From food all beings are born, all beings increase their bulk; all beings feed upon it, it feeds upon all beings.[24]

All beings are related to each other in what is called, in the science of ecology, a *community of interest*. This term describes a species' neighborhood in the ecosystem. In an essay published in 1887 called *The Lake as a Microcosm*, entomologist Stephen A. Forbes pioneered the study of ecosystems before that word was even in the scientific lexicon. In examining the interrelationships of the residents of a lake, Forbes points out "the necessity of taking a comprehensive survey of the whole as a condition to a satisfactory understanding of any part."[25] To understand the little black bass, for instance, (whom Forbes charmingly personalizes as 'our hero') one must first be aware of the rhythmic seasonal expansion and contraction of the lake due to its connection to other lakes, rivers and streams. In times of overflow, as in springtime, breeding grounds are increased for fishes, animals and plants so that everyone has enough to eat. The profusion of life keeps the lake community balanced, checking and reducing numbers through the predator-prey relationship. Fishes eat entomostraca (a subclass of Crustacea) who eat animalcules (microscopic protozoa). In the stew are also insects that the bass and crustaceans eat. Some fish eat mud and algae. Omnivorous crawfishes eat anything. But when the lake waters recede, writes Forbes, "the teeming life which they contain is restricted within daily narrower bounds and a fearful slaughter follows."[26] Then each animal must scramble for food and watch its back at the same time. The little bass faces predaceous fishes, water snakes, birds, and even gigantic bugs so that "fishes which reach maturity are relatively as rare as centenarians among human kind."[27] There are also competitors to deal with; for example, fish, including the bass, compete with a flowering water plant called the bladderwort to obtain the gourmet delicacy—entomostraca. The bladderwort has no roots and eats by means of a mass of little bladders which trap and gobble up the entomostraca. Yet this rivalry, says Forbes, is an example of how Nature regulates the population of each species. A balance in birth and death rates in each species allows for survival of the whole and constitutes a healthy community of interest, along with the force of natural selection which eliminates the unfit. Forbes warns, however, that ". . . the dependent species evidently must not appropriate, on an average, any more than the surplus and excess of individuals upon which it preys, for if it does so it will continuously diminish its own food supply, and thus indirectly but surely exterminate itself."[28]

The human being, as part of the web of life, is that dependent species who is appropriating resources beyond measure, inflicting pollution and habitat loss upon other species through predatory acts, while overpopulating the planetary ecosystem. In this regard, Cicero's assessment of man's real enemy is apt: "The enemy is within the gates; it is with our own luxury, our own folly, our own criminality that we have to contend."[29]

THE SOCIAL WEB

The interactive drama of interdependence and reciprocity distinguishes not only the biological web but the social web as well. Central to this social web is the family which forms the first community of interest. However, if you and I live on the same block, work at the same business, attend the same church or temple, or go to the same college these social bonds expand the community of interest.

In the non-human world, sociability and division of labor in the industrious ant colony is well known. Scientists have now found another insect with a social instinct—and in the most unlikely of candidates: the spider. We think of a solo spider hunkered down in his or her intricate, translucent web waiting to capture the next unfortunate passer-by. But the social spider *Stegodypus mimosarum*, has found a niche in the Kalahari desert of southern Africa where communal webs the size of a minibus are weaved and hung on trees and bushes. Skeletons of rats and birds have been found tightly wound in the webs. The security of belonging to a colony—in this case from 20 to

300 individuals—appears to develop and accentuate individual predisposi-tions (to aggression or docility, for example) rather than produce a bland behavioral conformity. A high level of teamwork among the spiders insures success. As one science writer, reporting on these small wonders, writes: "The spider communities gain their strength through a division of labor, with some members specializing in web repair, some in attacking and subduing prey. Still others tend to the young, regurgitating liquefied food right into an offspring's mouth and eventually *liquefying their own bodies to nourish the next generation* [italics are mine]."[30]

Primates, the order of mammals that includes humans, have a high degree of socialization. Their larger brains, extended developmental period, foraging and hunting techniques, and communicative skills such as facial expressions and vocal signals predispose them to group life. Our nearest primate relatives, the Great Apes, diverged from early humans and developed their own evo-lutionary lineage between four and eight million years ago. Anthropologists view the genus *Pan*—chimps and bonobos—as an early behavior model for the human species. Both chimps and bonobos find stability in family group-ings, food gathering expeditions, grooming rituals, and play.

Each species' pattern of social contact reminds us, in positive and negative ways, of human societies. The male-dominant chimpanzee groups show more

Figure 7.6.   Savanna chimpanzee (Pan Troglodytes), three juveniles swinging on a branch.
Courtesy of Juniors Bildarchiv GmbH/Alamy Stock Photo.

aggressive behavior and intergroup violence. Bonobos, on the other hand, whose female alliances are strong, use frequent (some might say promiscuous) sexual contact among all possible sex and age combinations except close relatives. These intimate interactions are used to prevent impending conflict over food or to defuse antagonistic encounters.[31]

Turning to human society we see that a social web is constructed by customs of family life, clubs and civic organizations, religious affiliations, trade and business partnerships, and shared political governance. These social ties balance the combative urge of individuals and groups for dominance. When the laws of interdependence and reciprocity are respected by the populace the social web is healthy.

In a simple egalitarian *band* of kin-based hunter-gatherers, like the San Bushmen of the Kalahari, survival depends on teamwork and sharing of the kill. *Tribes* stabilize their social groupings through constructing extended families called kinship systems of descent. These clans and lineages determine marriage partners and regulate allegiances through complex rules that everyone knows and obeys. For example, marriage outside one's descent group, or *exogamy*, has adaptive value by extending the social web to 'strangers,' converting them into friends and allies. Descent groups are either patrilineal (descent through the male line) or matrilineal (descent through the female line).[32] A tribal social web is perceived as a continuum of living and deceased members. It is expected that one knows the names of deceased forbears in one's lineage back 8 to10 generations to an *apical* (original) ancestor. The Old Testament has long litanies of *begats* that trace a patrilineage belonging to Jews, Christians and Muslims back to Abraham as their shared apical ancestor. What changes might result from a realization of this social web by practitioners of these three religions?

The tribal web can also extend into the future. Native American tribes believe that their actions must show responsibility to descendants and to the land seven generations into the future. The social cohesion of kin groups is reinforced in many tribal societies by non kin groups. For example, age mates bond for life after enduring puberty rites together. In American culture this broader affiliation compares to fraternity brothers and sorority sisters who form lifelong bonds in college.

When economics is woven into the social network a *socioeconomic* web is formed, from simple bartering all the way to multinational exchange of products. Trade exemplifies reciprocity through the distribution of wealth. Economic homeostasis is achieved when all parties (i.e., producers and consumers) have their basic needs fulfilled. So the mark of a healthy economic web is an equal distribution of wealth which in turn promotes cultural stability. The extent to which a tribe—or a nation—follows this path of reciprocity and keeps the web from getting too narrow, imbalanced and exclusive reveals cultural values. In New Guinea, for example, the tribal society of the Kapauku Papuans secures its livelihood by tending small gardens and raising pigs. The Kapauku choose a *big man* or *tonowi* to represent them. He achieves status through amassing wealth in the form of pigs—and then generously gives the pigs away in a ceremony called a *moka*. His aim is to first persuade his fellow Kapauku to help him accumulate pigs (it helps if he has oratory skills) and then to conduct a give-away that surpasses his tribal peers in generosity. The moka was instituted by Papuan tribes to stem warfare by providing a safe way for men to channel aggressive energies.

Among North Pacific Coast Indians, including the Salish and Kwakiutl, a cultural tradition called the *potlatch* ceremony requires wealthy men to give away blankets, food, and other household items. Power and influence are equated with generosity. Our thrift stores pale before this lavish giving which can have ecological as well as social benefits. Resources are rarely constant; the salmon aren't abundant every year. So if the local economy of one village is depressed another village with a different resource that is plentiful can convert its surplus food into prestige while also helping the other village.

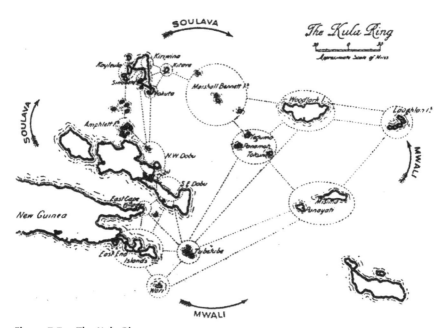

Figure 7.7.   The Kula Ring.
From *Argonauts of the Western Pacific: An Account of Native Enterprise and Adventure in the Archipelagoes of Melanesian New Guinea* by Bronislaw Malinowski (London: G. Routledge and Sons, 1922; reprinted by E. P. Dutton, New York, 1960–p. 158).

Perhaps the most intricate and original system of socioeconomic reciprocity is the *kula* of the tribal Trobriand Islanders. The kula was made famous by Bronislaw Malinowski who, in the 1920s, was the first anthropologist to do extensive on-site fieldwork. The Trobriand Islands are northeast of Australia, east of New Guinea. The entire culture of the Trobrianders revolves around the ritual exchange of beautifully crafted bracelets (*mwali*) and necklaces (*soulava*), some of which are prized for their great age and beauty—like our heirlooms. These treasures are circulated by tribal chiefs from all the islands who lead their vassal subjects on kula journeys in fleets of elaborately crafted canoes. Since the open sea may be treacherous a shaman blesses the ceremonial canoe and its occupants with magical incantations before it sets out. The bracelets travel counter-clockwise; the necklaces clockwise.

The ritual of giving and receiving is formal and stylized like a great drama. The kula journeys are often accompanied by trading of ordinary goods between islands (*gimwali*) but this activity is considered inferior to the ceremonial kula. Once a tribal chief receives a valued item from his partner in trade he may keep it, but only for a year; then he must pass it on. In this way valuables are always circulating and no tribe becomes wealthier or more prestigious than another. Possession of the valuable by the chief symbolizes his responsibility to serve the needs of his subjects. Peace is maintained between tribes by this elaborate system.

The Gift, by sociologist Marcel Mauss, is a study of reciprocal exchanges in archaic societies. Mauss' description of the kula evokes the ceremonial flourish of feudal lords and knights in medieval times. He writes:

> Trade is carried on in a noble fashion, apparently in a disinterested and modest way. Of an individual who does not proceed in the kula with the necessary greatness of soul it is said that he is 'conducting it like a gimwali'. . . . The recipients of one day become the givers on the next. . . . The giver affects an exaggerated modesty: having solemnly brought on his present, to the sound of a seashell, he excuses himself for giving only the last of what remains to him, and throws down the object to be given at the feet of his rival and partner. However, the seashell and the herald proclaim to everybody the solemn nature of this act of transfer. The aim of all this is to display generosity, freedom and autonomous action, as well as greatness.[33]

The United States is the most powerful industrialized, capitalist democracy in the world yet its socioeconomic web shows serious signs of imbalance and friction that denote greed and hoarding of wealth as dominant cultural values. The historical interplay between individualism and community is skewing towards the individual who finds himself progressively isolated and alienated from society when he doesn't succeed in a monetary way. The shrinking of the middle class, bouts of recession, and the shifting nature of the nuclear family unit, which was once part of a scaffold of extended family relations, accentuates the dilemma. If the United States could invent ways to adopt tribal solutions of communal exchange, molding them in modern context, the status quo, though entrenched, could give way. A change in values and a change in thinking are prerequisites.

A modern application of the tribal social web is the global Internet. Facebook and other social media provide numerous opportunities to connect with people one may never meet in person. In this new inclusive web a *sharing economy* has arisen. For example, Craigslist is a website that posts items for recycling and reuse. It enables seller and buyer to benefit from the transaction and, as a side benefit, reduces waste. Craigslist covers its operating costs from revenues that are generated by employers who must pay for posting wanted ads in certain cities. From the get-go the president of Craigslist, Jim Buckmaster, decided to emphasize a superior quality of user experience over making a profit.

At the grassroots level, with the help of the Internet, innovative local communities are forming DIY (Do-It-Yourself) networks where skills are traded and activities coordinated. These networks reinstate bartering—the customary exchange of goods that predated the use of money as currency. Baby-sitting co-ops, which save families money, and clothing-exchange parties which sidestep a trip to the mall to feed capitalist consumerism, exemplify this 'direct-trade economy.' These activities also build community ties. A collaborative lifestyle characterizes community gardens and CSAs (community sponsored agriculture), libraries where seeds and tools as well as books can be lent out, car and bike-sharing services, and housing complexes where modest private residences share public spaces and facilities in a spirit of mutual aid and fellowship.[34]

The prominent values of a culture are acted out in the social web. The environmental problems that now overwhelm human society were born in the global socioeconomic web of a distorted capitalist system informed by an anthropocentric worldview. When the belief in a unified Earth community consisting of diverse life forms becomes the worldview of a majority of global citizens then cultural institutions change to match this new worldview. In his Christmas Eve sermon in 1967 at the Ebenezer Baptist church in Atlanta, Georgia, Martin Luther King envisioned such a global community, dedicated to peace on earth. He states: "All life is interrelated. We are all caught in an inescapable network of mutuality, tied into a single garment of destiny. Whatever affects one directly, affects all indirectly. We are made to live together because of the interrelated structure of reality."[35]

The tribe has been defined as the smallest unit of a social web. In modern society, distinguished by the World Wide Web, the tribe becomes humanity itself. When humanity recognizes and lives its bond with the Earth then the smallest unit of the social web becomes the entire Earth community.

THE SPIRITUAL WEB

It could be said that the spiritual web corresponds to Bohm's implicate order. As the subtle generator and repository of energy its vibrations fuel the biological and social dimensions of the web. The spiritual web also corresponds to the mystical ground of all religions. Here, every creature is viewed as an expression of One Living Energy. Thus, every creature is related to every other creature. Interdependence is a spiritual law and reciprocity, encased in the Golden Rule, is the spiritual practice whereby interdependence is demonstrated. When human beings acknowledge this spiritual web they are motivated to act in ways that enhance every species' right to life. Abraham Heschel affirms this spiritual community when he says that "all existence stands in the dimension of the holy . . . Just as man lives in the realm of nature and is subject to its laws, so does he find himself in the holy dimension. He can escape its bounds as little as he can take leave of nature."[36]

Buddhist philosophy refers to a continuous *dependent co-arising* of sentient forms which, within an environment of constant flux and change, are necessarily impermanent. There can be no permanent self in Creation; however, the *buddha-nature*, inherent in all beings, is the constant amongst variables.

Hinduism encases its teaching of the unity of life in scriptures such as the *Eesha Upanishad* which states: "The Self is One. Unmoving, it moves . . . Out of Self comes the breath that is the life of all things. Of a certainty the man who can see all creatures in himself, himself in all creatures, knows no sorrow."[37]

How is it that seeing oneself in the other has the power to erase sorrow? Where does sorrow come from? If we examine our own experiences of sorrow we discover that it often stems from the feeling of being separate, cut off and alone. A feeling of isolation breeds depression, a prevalent marker of modern society and a primary cause of the recent upsurge in the United States of addiction to heroin and prescription painkiller drugs, particularly amongst teenagers.[38] By contrast, the experience of interconnectedness expunges negative feelings and, in biological terms, generates endorphins. For example, on a walk through the woods we can suddenly be immersed in a sensation of momentary bliss. An instinctive feeling of affinity for all life arises, producing a spiritual epiphany that bestows health.

Taoism teaches that the ultimate source of Creation is the *Tao* which is translated as the *Way*. The Tao is unfathomable. Human beings approach the Tao through its *ch'i* which is the energy that enlivens all beings. Lao Tzu writes in the *Tao Te Ching*:

> The Tao gives birth to all beings,
> nourishes them, maintains them,
> cares for them, comforts them, protects them,
> takes them back to itself,
> creating without possessing,
> acting without expecting,
> guiding without interfering.
> That is why love of the Tao
> is in the very nature of things.[39]

When the natural world is entered in awareness a mysterious alchemy can take place—a merging with all life that transports the spirit. This alchemy is captured in a poem by Mary Oliver called *Sleeping in the Forest*. The poet writes:

> I thought the earth
> remembered me, she
> took me back so tenderly, arranging
> her dark skirts, her pockets
> full of lichens and seeds. I slept
> as never before, a stone
> on the riverbed, nothing
> between me and the white fire of the stars
> but my thoughts, and they floated
> light as moths among the branches
> of the perfect trees. All night
> I heard the small kingdoms breathing
> around me, the insects, and the birds
> who do their work in the darkness. All night
> I rose and fell, as if in water, grappling
> with a luminous doom. By morning
> I had vanished at least a dozen times
> into something better.[40]

The web of life is a layered and living phenomenon distinguished by three dimensions: biological, social and spiritual. The accelerating disturbance of the web in its biological aspect indicates that we human beings have forgotten the necessity of maintaining the health of the elements of air, fire, water and earth of which the vast network of Earth's ecosystems, including our human bodies, are constituted. That forgetting proceeds from a deeper forgetting of the social and spiritual bonds that connect all life forms. Indigenous peoples, who remember their bond with Nature, view the web in its entirety as a prototype of Earth as sacred space. Before exploring this ancient vision of the world you are invited to try an exercise in sensory awareness that can precipitate an expansion of consciousness such as Mary Oliver experienced. This exercise is a type of meditation which encourages a deep and visceral connection to the natural world.

EXERCISE IN IDENTITY: WHO AM I?

Sit down preferably outside in a natural setting.

Begin by coming into the present moment through opening each of the senses and allowing mental energies to subside. . . .

See what is in your sight, listen to the sounds around you; feel your body as part of the physical landscape. By attention to the senses the mind becomes quiescent . . . .

Now choose a life form (such as plant, animal, tree, insect, grass, water, or sky) and contemplate this subject for two or three minutes. Just be with the life form in the neutral state of observation. . . .

Next, examine this life form on three levels: physical (bodily processes), mental-emotional (intelligence, feelings), and spiritual (essence). At each of these three levels ask yourself, how am I similar to and different from this life form? You may want to jot down responses in a journal. . . .

When you are finished review your notes and ask yourself, what is this life form teaching me?

Chapter Eight

Perceptions of Earth as Sacred Space

. . . this goodly frame, the earth . . .this most excellent canopy, the air, look you, this brave o'erhanging firmament, this majestical roof fretted with golden fire. . . .

—Hamlet, *Hamlet* II:2

From time immemorial peoples of diverse cultures around the world have perceived the Earth as sacred space, either in the pristine beauty of certain geographic features—such as the Himalaya Mountain range—or as a specific location to which sacredness is attributed. At the top of a mountain in Bighorn Canyon, Wyoming rests the Great Medicine Wheel, a circular design of stones 80 feet in diameter. Built to honor the Great Spirit by unknown ancestors, the medicine wheel is considered sacred to Native Americans. To this day tourists and native peoples still travel the seven mile trek up the mountain to visit this sacred site where earth meets sky. For centuries medicine wheels have served as holy places that teach indigenous knowledge of the cosmos. Here the tribal community gathers to pray, give thanks, and conduct ritual ceremonies that call upon the spirit powers for guidance and healing both personal and collective.

In the middle of The Great Medicine Wheel a cairn of piled rocks marks the center or heart of the world, the abode of the Creator, from which twenty-eight spokes, suggesting the lunar cycle, radiate to the outer sphere. The traditional design of a medicine wheel features a Creator stone at the center surrounded by seven other stones which symbolize the foundational forces that build and sustain the Creation like Father Sky, Mother Earth and even Star Nation. The four cardinal directions are marked by special stones called Spirit Keeper stones. They honor certain energies such as healing (South) or

Figure 8.1.   The Great Medicine Wheel.
Courtesy of US Forest Service.

wisdom (North) and are guarded by specific animal powers. The energy of
the North, for example, is generated by White Buffalo spirit. According to
the Lakota Sioux, Buffalo spirit took human form in 1780 as White Buffalo
Calf Maiden, an incarnation of Whope, the ancestral embodiment of female
energy. She came as a messiah to assuage the people's spiritual wounds, suffered at the hands of white oppression; she delivered the wisdom of the seven
sacred rites and the sacred pipe. The latter is housed in a special place, the
Lakota *Holy of Holies*.

Sacred sites often reflect in their structure the rich and ancient meanings
associated with certain numbers. In esoteric numerology wholeness (as
perfection) is signified by the number 1. The circle and its center represent
wholeness, perfection, the natural state of health that permeates the Creation
and unifies all beings as interconnected souls born of the Creator. For Native
Americans the circle is holy. It is the round form of sacred Mother Earth and
expresses her cyclical rhythms. As Lakota shaman Black Elk states: "'Everything the Power of the World does is done in a circle. The Sky is round and I

have heard that the earth is round like a ball and so are all the stars. The Wind, in its greatest power, whirls. Birds make their nests in circles, for theirs is the same religion as ours. The sun comes forth and goes down again in a circle. The moon does the same, and both are round.'"[1]

All cycles that govern life on Earth—the seasons, day and night, phases of the moon, life-death-rebirth, in fact all facets of time and space—are circular. Yet sacred sites such as this medicine wheel—or any designated sacred site be it mosque, cathedral or temple—simultaneously transcend the time-space continuum. Therefore, sacred time and sacred space are not limited to this earthly dimension but reflect a transcendent unity. Sacred time is timeless; sacred space infinite. Thus the circle dissolves its boundary and becomes the mystical symbol for a divinity "whose center is everywhere, whose circumference is nowhere."[2]

The seven powers that surround the Creator Stone, like angels around God's throne, enact the creative process of making and sustaining the world. The number 7 signifies a series of successive steps that complete an event. The seven days of the week, the musical octave, and the powerful drama of the Book of Genesis which describes how God created the world and then rested on the seventh day, exemplify the energy of 7 in action.

The medicine wheel is a quadrated circle with each of four lines extending from the spirit keeper stones to the center, creating a cross. The number 4 represents the material Creation which mirrors the perfection of the celestial realm represented by the circle. This correspondence is the *hermetic metaphor*: as above, so below. The efforts of tenth century alchemists in Europe to change lead into gold was a metaphor for the work of spiritual transformation. They were haunted by the concept of squaring the circle which had to do with developing and realizing the divine potential inherent in the earth-bound human being—in other words, with actualizing the hermetic metaphor. The four lines of stones leading from the outer circle to the inner circle represent spiritual paths that one can travel in the work of transforming one's life from ordinary to sacred. These paths may include a deep acquaintance with the elements of air, fire, earth and water at their subtle and spiritual levels, physical and psychic cleansing, and an opening of the heart to a loving relationship with all creatures.

A medicine wheel is a picture of the universe that represents the interpenetration of cosmic, earthly and human energies. This universe is perceived as alive, intelligent and essentially benevolent, exacting only gratitude from humanity as the self-aware species who honors Mother Earth and serves all creatures as kin. Achieving the right relationship with all beings in the natural world is the human function. This right relationship happens naturally when the realization of nonduality dawns. In those moments when the sense of egoic separateness yields to an awareness of interconnectedness love arises, erasing all boundaries. One sees with the eyes of an enlightened mind and heart. The innate memory of wholeness—that which psychologist Stanislav Grof calls the *holotropic mind*—is activated. As this love widens and deepens to encompass the merest ant or the farthest star, the experience of relationship dissolves into an underlying unified consciousness.

The spiritual language may differ but this royal path to self-discovery is a common theme in all mystical traditions. The path begins with the perception of Earth and earthly creatures as sacred. In the story of St. Francis and the wolf, it is said that because of the saint's affinity with animals and plants he is approached by the villagers and asked to confront a wolf who is devouring the children of the village. Because Francis speaks the language of all-inclusive love, or *agape*, he is able to lovingly admonish the wolf while changing the beast's desires. He promises the wolf daily meals as the village pet if he stops his predatory behavior. Since the major predator of the world is now the human being, how shall he be persuaded to desist from destructive actions that consume and deplete the planet, our common home?

While diverse civilizations have in some manner differentiated the ordinary or secular plane of existence from the non-ordinary or sacred plane, it is also clear, from the historical review of Western cultural history presented earlier, that the idea of Creation itself as the sacred projection of a Creator was espoused until the era of the Scientific Revolution. The intermediary who accomplished this divine intention in Greek and medieval philosophy was anima mundi.

In order to appreciate the ways in which diverse cultures have conceived of Earth as sacred space we begin with the Greek concept of *chora* and then extend the investigation into the indigenous worldview which reveals a distinct blurring of the line between secular and sacred realms. To the indigenous eye all life forms are perceived as alive and equally ensouled—even rocks and mountains, water and air. A close-up of the Navajo and Aranda worldviews will highlight the intimate relationship that indigenous peoples have cultivated with Mother Earth, followed by a discussion of antidotes for the diseased state of disconnection from the Earth which afflicts modern society. These remedies can be found in two indigenous cures: soul-retrieval (and its modern equivalent, ecopsychology) and the cultivation of an *ecology of mind*.

CHORA

The Greek civilization conceived of two words for place—*topos* and *chora*. From *topos* comes our word *topography*. *Topos* is concerned with location exactly measured and mapped. Whenever we use a GPS system we are in the realm of topos. *Chora* is qualitative rather than quantitative. It is the energizing force that renders a site sacred to the viewer. That place is perceived as sacred space. For example, Starbucks is a famous topos, a mecca for good coffee. But if a proposal of marriage happens at a table where two lovers sit, drinking their good coffee, then that place may become chora for them. In the *Timaeus* Plato speaks of the creation of the universe as an emanation of divine energy that moves down into a receptacle which is chora, a vessel of becoming that entails the translation of sacred geometric forms—the Platonic solids—into manifest form: Earth as constituted of the five elements.

A similar design appears in Jewish mysticism. According to the Kabbalah the unnameable No-Thing, *Ayin*, begins to manifest its glory in created form through Light, *En Sof*, which emits a network of emanations of divine energy. This energy flows downward through successive levels of reality, finally imbuing Shekhinah, the material Earth, with vibrations of the divine feminine. As Psalm 19 states: "The heavens declare the glory of God; and the firmament sheweth his handywork. . . . Their line is gone out through all the earth, and their words to the end of the world."[3] By contemplation of these emanations, called the Divine Names, which are celestial qualities like Wisdom or Beauty, one's being is purified. This journey is mapped out for the devotee as a mystical ladder called the *sefirot*. God descends and man ascends in waves of interpenetrating energy: as above, so below. According to Celtic spirituality the Creation is a theophany or manifestation of God, a holy place where, in the words of Celtic poet Kenneth White, one is "'taking off the clothes of the mind/and making love/to the body of reality.'"[4]

When ritual activity, performed from the heart, consecrates a place in Nature—such as the mountain where The Great Medicine Wheel resides—a topos becomes chora. For example, the Huichol Indians of Mexico make a ritual pilgrimage every year to Wirikuta, their ancestral holy land. Here peyote is harvested and ingested ceremoniously to renew communion with the Creator. The Huichol believe that if they fail to perform this sacred journey the world will collapse. A primeval sense of connection to the elements, particularly Grandfather Fire and Mother Earth, inspires their belief and practice. The idea that one has a sacred duty to uphold the world may, from a modern perspective, appear naïve, even superstitious. But if it is acknowledged that in ignoring the truth of interconnectedness we have become irresponsible and dangerous to the survival of the world then the remedial actions of the Huichol appear wise and our imprudent actions foolish.

Geographer Yi-Fu Tuan calls the bonding with certain places in the landscape *topophilia* (love of *topos*). We become rooted to a habitat that enjoins our affections—be it the skyline of New York City or the plains of Kansas. The Western Apache exemplify topophilia in their association of geographic locations with stories of past events that occurred at those places. In the vicinity of the Cibecue Valley as many as 296 place-names have been collected by ethnologist Keith Basso. These places serve as a repository of tribal history for future generations of children whose education depends upon an oral tradition. By remembering and relating stories recorded in the geography of the land tribal members affirm their solidarity in both present and past time. For example, a place called *men stand about above* refers to a point on a low ridge overlooking the valley where Apache men stood as lookouts to guard against surprise attacks from enemy tribes and from the United States Sixth Cavalry. While these places may or may not be tinged with a sacred aura they do represent a sacred trust of Western Apache identity that constitutes a blend of topos and chora. An American example of a place-name that carries poignant historical meaning is the Tomb of the Unknown Soldier at Arlington National Cemetery, Virginia. Day and night army sentinels in full dress uniform rotate on a 24-hour cycle, 'guarding' the tomb by walking in front of it in a specific, cadenced way. This ceremonial rite commemorates the wartime service of countless men and women whose names may be lost to history but whose sacrifice is enshrined in our shared cultural memory.

More inclusive than topophilia is biophilia, a word coined by biologist E. O. Wilson that means *love of life*. Wilson suggests that biophilia emerges from an archaic imprint in the brain that records the millennia of human evolutionary experience vis-à-vis the natural environment. This innate impulse of emotional connection to the natural world surfaces in early childhood and pervades cultural patterns which show a preference for green spaces, whether it be home landscaping, a city park, or access to wild places like rivers, forests and mountains. In indigenous cultures the natural affiliation of human beings with the Earth is retained as a philosophical and practical given. The perception of a web of life bound by reciprocal relations is also at the crux of ecological studies and modern physics which demonstrates the interpenetration of energy fields. The whole is truly larger than the sum of its parts.

The intimation of a deep bond shared by all living systems corroborates Edmund Husserl's phenomenological contention that all species participate in each other's experiences in an intersubjective way. Though modern industrialized man may try to impose himself as the dominant subject that manipulates a passive and subordinate Earth as object there is in truth no subject/object relationship but rather two subjects conversing through a subtle energy exchange. The landscape participates as a player in the experiential interplay between viewer and viewed. For example, when one is viewing the brilliant reds and pinks of a sunset the interaction gives rise to a peaceful feeling. It is as if the peace is a shared experience.

The indigenous conviction that Nature is alive and 'converses' with humans if they are listening is poignantly expressed by Walking Buffalo, a Stoney Nakota Indian from Canada, when he says: "'Did you know that trees talk? Well, they do. They talk to each other, and they'll talk to you if you listen. Trouble is, white people don't listen. They never learned to listen to the Indians so I don't suppose they'll listen to other voices in nature. But I have learned a lot from trees: sometimes about the weather, sometimes about animals, sometimes about the Great Spirit.'"[5] Even a devastating landscape can arouse feelings of reverence and empathetic union. Abraham Lincoln, for example, described the blood-soaked earth of Gettysburg as 'hallowed ground' because it received the bodies of soldiers who, regardless of their allegiance to the Union or the Confederacy, sacrificed their lives for a cause they considered just. Similarly, a visit to the Ground Zero Museum and Memorial in Lower Manhattan evokes in the viewer an emotional mix of sadness, veneration and solidarity with the victims.

According to the Maori, an indigenous people of New Zealand, every sentient being possesses a *toiora* or *soul* emanating from *Io*—God. In like manner, the Lakota Sioux define *ton* as that spiritual essence which is shared by all life forms. If the Maori and Lakota are right and all life forms are essentially spirit, then the entire Earth is chora—and beyond the Earth, the whole pulsating universe. When theologian Teilhard de Chardin speaks of human evolution as a conscious movement towards the Omega Point and Thomas Berry describes the human being as the universe becoming self-aware they are mapping out the pivotal human task of transcending self-imposed mental-emotional limits so that a radical shift in perception reveals the divine essence in all life forms. The problem for modern *Homo sapiens* is that the *doors of perception*—as Aldous Huxley calls the senses and mind—are closed. As Jesus says in the Gospels, "they seeing see not; and hearing they hear not, neither do they understand."[6]

These doors are opened through the practice of sensory awareness.[7] When mind through the faculty of attention is linked to sensory input we are present: we truly see, touch, taste, smell and hear. In turn we are seen, touched, tasted, smelled and heard by our next of kin in the natural world. When this exchange happens we feel chora everywhere. We feel the vibration of subtle awareness that suffuses all life and we are freed from a worldview that dismisses matter as lifeless. We are released also from an aggressive behavioral pattern that in recklessly stripping the Earth of resources causes environmental degradation.

"The wild mind of the planet blows through us all," remarks David Abram.[8] Thus, "each entity participates in this enveloping awareness from its own angle and orientation, according to the proclivities of its own flesh."[9]

And while "a praying mantis's experience of mind is as weirdly different from mine as its spindly body is different from mine" we jointly tell Earth's story and live her mystery.[10]

REMEMBERING OUR INDIGENOUS HERITAGE

Perception and conception work in tandem; we see what we think we see. Perception begins as a collective activity, an enculturated *worldview* that humans grow up with, are conditioned by, and adhere to through a system of values or cultural *ethos* that translates into customary behavior. The worldview informs and forms cultural institutions which in turn reinforce the worldview. Anthropologist Clifford Geertz describes the process as a congruence between "an assumed structure of reality" (worldview) and "an approved style of life" (ethos) that "complete one another and lend one another meaning."[11] For most of us reality is negotiated by habitual patterns of thought, personal and cultural constructs in mind that accrue over time and appear automatically in our words and actions. Only the practice of awareness can arrest the treadmill of these mental patterns.

Engrained in Western industrialized culture is the worldview that Earth is a commodity to be bought and sold, a thing to be exploited and denuded of its resources indiscriminately. When polluted water, contaminated air and depleted soil are left as detritus of our actions there is no compunction *because these entities are not perceived as alive.* Land is property. The goods of the land, the inner wealth of its energy, belong to whoever has enough money and power to take them.

The worldview of indigenous cultures is starkly different. Earth is the sacred Mother and all creatures are kin. Therefore, extraction of Earth's resources by any method is a violation of Her Living Body and a sacrilege. The solidarity that indigenous peoples feel with their environment reflects a conceptual universe built on respect for Nature accompanied by a healthy fear. Man does not control nature. He must live rightly. If trouble arrives such as a poor hunting season the tribe must examine their behavior for signs of offense to the Mother. In *Primitive Man as Philosopher* anthropologist Paul Radin describes the connection the native feels with Nature as ". . . an attraction, a compulsion. Nature cannot resist man, man cannot resist nature. A purely mechanistic conception of life is thus unthinkable . . . the material form taken by objects in nature are mere symbols, *simulacra*, for the essential psychical-spiritual entity that lies behind them."[12] This connection is broken in modern man; therefore only a 'mechanistic conception of life' is conceivable. He thinks and acts through the narrow lens of technological mind.

By contrast, an *ecospiritual* vision determines the actions of indigenous peoples. For example, the Mbuti pygmies are hunter-gatherer tribes who have lived for centuries in the Ituri rainforest of the Republic of the Congo. Utterly dependent upon the forest for their survival they perceive the forest as Mother, Father, Lawgiver, Friend, Lover, and God. The forest provides food—game, berries, and honey—and shelter in the form of leaves and sticks to build thatched huts. The pygmies call themselves *the children of the forest* and, unlike the Bantu villagers with whom they trade goods, they feel no fear in traversing the thickly leaved forest floor because they believe that the forest protects them from all harm. As described by Colin Turnbull in his ethnography of the Mbuti, *The Forest People*, these 4-foot tall muscular people move like sprites, quiet and alert, through their beloved forest landscape. Every day is Earth Day to the Mbuti. In their main ceremony, called the molimo festival, the Mbuti gather around a fire in the evening and sing love songs to the forest to the accompaniment of a flute made out of bamboo—the molimo. This instrument is playfully described by the Mbuti as a mysterious 'animal' who sings its ethereal song in the secretive shadow of the forest.

Towards the end of his stay with the pygmies Turnbull witnesses a moving event that highlights for him the intimate relationship that the Mbuti have with the forest—with the 'real world' as his informant Kenge puts it. Turnbull writes:

> One night in particular will always live for me, because that night I think I learned just how far away we civilized human beings have drifted from reality. The moon was full, so the dancing had gone on for longer than usual . . . in the tiny clearing, splashed with silver, was the sophisticated Kenge, clad in barkcloth, adorned with leaves, with a flower stuck in his hair. He was all alone, dancing around and singing softly to himself. . . . When I asked him why he was dancing alone he looked at me as if to say how stupid I was, and said 'But I'm not dancing alone, I am dancing with the forest, dancing with the moon.'[13]

Another classic study of indigenous peoples is that of the Danish anthropologist Knud Rasmussen who did research on the Inuit Eskimo in the early 1900s. He observed how the Inuit think and behave, especially when faced with calamity. The Inuit believe that their survival depends upon a healthy relationship with the Sea Goddess who supplies them with sea animals in the harsh Arctic environment. During a famine Rasmussen attends a ritual in which the shaman goes into a non-ordinary state of consciousness and, through an out-of-body experience, travels to the bottom of the sea to persuade the Goddess to forgive tribal sins which are sullying her body with impurities. Through the cooperation of tribal members, who chant prayers while the shaman does his conciliatory work, the Goddess relents and releases the game. In the twenty-first century, as droughts, floods and storms increase in severity, threatening to devastate crops around the globe, where are our rituals, our acts of contrition to avert calamity?

Once upon a time all humans were indigenous peoples. An instinctual ecological understanding governed our actions. Our behavior in relation to the land was respectful, even reverential, for the land served our basic needs of food, medicine and shelter. It still performs these functions but the memory of an intimate connection has faded. As hunters and foragers we were utterly dependent on Earth's bounty, and our knowledge of the environment was keen. When the idea of planting wild seeds led to the dawn of the Agricultural Revolution in the Fertile Crescent we did not forsake Mother Nature but based our spirituality in the fertility of the Earth Goddess. In the Americas the history of Native Americans reflects a reverence for the plant and animal beings whose sacrificial offerings to humans must be reciprocated by ritual ceremonies of thanksgiving and respect. For example, corn or maize was perceived as a gift of Mother Earth. Treated as a sacred being, each corn plant was nursed into full 'adulthood' with sacred songs and the gentle touch of maternal hands. As one Navajo puts it: "'Corn is the same as a human being, only it is holier.'"[14]

At the heart of indigenous spirituality is the belief that all created forms on Earth and in the cosmos are animate and ensouled. This belief system is called *animism*. Because all religions were originally indigenous it follows that reverence for the Earth is still rooted in this spirituality. It is the Eastern religions in particular which have retained the indigenous remembrance of Creation as sacred matter. For example, in the holy Vedas of Hinduism the great powers of the five elements of Creation are described as deities: Fire (*Agni*), Air (*Vayu*), Water (*Jala*), Space or Ether (*Akasha*), and Earth herself, the goddess *Prithvi*.

Geographical features of the landscape, such as Mother Ganges and the lofty Himalaya mountains, are perceived by Hindus as spiritual beings. Ritual ceremonies of propitiation and thanksgiving are still enacted to honor all the divine forces that populate the natural world. As Krishna tells Arjuna in the *Bhagavad Gita*: "He who can see the Supreme Lord in all beings, the Imperishable amidst the perishable, he it is who really sees. Beholding the Lord in all things equally his actions do not mar his spiritual life. . . ."[15]

Jainism, which preceded Hinduism, dates back to a distant indigenous past. It remains a minority religion in India but has about six million adherents around the world. Jains share with Hindus the belief in the interdependence and equality of created forms as well as the practice of compassion and non-violence (*ahimsa*). These philosophical tenets determine diet (vegetarian), inform a regard for animals who are often rescued from slaughter, and guide

Figure 8.2. "Travelers Through Mountain Passes" by Dai Jin
(1388–1462), Ming Dynasty.
Courtesy of Palace Museum, Beijing.

the spiritual practice of meditation. Before sitting down to meditate Jains may sweep the area gently with a small broom so as not to crush minute forms of life such as insects.

Buddhism shares with Hinduism and Jainism a deep regard for other species. For the Buddhist the practice of ahimsa is a natural outcome of the belief that the whole universe is Buddha's Body (*Dharmakaya*). All sentient beings evolve together and depend upon each other through the pervasive *buddha-nature* which each organism expresses in a species-specific way. The practice of mindfulness gives rise to compassion because mindfulness reveals interdependence as a fact of life. The mindfulness trainings that Buddhist teacher Thich Nhat Hanh devised for the monks and laypeople of his monastic order begin with two promises: "I vow to develop my compassion in order to love and protect the life of people, animals, plants and minerals. I vow to develop understanding in order to be able to love and to live in harmony with people, animals, plants and minerals."[16]

Finally, Taoism acknowledges Nature and natural law as an expression of the mysterious Tao that creates and pervades every life form. The human species is perceived as embedded in the natural world. In Chinese landscape painting there is always a difference in size between man and his artifacts and the overpowering, lush presence of the Great Mother.

TWO INDIGENOUS WORLDVIEWS: A CLOSE-UP

Out of the many examples which elucidate the indigenous worldview and ethos the Native American Navajo and the Aboriginal Australian Aranda present rich symbolic systems that show the animistic perception of Earth as sacred space. These two peoples share certain cultural concepts such as a belief in powerful spiritual energies residing in material form and the potency of song to penetrate those spiritual energies and make them available for human use. Each offers a unique expression of these shared concepts, reflected in ritual practice.

Before proceeding to study their respective traditions it is well to acknowledge our own prejudice as Westerners, enculturated as we are in Cartesian logic, empirical science and materialism. The beliefs and customs of both peoples, but especially the Aranda, may seem exotic to us. Indeed, for his beliefs the Aboriginal Australian continues to suffer from ethnocentric bias. But there is growing recognition that the idea that matter derives from and expresses spirit—an idea which indigenous peoples see playing out in the 'empirical facts' of geography—does not arise from childlike imagination or a 'primitive' use of mental faculties *but from a different kind of thinking.*

The indigenous brand of intelligence favors those faculties of free-roaming instinct, intuition and imagination that cut through, like a sharp knife, the inner reality of Earth to reveal living spirit.

In the West, as modern sensibilities to the land dulled and reliance on book-learning, followed by mechanized educational tools like television and computers, removed human beings from Nature's magic, even empirical science, which can provide access to Nature's hidden realm, was barred entrance until the onset of modern physics because of a cultural mindset that still perceives what is observed and handled as dead matter.

Navajo

The Navajo tribal people inhabit and manage 27,425 square miles of desert terrain atop the Colorado Plateau situated in the southwestern United States. The Navajo joined the United States as the result of a treaty signed by their chiefs and President Andrew Jackson in 1868 by which they acquired the status of a semi-autonomous entity which governs its own territory known as the Navajo Nation. The Navajo worldview revolves around the concept of *hózhó* which means beauty, order, harmony. One version of a Navajo prayer reads: "Now I walk in beauty; beauty is before me; beauty is behind me, above and below me." These simple words describe the human being as embedded in a sacred cosmic circle where there is nothing but beauty everywhere, punctuated by the four cardinal directions. Even the traditional humble home of a Navajo—the hogan—is a microcosm of this heavenly design. Made of mud and logs, its simple circular perimeter and curved roof is meant to imitate the dome-shaped sky and the flat earth out of which First Man and First Woman emerged to create the world. The four wooden pillars that support the roof are aligned with the four directions. The doorway faces east, the direction of sunrise and awakening, both physical and spiritual. Every hogan is the center of the world, an *axis mundi.*

Whenever the Navajo prays within a hogan he or she walks in a sunrise direction to augment the natural forces of equilibrium. In the natural state the human being and the cosmos are in perfect resonance because the Great Spirit created a world based in hózhó through the agency of the Holy People—the Navajo primordial ancestors. All life forms are interrelated manifestations of hózhó. Through aligning one's words and actions with hózhó one unites the realm of the ancestral Holy People with the earthly people, the celestial with the human, the inner with the outer: as above, so below.

For the Navajo ritual ceremonies are necessary instruments through which hózhó is maintained. The Navajo are enjoined to chant the world into existence every morning just as the Holy People did on the first day of Creation.

In this morning ritual sacred songs and prayers are intoned, flowing out into a spacious landscape of desert scrub and towering red cliffs. These chants, learnt by heart as part of an oral tradition, enable the Navajo to recall and celebrate tribal history and to recreate the holy balance of hózhó through the intercession of the holy ancestors. When hózhó is disturbed by offensive acts, sickness or any other tribal disharmony a shaman must mend the tear in the sacred fabric of Creation by a series of ritualized actions of healing that put things back into their proper places. Every individual action—even if the harm done is unintentional—has a wider consequence. The Navajo believe that the effects of a ritual healing ceremony, properly performed, can rejuvenate the Earth and even have a cosmic effect. As David Suzuki and Peter Knudtson state in *Wisdom of the Elders*: "The over-arching purpose of Navajo ritual is to maintain or restore hózhó. Its central theme, with countless variations, appears to be environmental renewal—the revitalization and restoration of all of nature, from the earth's mortal inhabitants and stone-strewn southwestern landscapes to the outer celestial reaches of the cosmos."[17] For such a vast undertaking the accumulation of prayers and songs based in mythical history accompanied by ritual procedures are safeguarded in the shaman's memory, to be passed down through the generations.

Navajo healing rituals make use of sand paintings. A healing ceremony called *hózhóóji* or *Blessingway* is the model of all the healing 'ways' that are available to the shaman to treat various physical and mental ailments. The *Blessingway* is described as "'the spinal column of all songs.'"[18] Each way has its own songs and sand painting. A ceremonial hogan is the site of the ceremony. Preparations may last several days as the shaman purifies himself in a sweat lodge and gathers into the hogan sacred objects which are considered animate such as a drum, rattles, feathers of eagle or hawk, and his medicine bundle. These are placed on the holy ground of the hogan where a sand painting is then constructed by the shaman to serve as a kind of altar of supplication and a repository of energies. The shaman must study to understand the subtle meanings of the images portrayed and attain the skill needed to apply with the fingers the different colored sands that make up the picture. The artwork requires attention and patience.[19] The final product is a mandala which, in featuring images of the ancestral Holy People, is believed to contain subtle power.

In the healing ceremony the patient is seated on the painting. The shaman begins to 'sing over' him or her. A long, complex repertoire of chants, to the accompaniment of drum or rattle, invoke the intercession of the sacred ancestors whose energies will descend through a hole in the top of the hogan to penetrate the painting and the patient. Central to the Blessingway rite is the Navajo Prayer to the Internal Forms of the Earth or simply the 'Earth's

Prayer' in which the shaman addresses and communes with spiritual energies that inhabit and sustain all physical forms placed on Earth by the Holy People at the dawn of Creation. If the recitation of these sacred verses is properly intoned it is believed that not only the patient but the natural environment will transmute into its original purity: hózhó. The shaman may dance and make sounds which resemble the shaman's power animal whose spirit is assisting him. Finally, when the shaman touches the patient's body in particular places with his sacred objects it is as if an infusion of energy from Spirit—Sky—into Earth unites the earthly with the divine. The patient is made whole again, identified with the harmonious energies alive within the Earth as in primeval times. This healing reverberates into the Navajo community in a holographic way; as Suzuki and Knudtson put it, "Through the reenactment, the original acts of creation are repeated and the world is re-created."[20] At the end of the ceremony the sand is collected and removed from the ceremonial hogan; the painting has done its work by absorbing negative energies of the patient's sickness.

Aranda

The Aranda are one of the indigenous peoples of Australia known as Aboriginal Australians. There are close to 500 distinct Aboriginal tribal groups each possessing an ancestral language. Traditionally Aboriginal Australians were hunter-gatherers who roamed the vast continent. Today they occupy reserves allocated by the Australian government. The reserves are distributed mainly to the northern, central and southern parts of the country; the Aranda live in the central part.[21]

In parallel fashion to the prejudicial attitude of white settlers towards Native Americans (still extant in the American cultural ethos), the Aboriginal Australians have long been considered a lesser race, beginning with the belief by British colonists that access to human rights was determined by one's racial identity. The idea of *race* and racial hierarchies has been disproven as a fallacious cultural construction; nevertheless, a widely endorsed referendum to the Australian Constitution in 1967, while recognizing Aborigines as citizens who should be included in the census and protected from racial discrimination by the federal government, has not in practice delivered all the benefits of citizenship. Even standard documents such as birth certificates are not available to many Aborigines.[22]

Two essential themes of Aboriginal spirituality are the perceived symbiosis between human beings and the land and the interwoven nature of spirit and matter. As in Navajo spirituality there is a belief that all life in its diversity emerged from the womb of Mother Earth through the agency of ancestral powers. Many

Aboriginal myths relate how animals, plants and humans all came from the same original ancestor—an interesting resemblance to the modern theory of evolution which traces species' lineages from ancestral forms. Aboriginal tribal identity is totemic: that is, the tribe associates itself with a certain animal or plant species that is believed to have emerged from the land and taken on human form. There is a kind of mysterious shapeshifting, a holistic sharing of life and death and reincarnated life between animals, plants and humans which defines the Aboriginal concept of kinship. It is by learning about a tribe's particular totem and how the land was created and sacralized by that ancestor that one learns about oneself and adopts responsibilities to the land. The Aranda, for instance, trace their totemic ancestry to the red kangaroo who graze among the scrub mulga woodland and desert plains. No place is more sacred to the Red Kangaroo clan than a natural spring known as Krantiji where the original totem ancestor or 'chief' named Krantijirinja emerged during Dream Time.

Central to the Aboriginal sense of personal and collective identity is this unique concept of Dream Time or *altjira*, a primeval time when the Creation was first sung into existence as a perfect material reflection of spiritual authority. In this 'Garden of Eden' the totemic ancestor emerged from a specific location and, in the process of creating the landscape, marked its passage with signs of its presence in the shape of boulders, caves, springs, and trees. These natural haunts are consecrated by all Aboriginal tribes through the placement of sacred objects, called *churingas*, at these locations. As the ancestor moved across the landscape he sang songs; each trail of his footprints translated as a musical score. The Aborigine knows the songs and sings them as he too travels the landscape. By doing so he recreates and rejuvenates the original abundance of a mystical providence that he trusts will always be available to him as a timeless gift and enjoinder to perform the human role of maintaining the abundant fertility of all species according to ritual prescriptions handed down through the generations. Like the Navajo concept of *hózhó*, which demands of humans a role in maintaining the original balance and reciprocity of the Creation, so allegiance to the perfect design of the world programmed during Dream Time and manifest in the natural environment is each Aborigine's sacred duty. As anthropologist W. E. H. Stanner states:

If life has a mystical foundation, and if its design was fixed once-for-all, what else should rational men do but maintain and renew that design? . . . Part of their religion seems to be like a return of equivalent or compensatory signs to the mysterious domain whence they came . . . which suggested a conscious attempt by men to bind themselves to the design in things they saw about them, and to the enduring plan of life as they experienced it."[23]

For the Aranda, the presence of Krantijirinja still animates the holy spring of Krantiji where lush grasses and pure water are preserved and protected for the red kangaroo's exclusive use. Certain underwater stone slabs, revered as churinga, symbolize pieces of the original flesh of Krantijirinja who embodies "the *living essence* of the Dreamtime unity of the two species."[24] The Aranda believe that this site holds the mysterious reproductive potential for both human and kangaroo whose interchangeable forms are regenerated through fertility rituals called increase ceremonies or *intichiuma*.

Aboriginal tales about the red kangaroo show a sophisticated ecological understanding of the kangaroo's population dynamics, diet and habitat preferences fused to a spiritual affinity with and respect for the animal as kin, and more than kin—as alterego. T. G. H. Strehlow's deep study of the Aranda, related in his classic 1947 ethnography, shows that the protected spring and other sacred places where the drama of Creation was enacted by Krantijirinja are perceived as repositories of his living cells. These cells are disguised as features of the landscape, ready in embryonic form (like stem cells?) to be born again. Thus, says Strehlow, the hunter works in harmony with this force so that he summons his own alchemical capacity to "'create the animals he needs with ease, simply by rubbing a portion of the rock representing the changed body of the ancestor with a stone; for every atom of that rock is a potential animal'"—the law of attraction at work.[25]

The complexity of the Aborigine symbolic rites, particularly regarding the prescribed duty of generating the fecundity and growth of all species, reveals an implicit and explicit *ecological conscience* (Aldo Leopold's term), a recognition of the need for conservation practices based on respect for life. Stanner notes: "The known evidence suggests that Aboriginal religion was probably one of the least material-minded, and most life-minded, of any of which we have knowledge."[26] Yet the material result—fecundity—is certainly the goal, and it is achieved, says the Aborigine, through spiritual agency.

This subordination of matter to spirit, or more accurately the fusion of matter and spirit, is shown in two related ways: the belief in spirit impregnation of women and rites of fertility or *intichiuma*. As to the former, when a woman wants to have a child she visits one of the sacred places which the totemic ancestor in Dream Time sang into being. The totem's spiritual force enters and impregnates her. Thus each fetus is an incarnation of the land, living temporarily in human form. The Aboriginal Australians are not ignorant of the biological means of reproduction between man and woman, but they believe it is the *spiritual* consummation provided by the land that actually engenders life.[27] The second means by which Aborigines fuse matter and spirit is participation in the intichiuma. These rituals are believed to have the power to unlock spiritual energy preserved in the sacred geography. A totem clan will travel to a holy site and bless that site by singing and dancing. In some cases a man may even cut his arm and release blood onto the sacred ground, with the intent of replenishing the fertility of the totemic ancestor—and by extension all species of the land upon which Aborigines depend for sustenance. Killing and eating the totem, especially around ceremonial sites, is usually forbidden.

Max Duramunmun Harrison is an aboriginal elder and teacher of the Yuin Nation. In a 2012 television interview he speaks of how Mother Earth not only sings the world into existence every moment but speaks to human beings through features of the land. He says: "This tree, this rock is recording and holding what I am saying, just like the TV is holding my image now."[28] Max Duramunmun bemoans the dissociation between people in the industrialized West and the natural environment, particularly the loss of connection between what we eat and where it comes from. He states:

> Where does a tin of peas come from, before the supermarket? Take it back to where food comes from. Some kids don't know where milk comes from—a carton. This is a big problem. We have to start respecting Mother Earth who will rebirth us. How do we teach these kids this concept when teachers themselves don't remember. I open up a tin and say 'thank you for birthing this,' both the peas and the tin. It's all birthed from the Mother.[29]

SOUL RETRIEVAL AND ECOPSYCHOLOGY

The indigenous worldview associates health, both individual and collective, with wholeness, with feeling connected to the land as home and to the sacred forces that created everything. Physical and/or mental sickness is perceived as a loss of this wholeness, a loss of soul due to a disconnection from the inherent harmony between man and the universe. Disease therefore has a spiritual origin. When a member of the tribe becomes sick a shaman or medicine man is called upon to retrieve the lost portion of his or her soul from the spirit world and return it to the patient, often by forcefully blowing the subtle substance back into the body. The Navajo healing rituals exemplify this method of restoring wholeness. This approach to illness may strike us as strange; yet it may also urge us to ask whether modern man has lost a part of his soul, that part that once knew its close familial relationship to the natural world. If that loss is acknowledged, can we be our own shamans and, through knowledge of the loss, self-administer the cure? Sensory awareness initiates the cure by beginning the work of retrieving our lost identification with the natural world and then establishing our rightful place in that world.

Bill Plotkin, founder of Animas Valley Institute which offers guided wilderness training, describes soul as one's *ultimate place* in the world and "locus of authentic personal power—not power over people and things, but power of partnership with others, the power to co-create life and to cooperate with an evolving universe."[30] The hero's quest, relayed in Greek mythological tales of adventure, is to discover this *psycho-ecological niche.*[31] Interestingly the Greek word *psyche* is translated as *soul.* Everyone, says Plotkin, is "born to occupy a particular place in nature—a place in the Earth community, not just in a human society. You have a unique ecological role, a singular way you can serve and nurture the web of life. . . . You have a specific way of belonging to the biosphere, as unique as that of any birch, bear, or beaver pond."[32]

Sandra Ingerman, shamanic practitioner and author, discusses soul retrieval at the level of planetary sickness. Toxins that infect human beings and the environment can be neutralized, she says, when humans consciously reconnect to their earthly home. "We can't transmute environmental pollution," says Ingerman, "until we once again understand our connection with nature, the cycles of the moon, the seasons, the elements, and all of life. Harmony with the earth's cycles and the forces of nature is essential, since disconnection and disharmony with nature create disease."[33]

In his autobiography, *Of Water and the Spirit,* African shaman and teacher Malidoma Patrice Somé relates the way in which his soul was contaminated by indoctrination into the white world represented by the Jesuit school and seminary where, after being abducted from his tribal village at the age of four, he was confined for fifteen years. At the school Malidoma was called by his Christian name Patrice and was forbidden to speak Dagara, his native language, under threat of beatings and other abusive punishment. He was forced to learn and speak French and was subjected to a Western education in which his own indigenous culture was belittled as backward because it taught that the spirit world, accessible through dreams and visions, was more important than the material world known by logical empiricism. The elders of his tribe, particularly Malidoma's grandfather, a visionary shaman, understood that the young boy's mission in life was to be *friend to the enemy, the stranger* which is the meaning of the name *Malidoma.* He was destined to be a bridge between two worlds by communicating tribal wisdom to the West; therefore Malidoma's Western training was necessary. Nourished and guided by his grandfather's spirit during these hard years of incarceration Malidoma finally escapes and finds his way back home. At his arrival the elders are alarmed and fearful because Malidoma has absorbed the white man's aggression and anger; he has been poisoned by the colonialist mindset and has lost part of his soul or *siè.* This poison could infect the village so the elders decide that only through participation in the rigorous and even dangerous puberty initiation—the month-long Baor—could Malidoma's true soul be retrieved, making him whole again. A critical element in Malidoma's transformation is his realization that he must let go of the narrow analytical mindset of his Western education and awaken to a higher reality of visionary, non-rational experiences. This entry into the spirit world is initiated late one night when, sitting around a blazing communal fire with his agemates and elders, singing tribal songs to the beat of a drum, he feels an inner release followed by an emotional connection to the natural world of trees, grass, sky and stars perceived as fellow animate beings. This breakthrough begins a process of soul retrieval; the catalyst is Nature as healer and teacher.

The contemporary field of ecopsychology can be viewed as a modern derivative of soul retrieval that has arisen to treat a growing number of children and adults who are psychologically sick due to a spiritual breach between humanity and the natural world. In his classic study, *The Voice of the Earth*, psychologist Theodore Roszak examines the disability suffered by human beings who have grown deaf to the voice of the Earth. He attributes the abuse of the planet to an ignorance—an ignoring—of the elemental structure of the human mind. "The core of the mind," says Roszak, "is the ecological unconscious. For ecopsychology, repression of the ecological unconscious is the deepest root of collusive madness in industrial society; open access to the ecological unconscious is the path to sanity."[34]

Roszak asserts that the ecological unconscious holds within it the deep living record of cosmic evolution which in turn contains the species-specific evolution of *Homo sapiens*. There is, he says, a "synergistic interplay between planetary and personal well-being."[35] In order to unlock this repressed memory and restore consciousness of the interconnected whole in which humans have evolved ecotherapy is needed. Experiences that can reawaken and develop this connection to the whole—to the nondual ground of all experience—include wilderness-based work, shamanic work and sensory-based educational techniques which may involve simply reintroducing the patient to the natural world through sensory exploration.

The repression of the ecological unconscious has been reinforced, argues Roszak, by the prevalence of male character traits which historically have emphasized the domination of Nature, particularly through the political, economic and social structures that emerged and solidified during the Industrial Revolution in the West. Nature mystics and Romantic poets have traditionally offered an alternative worldview in which, as Wordsworth puts it, Nature is "the anchor of my purest thoughts, the nurse / The guide, the guardian of my heart, and soul / Of all my moral being."[36]

The root of the words *human, homo* and *humus* translates as *of the Earth*. When humans are displaced from their larger home, the natural world, a psychological malaise develops. When, says John Muir, people fear Nature's solitudes it is "'like very sick children afraid of their mother.'"[37] The well-spring of love and reverence for Nature, common to native peoples, is the *natural* response of biophilia which bestows health. Not only is it uncommon in modern society to feel this response. We don't even recognize our own bodies as smaller versions of Earth's body, made of the same elements, subject to growth and decay. Is it any wonder that contemporary human lives are beset with systemic diseases of body-mind like depression, addiction, obesity, cancers, diabetes, and the increasing number of children diagnosed with ADHD?

Two other maladies can be added to the above list: solastalgia and biophobia. Solastalgia is a longing for the restorative health and safety that a healthy planet provides. Those of us who care deeply about the Earth may feel solastalgia as we watch the Earth absorb the deformities inflicted on her. Biophobia, a term coined by educator and environmentalist David Orr, means *fear of life*. Feelings of estrangement from Nature as alien and threatening, fear of dark woods and wild places—these revulsions revisit Puritan fears of the wilderness as evil. Muir intuited this problem even in the nineteenth century when he said: "Most people are *on* the world, not in it—have no conscious sympathy or relationship to anything about them—undiffused, separate, and rigidly alone like marbles of polished stone, touching but separate."[38]

David Orr speaks of the malaise of homelessness that besets modern man as a devaluation of place. He writes:

> In contrast to 'dis-placed' people who are physically removed from their homes but who retain the idea of place and home, we have become 'de-placed' people, mental refugees, homeless wherever we are. We no longer have a deep concept of place as a repository of meaning, history, livelihood, healing, recreation, and sacred memory . . . places have become just the intersection of two lines on a map. . . .[39]

Even as today's progressive towns and cities insert parks and other green spaces into their design, the pervasive landscape of many urban centers is black top. Parking lots and strip malls replace meadows. New housing developments and condos replace vacant lots where children once exercised their creative imagination in the unstructured play of building forts and castles. Progress has emphasized an enclosed life indoors—at home, in the office or classroom—where one is protected from feeling the wind against one's face or smelling the rain-soaked earth. Without a tactile, sensory awareness of the outdoors environment the subliminal connection of human beings to the natural world atrophies. Energy is redirected to sitting in front of a computer screen; the impetus to self-discovery and self-renewal that Nature offers is forfeited. In a playful diatribe against the digital age Kurt Vonnegut describes the illusion of fulfillment through computers. "We have contraptions like computers," he says, "that cheat you out of becoming. Bill Gates says, 'Wait till you can see what your computer can become.' But it's you who should be doing the becoming, not the damn fool computer. What you can become is the miracle you were born to be through the work that you do."[40]

It is important to ask whether our adulation of technology includes any technological invention or virtual reality mechanism that can replace a walk in the garden or nearby woods, a child's recess at school, a canoe trip down a pristine river, or a family camping trip. As Muir said of the tourists who in 1898 were seeking out the mystical medicine of mountains and forests: "'Thousands of tired, nerve-shaken, over-civilized people are beginning to find out that going to the mountains is going home.'"[41]

This isn't to say that urban life necessarily deprives a person of a connection with Nature. City parks and community gardens beckon the urban dweller. Even a row of potted tomato plants placed on a fire escape landing, with morning glory vines wrapped around the railing, can be one's personal green space—with the added bonus of providing fresh tomatoes to make grandmother's special spaghetti sauce. Even a small dose of natural beauty can delight the soul.

Nature is a natural medicine. This fact began to be quantitatively measured in the work of Swedish behavioral scientist Roger S. Ulrich who in 1979 found that natural scenes elicit positive feelings of elation and affection in subjects tested whereas urban views produce anger and sadness. The former response is correlated with the release of serotonin, an antidepressant, in the brain. Ulrich's subsequent study in 1984 showed that people who had undergone identical surgeries but were placed in recovery rooms with differing window views—a brick wall versus lush trees—showed dramatic differences in recovery rate and pain threshold. A complementary experiment was initiated in 1982 by the Forest Agency of the Japanese government. Citizens were offered a program that encouraged them to get out into the great outdoors. It was called *shinrin-yoku* which means *basking in* (*yoku*) the *forest* (*shinrin*). In 1990 a study by Dr. Yoshifumi Miyazaki corroborated the good sense of this program by discovering that people who took advantage of *shinrin-yoku* showed reduced levels of stress hormones such as cortisol as well as lower blood pressure.

Subsequent studies confirm these earlier forays using new technologies such as MRIs which allow researchers to pinpoint portions of the brain triggered by natural versus urban scenes. When natural scenes are presented opioid receptors are fired up, stimulating feelings of wellbeing; in contrast, urban scenes excite the amygdala, a site associated with fear. A 2009 study by psychologist Peter H. Kahn of the University of Washington involved putting simulated natural scenes on 50-inch high-definition televisions that were attached to the interior walls of windowless offices. Office personnel reacted positively to the scenes but a later study showed a striking difference in the measurement of heart-rate recovery from stress of workers given only these virtual scenes versus those whose offices contained actual windows that looked out on natural green scenery. These results strongly suggest that being in the natural world soothes the mind and is necessary to mental health. Because trees are an elemental part of Nature it is clear that deforestation, besides being a major contributor to global warming, is also a hazard to mental-emotional health.

We can relearn a living engagement with Nature from children, says Roszak, because children see Nature as alive; they display the innate animistic nature of *Homo sapiens*. Bill Plotkin elaborates on the child's enchantment with wild Nature. He writes:

> Through his interactions with wild nature the child is granted the widest and deepest trove of resources with which to flesh out a self. Unselfconsciously, he discovers some of his own possibilities in the animals: the grace and stealth of cat, the cunning of fox, the lighthearted spirit of butterfly, the rowdiness of coyote, the fluid grace of trout, the power and roar of bear, the joy and song of wren. He catches glimpses of the possible self in the rootedness, open arms, and tall-standing nature of tree, the beauty and delicacy of flower, the solidity and patience of rock, the enfolding snow, the Sun's warm countenance, the shape-shifting of clouds, and the hope and endurance of stars.[42]

At the forefront of a new educational framework for children (and parents) that emphasizes a renewed friendship with the natural world is journalist Richard Louv. His first book, *Last Child in the Woods*, became an instant classic because it presents both the research that clarifies the modern alienation of people, including children, from an engagement with the natural world and offers remedies. Louv argues that from an early age "Nature's Ritalin" nurtures us with her beauty and serenity.[43] Yet today "the life of the senses is literally electrified" so that a computer provides a virtual education about Nature but cannot provide an authentic learning experience based in sensory contact.[44] This "denaturing of childhood" is creating what Louv calls Nature Deficit Disorder or NDD which "describes the human costs of alienation from nature, among them: diminished use of the senses, attention difficulties, and higher rates of physical and emotional illnesses."[45]

At the root of NDD is a faulty perception of the natural world as dangerous and alien; this fear leads parents to keep children inside. While protection of a child's safety is essential, says Louv, one must also ask "where's the greatest danger? Outdoors in the woods and fields? Or on the couch in front of the TV?"[46] While Louv does not advocate 'unplugging' children from the pervasive intrusion of technology he believes that regular immersion in the natural world brings balance.[47]

DEVELOPING AN ECOLOGY OF MIND

If we listen to the unaffected native and follow the child into the woods it is possible that all species, including our own, could be delivered from the destructive effects of alienation from the natural world. We could relearn an indigenous practice known as *ecology of mind* through which, says psychologist Christopher Bache, we "gain access to what could be described as the universe's inner experience of itself." [48] This adaptive mindset remembers the interdependence of all organisms and fosters actions that obey the natural harmonies of the universe.

The Gabra of the Sahara desert, for example, are a nomadic herding people who raise goats and travel by camel. The goats and camels are treated as part of the tribal family. Goats need pasture; therefore the Gabra have named and learned the use of 450 species of desert grass. To survive in this inhospitable environment the Gabra practice *finn* which translates as *ecology of mind*. Finn means knowing how all species depend on each other and work together. Man is one of these species who must, as one tribal elder tells his son, "bend with the wind or you will break because things always change."[49]

Cultivating an ecology of mind requires a conscious experience of being embedded in the natural world so that we see, hear, smell, taste and touch our fellow animate beings. David Haskell, biologist at the University of the South in Sewanee, Tennessee, guides us into an ecology of mind by his habit of strolling the hardwood forest on the edge of the Cumberland Plateau, listening and looking in silent meditation at patches of earth which, when examined carefully with a hand lens, hold, says Haskell, a holographic vision of the whole forest. "'Science deepens our intimacy with the world,'" says Haskell, "'but there is a danger in an exclusively scientific way of thinking. The forest is turned into a diagram; animals become mere mechanisms'" whereas, in truth, these squirrels sprawled on the limb basking in the sun "'are our cousins.'"[50]

A conscious immersion in Nature stimulates the emotion of awe. Psychologists Dacher Keltner and Jonathan Haidt have found that when a person witnesses events that elicit awe, like the birth of a baby or the vastness of the Grand Canyon, their habitual mindset gives way to a sense of humility, a quieting of the mind, and a desire to help others. Abraham Heschel elevates this phenomenon of awe into a mystical experience when he writes:

Awe is an intuition for the dignity of all things, a realization that things not only are what they are but also stand, however remotely, for something supreme. Awe . . . enables us to perceive in the world intimations of the divine . . . to sense the ultimate in the common and the simple; to feel in the rush of the passing the stillness of the eternal. What we cannot comprehend by analysis, we become aware of in awe.[51]

A legend from the Hindu scripture *Srimad Bhagavatam* tells of the god-man Krishna who, as a baby, is found by his foster mother Yasoda sitting on the earth, eating mud. She scolds him for playing with dirt and getting himself dirty. She asks him to open his mouth so that she can extract the mud. When he does so Yasoda sees the whole universe within the mouth of Baby Krishna. Bewildered and overcome with awe Yasoda exclaims, "'Is this a dream or an hallucination? Or is it a real vision, the vision of my little baby as God himself?'"[52]

By returning to our soul-place in Nature and practicing ecology of mind we are poised to take the next step—to work diligently for cultural transformation so that all species can enjoy a sustainable future. Will we take this step? That is the subject matter of the next chapter.

Chapter Nine

A Fork in the Road

To be or not to be, that is the question

—Hamlet, *Hamlet* III:1

We human beings create and sustain the current mindset of a felt separation from the natural world whenever we perceive Nature as a thing, an object to be manipulated for human gain. This *anthropocentric* worldview also legitimizes a world where the powerful dominate the powerless—be it the natural world or native peoples.

There is an alternative worldview that is *ecocentric.* This worldview is very old, nestled in the indigenous perception of peoples like the Navaho and Aranda. Earth is viewed as Mother, and all creatures are kin. According to this egalitarian perspective all life sprouts from and belongs to the Earth as chief provider. Modern man has chosen to reverse the order of dominance by insisting that the Earth and her resources, as lifeless commodities, belong to man.

Nature mystics, as well as certain poets and philosophers, share the indigenous worldview. They perceive the natural world as grand, mysterious, even fearful, but also as caring, protective, and conducive to flights of spiritual ecstasy. American transcendentalist philosopher and essayist Ralph Waldo Emerson sheds his brilliant intellect momentarily to indulge in a moment of rapture while walking in the woods. He writes:

> Standing on the bare ground—my head bathed by the blithe air, and uplifted into infinite space—all mean egotism vanishes. I become a transparent eye-ball. I am nothing. I see all. The currents of the Universal Being circulate through me; I am part or particle of God. . . . In the wilderness, I find something more dear and connate than in streets or villages. In the tranquil landscape, and especially

in the distant line of the horizon, man beholds somewhat as beautiful as his own nature. The greatest delight which the fields and woods minister is the suggestion of an occult relation between man and the vegetable. I am not alone and unacknowledged. They nod to me and I to them.[1]

In the following poem by Emily Dickinson the maternal face of the natural world is captured:

> Nature—the Gentlest Mother is,
> Impatient of no child—
> The feeblest—or the waywardest—
> Her Admonitions mild—
>
> In Forest—and in Hill—
> By Traveller—be heard—
> Restraining Rampant Squirrel—
> Or too impetuous Bird—
>
> How fair Her Conversation—
> A Summer Afternoon—
> Her Household—Her Assembly—
> And when the Sun go down—
>
> Her Voice among the Aisles
> Incite the timid prayer
> Of the minutest Cricket—
> The most unworthy Flower—
>
> When all the Children sleep—
> She turns as long away
> As will suffice to light Her lamps—
> Then bending from the Sky—
>
> With infinite Affection—
> And infiniter Care—
> Her Golden finger on Her lip—
> Wills Silence—Everywhere.[2]

These two conflicting worldviews—*anthropocentric* and *ecocentric*—represent a contemporary fork in the road of human cultural evolution. Will the dominant anthropocentric worldview continue to gain supremacy? In *A Study of History*, published in 1946, Arnold Toynbee addresses this very question. He is discussing ways in which the response of societies to environmental or cultural challenges either further their growth (which he defines as an inner maturity in the art of self-determination) or lead to their destruction. In a prescient inquiry regarding the future use of industrialism and democracy in Western society Toynbee writes:

> It may be that in every age of every society some moral issue is always the challenge that is fateful for the society's future. . . . Is the new social driving power of Industrialism and Democracy to be employed in the great constructive task of organizing a Westernized World into an ecumenical society, or are we going to turn our new power to our own destruction?[3]

The act of choosing one path or another assumes that the chooser is awake and aware that there are alternatives. If we are asleep—that is, living mechanically, without conscious awareness—how can we see that we have a choice? Thomas Berry lays out the critical choice humanity now faces. Human beings can either continue the *Technozoic Era*, based on the anthropocentric worldview, or change course and usher in an *Ecozoic Era* which affirms life and heals the planet. Berry predicts that if humanity pursues technological advances without a shift to the inclusive ecocentric worldview the result will be ecocide—a kind of self-mutilation since humans will surely be part of the massive disaster. Science and technology must be redirected to the service of Earth and all her creatures. Just as fighting Nazism was the task of the previous generation, Berry defines the Great Work of this generation as that of establishing new policies and practices that are ecologically sustainable and beneficial to all species.[4] In the 1940s the war effort aroused a communal sense of mission. Now the human task is to become aware of the environmental damage we are causing and, using restraint, undue that damage and rediscover our proper ecological niche. Whereas other species have predators that limit the capacity of any one species to overextend its influence, we humans must self-limit. The only enemy is our own myopic self-regard. Berry writes:

> Survival of any group of living beings in relation to other groups depends on the recognition of limits in the actions of each group. This law of limits is among the most basic of all cosmological, geological, or biological laws . . . In the Hindu world this law of limits is recognized as *rita* [restraint] in the cosmological order or as *dharma* in the moral order.[5]

Humanity is mentally trapped in false ideas and beliefs. Sufficient awareness allows us to reject the falsehood of human superiority and expand our vision to encompass the whole. Action is then taken for the benefit of this whole. Bill McKibben puts the choice in stark terms:

> As birds have flight, our special gift is reason. . . . Should we so choose, we could exercise our reason to do what no other animal can do: we could limit

ourselves voluntarily, choose to remain God's creatures instead of making ourselves gods. What a towering achievement that would be, so much more impressive than the largest dam (beavers can build dams) because so much harder. Such restraint—not genetic engineering or planetary management—is the real challenge, the hard thing. Of course we can splice genes. But can we *not* splice genes?[6]

Rachel Carson, biologist and ecological pioneer, wrote in 1962 about this fork in the road in her seminal book *Silent Spring*. Trained in genetics and marine biology she became concerned about evidence that the new miraculous insecticide, DDT, was found in the fatty tissue of birds and fish far from spraying areas. Though the common household fly had developed immunity to DDT wild birds were dying by the hundreds. Carson explains the chain of concentration: DDT sprayed on elm trees (which were dying of Dutch Elm disease) became lodged in the soil; earthworms ingested the poison; birds ate the worms. She argues for the replacement of toxic pesticides and insecticides with natural biotic controls which do not harm the web of life. Even as Carson's work galvanized the nascent environmental movement it also enraged the company that invented and marketed DDT. The pushback was sexist; her findings were questioned because she was female.

Another incident in Sheldon, Illinois involved spraying Japanese beetles, who were eating the leaves of certain plants, with dieldrin, a toxic pesticide which is fifty times as poisonous as DDT. Carson reports that wildlife and pets were affected and died in droves. All the while a bacterial disease, Milky Spore Disease, that only targets and kills Japanese beetles, had been discovered and was introduced successfully in fourteen eastern states without adverse effects on other forms of wildlife. This natural solution could have been used in Illinois. Carson writes:

> Incidents like the eastern Illinois spraying raise a question that is not only scientific but moral. The question is whether any civilization can wage relentless war on life without destroying itself, and without losing the right to be called civilized . . . By acquiescing in an act that can cause such suffering to a living creature, who among us is not diminished as a human being?[7]

Carson goes on to describe the choice we have:

> We stand now where two roads diverge. But unlike the roads in Robert Frost's familiar poem, they are not equally fair. The road we have long been traveling is deceptively easy, a smooth superhighway on which we progress with great speed, but at its end lies disaster. The other fork of the road—the one 'less traveled by'—offers our last, our only chance to reach a destination that assures the preservation of our earth. The choice, after all, is ours to make. . . .[8]

The aim of science is to discover the lawful, mechanical workings of Nature and probe her mysteries. This inquiry, however, has been sidetracked by an excessive exploitation of Nature, guided by the dominant anthropocentric worldview. Nevertheless, discoveries in the sciences of ecology and modern physics are drawing us towards an ecocentric worldview. There is now no denying the interconnected web of energy that regulates the subatomic world, defines ecosystems, and even manifests as the worldwide web of instant communication. But our socio-economic and other cultural institutions lag behind the incontestable fact of this subtle interrelatedness.

David Bohm's assertion that we live in a "'sacred web of relations'" suggests that the root of science and spirituality is the same.[9] Both inquiries grow out of deep existential questions that are as old as the emergence of *Homo sapiens*: questions like 'what is this Creation?', 'how does it work and to what purpose?', and 'what is my role in it?'.

In order to find permanent solutions to human-induced climate change we must ask these existential questions once more, listening for new answers that spark an enlightened response to the crisis we face. For example, rampant deforestation is associated with the detrimental effects of global warming. If we ask the question 'what is a tree, how does it live, what is its significance, and what is my relationship to it?', Newtonian science can tell us about the tree, how it lives and reproduces, how it adapts to and uses its environment. But this factual information cannot help us to truly *know* the tree because we are hindered by the fundamental Cartesian premise at the core of Newtonian science (and the anthropocentric worldview) that we are separate from, different from and better than other life forms. Empirical science argues that man must distinguish himself from what he sees, even though he is part of Nature, in order to examine and understand what is observed. Up to a point this may be true, but can we not observe, examine, and simultaneously realize our connection to what we see—as Heisenberg did in observing the effect of his presence on the behavior of subatomic particle-waves? How can we know the true identity of a world which is separate and different from our own awareness? How can we understand a world to which we have no communal relationship? Does not the very air we breathe belong to the whole biosphere? What part of it is yours or mine? Empirical science can only take us so far in the quest for knowledge. This is not a failing of science; it is simply its limit. Other dimensions of mind such as intuition and empathy must accompany rationality in order to begin to penetrate beyond the level of physical appearance to a subtler level of being so that the relationship between self and Nature is intuited and experienced.[10] Rumi expresses this enfolding of *knowing* into *being* in a short poem that reads: "I have lived on the lip / of insanity, wanting to know reasons, / knocking on a door. It opens. / I've been knocking from the inside!"[11]

While personal experiences of transcendence cannot be proved empirically they are still, insisted William James, a valid measure of truth. In collective form, these expanded faculties of mind and heart can trigger a change in worldview. James writes:

> 'Our normal waking consciousness, rational consciousness as we call it, is but one special type of consciousness, whilst all about it, parted from it by the filmiest of screens, there lie potential forms of consciousness entirely different. . . . No account of the universe in its totality can be final which leaves these other forms of consciousness quite disregarded.'[12]

When Albert Einstein died his brain was autopsied. Scientists were curious to see whether his extraordinary mental capacity would show up in the brain tissue. They were disappointed; his brain looked like any normal brain. It is interesting that Einstein begins his autobiography by asking an existential question: 'what is thinking?' By implication he is asking about the proper use of the human mind. His question is taking us beyond the limitations of technological mind.

Einstein knew that true thinking is not what we think it is. He believed that the right development of human mental capacities could elevate the human species by releasing us from the delusion of separateness. This delusory thinking, he said, is "a prison for us" and is erased by "widening our circle of compassion to embrace all living creatures and the whole of nature in its beauty."[13] Einstein relates that when the fine energy of thinking—which he seems to identify with quiet reflection—is liberated from personal desires and habits which constrain and pollute thought, not only is the scientific imagination set free but also human virtues such as humility and equanimity. Although Einstein never claimed possession of these virtues the fact that others observed them in his behavior suggests an expansion of mind that not only induced scientific insights but also promoted a balanced, virtuous life. This multiple release of qualities of mind and heart suggest a more holistic vision of mind. It is interesting that in many indigenous cultures mental functions are thought to originate in the heart, not the head.

Einstein describes thinking as multi-faceted; it is logic but it is also intuition. Real thinking, he says, exhibits a willingness to discard entrenched ideas and cherished opinions. Thus Einstein's discoveries of laws that shook the Newtonian paradigm were an outgrowth of the courage to dig deeper and, without negating mechanical laws like gravity or cause and effect, unveil deeper laws that reveal matter as essentially energy in a world of energy relationships—a world of relativity. He believed that a sense of wonder was essential in scientific investigation because wonder invites the mysterious, incomprehensible universe to bend to human inquiry and reveal an order both comprehensible and rational while simultaneously eliciting a non-comprehensible "cosmic religious feeling."[14]

Einstein's expansive view of the universe generated discoveries in modern physics that affirm a living, interconnected cosmos that mind *in its fullness* might begin to understand. As such, Einstein remains a model for the ecocentric vision that will induce cultural transformation.

In order to discern the way by which a cultural worldview based in anthropocentrism can be replaced by the kind of holistic thinking that Einstein espoused this chapter will look for clues in Thomas Kuhn's theory of paradigm shifts. Then, as an illustration of the current struggle between anthropocentric and ecocentric perspectives, the long-standing debate in the United States about land use will be examined. This debate exposes a deep-seated ambivalence in the cultural mindset about the conversion of Nature's wilderness into developed land. Lastly, the transition to an Ecozoic Era needs mentors who can inspire the vital but difficult work ahead. To serve this need a brief sketch of three historical figures in American history whose life work was dedicated to ecological principles is offered.

KUHN'S THEORY OF PARADIGM SHIFTS

The Scientific Revolution, in its overhaul of the medieval worldview, has had a steady, incremental effect on the way Western man thinks and acts. Its reverberations continue to energize our infatuation with material progress made possible by harnessing science to industry. In his innovative study, *The Structure of Scientific Revolutions*, physicist and philosopher Thomas Kuhn examines the means by which dramatic shifts in worldview take place. He identifies and explains a mechanism of change which he calls a *paradigm shift*. Kuhn's theory of paradigm shifts elucidates the path by which humanity can create an Ecozoic Era.

Kuhn proposes that the history of science shows a dynamic progression of conceptual revolutions, big and small, which interrupt longer periods of cultural stability. Such revolutions arise as necessary responses to crisis and appear as a differentiation between the operations of *normal science* and those of *extraordinary science*. Normal science is cumulative and selective, adding data which fit and clarify the existing paradigm or customary way of thinking which extends beyond science to inform all cultural institutions. Extraordinary science invites paradigm change when the existing worldview no longer supports new facts.

Sometimes a radical change in worldview is facilitated by the invention of new tools. For example, in the early seventeenth century, Galileo's telescope gave credence to the Copernican theory of a heliocentric universe and helped galvanize the Scientific Revolution. An ancillary result of the rejection of the geocentric paradigm was the unraveling of medieval society. In this century a number of technological breakthroughs provide the practical means for a paradigm shift towards sustainability. One of these is the invention and patenting in 2017 of a new improved type of battery by physicist John Goodenough, ninety-four-year-old co-inventor of the lithium-ion battery which is used in cars, laptops and cell phones. By applying a discovery made by a Portuguese physicist of a type of glass that replaces the lithium-ion battery's volatile liquid electrolytes Goodenough has created a battery that is lightweight, inexpensive and much safer than the previous model. A long-standing crusader for energy efficiency, Goodenough was inspired during the energy crisis of the 1970s to find a way to help society kick the fossil fuel habit by switching to electric cars. In an interview Goodenough explains that his success has been due to a faith-driven mission to eradicate pollution, a talent for synthesizing important ideas relative to that mission, and a serendipity of events that he describes as instances of synchronicity, stating: "I'm grateful for the doors that have been opened to me in different periods of my life . . . At just the right moment, when I was looking for something, it walked in the door."[15]

As a conceptual crisis builds, says Kuhn, a Copernicus or an Einstein is induced to perceive problems arising in his discipline in a new way. There is a willingness and determination to see old facts anew and to greet new facts without presuppositions because the latter will influence the answers called forth. In other words, a fresh perception is required because the questions posed by normal science "presuppose a world already perceptually and conceptually subdivided in a certain way."[16] A flash of intuition may precipitate the new vision.

When irregular or puzzling data grow in number and significance (Kuhn calls these data *anomalies*) the conditioned state of mind which is locked in habitual thought patterns is perceived by a few innovative scientists as dysfunctional. This realization stimulates an alternative view that answers the anomalies which then fit easily into the new paradigm that is vibrating at a higher theoretical level. The process resembles Hegelian dialectic in which thought evolves through phases of contradiction and negation, always moving towards a higher unity.

Kuhn states: "What a man sees depends both upon what he looks at and also upon what his previous visual-conceptual experience has taught him to see.'"[17] This perceptual bias is the power of enculturation, the process by which all humans incorporate a cultural worldview. That worldview to a large extent determines perception, valuation, and action in individuals and in the social institutions they construct. If this cultural armor becomes intractable only a change in thinking—a paradigm shift—can dismantle it.

Discontent usually grows at the margins of society where countercultural elements simmer and gain strength, especially if injustice is perceived. Kuhn explains how a conceptual revolution can percolate beyond science to stimulate political and social revolutions, especially if cultural institutions are experienced as malfunctioning. An example would be the power of Enlightenment ideas of liberty, justice and equality to galvanize the American Revolution. Confronted by what was perceived as oppressive British rule key figures of the thirteen colonies were inspired to fight for and form a democratic government. This revolution in thought and action has stimulated subsequent efforts to refine the implementation of democratic values. The phrase *justice for all* from the Pledge of Allegiance, for example, is now embodied in the concepts of *climate justice* and *social justice*. Some environmental groups tie these two concepts together. They point out that the destructive and unjust effects of climate change in the form of droughts, rising seas, and severe weather events affect people's lives.

A paradigm shift is a complex historical process involving a number of factors that accumulate and converge to produce events that shatter tradition. The cultural explosion may appear to be a relatively sudden change in worldview; in fact, however, the roots of discontent are long and often gnarled. As the breakdown of the status quo progresses history enters a transition in which the old paradigm descends in conscious awareness—even as voices of resistance to its demise are interjected—while the new paradigm ascends, triggering a gestalt switch. We as a global society are now experiencing a transition in which climate change deniers who benefit from the status quo are voicing dissent even as the scientific proof of global warming and its visible effects strengthen. The scrambling to find technological solutions for global warming, even if those solutions are recognized as temporary, inadequate, and irrational exemplifies Kuhn's argument that defenders of an entrenched paradigm, such as oil companies with a vested interest in the profits accrued by means of the economic status quo, will ratchet up their resistance. Even as the old paradigm becomes dysfunctional and plagued with anomalies they will "devise numerous articulations and ad hoc modifications of their theory in order to eliminate any apparent conflict."[18]

"After Copernicus," says Kuhn, "astronomers lived in a different world."[19] So did everyone else. With the gain in scientific knowledge, however, came the loss of an animate, ensouled world that bestowed security and meaning. Without assurance of a finite and fixed universe, created and guarded by God and his angels, and enlivened by anima mundi, the human being must have felt displaced and disoriented. A Deist God had set the clock of the universe in motion, stepped aside, and left His most valuable stewards homeless in a vast, inexplicable cosmos. Just as Earth was set adrift as an infinitesimal speck of dust in an infinite universe, so the human being as a mere earthly creature was diminished. Therefore, he must compensate; he must prevail through his own wits. Still assured of a God-given power of reason (which Bacon and Descartes had confirmed) man's need to control an objectified Nature through technology grew stronger.

That need has only increased. Instead of the Great Chain of Being, where the human being is placed just below the angels, he now occupies the top slot of a food chain. But the chain weakens and is set to break if the anthropocentric paradigm introduced by the Scientific and Industrial Revolutions is not rejected.

PRESERVATION VERSUS DEVELOPMENT

The choice as to whether the human species retracts further into the anthropocentric paradigm or realizes the danger of that trajectory and ventures out into a sustainable ecocentric paradigm is presenting itself through a number of volatile issues. One of the issues in which protagonists and antagonists are drawing battle lines is the controversy over land use. As the global population grows and available resources shrink or are monopolized by corporate interests, the question arises: how much of Nature's bounty should we, as 'civilizing' agents, convert to human use? Where is the line to be drawn between encroachment and enhancement, and who draws the line? Are we willing as a global community to clean up the polluted water, air and soil while converting to renewable sources of energy that do not harm the planet? Finally, is a joint partnership between man and Nature that balances actions that preserve, conserve and develop the natural world possible?

When our ancestors came to the shores of the New World they were introduced to a boundless and richly endowed geography, perceived as wilderness—Nature in its pristine state. Decisions had to be made about what to do with this abundance and how to develop it. A debate ensued between those Americans who wanted to preserve great swaths of natural wilderness, through campaigns and legislative acts such as allocating national parkland up to and including the Wilderness Act of 1964, and those who favored conservation mixed with economic growth. In his classic study, *Wilderness and the American Mind,* Roderick Nash notes a common thread of ambivalence towards the wilderness in the unfolding of American cultural history. He detects a dualistic underpinning of thought by which Nature was perceived by some settlers, particularly the Puritans of New England, as wild, primitive and chaotic, in need of human civilizing influence and control; and, by others, as a sanctuary, a refuge from the stresses of an increasingly mechanized, urbanized, and orderly lifestyle. Well into the nineteenth century a utilitarian perspective held sway as the wild frontier necessitated backbreaking work to clear land and establish homesteads. As the frontier moved west the idea of the conquest of the wilderness and its abundant resources in the name of Progress—and profit—gradually heightened the commercial view of Nature as an object for human manipulation.

In a painting by John Gast an over-sized, goddess-like woman hovers above a landscape dotted with covered wagons, people, and trains, all moving westward.

The use of an idealized woman to symbolize progress engineered by industry is perplexing in light of the cultural identification of female energy with untamed wilderness. It is also ironic that women's status did not begin to progress until the suffragettes' effort to win the vote was finally rewarded in 1920 with the passage of the 19th amendment.

Not until the seminal writings of Henry David Thoreau, John Muir and Aldo Leopold did the pendulum swing towards respect for Nature as a source not just of material gain but also of philosophical and spiritual enrichment. As Muir wrote in his journal in 1872: "In God's wilderness lies the hope of the world—the great fresh, unblighted, unredeemed wilderness. The galling harness of civilization drops off, and the wounds heal ere we are aware. . . . One day's exposure to mountains is better than cartloads of books."[20]

Figure 9.1. "American Progress" by John Gast, 1872.
Courtesy of Library of Congress.

Theodore Roosevelt, twenty-sixth president of the United States (1858–1919), embodied his countrymen's unsettled attitude about wilderness. As the population and its needs grew, Roosevelt tried to straddle the national ambition to clear forests and develop American's abundant resources with a personal love for untouched wilderness. He approved of the idea prevalent among preservationists like John Muir and artists like George Catlin that America's greatest asset was her magnificent landscape. For these naturalists the treasures of the land rivaled in grandeur the man-made beauty of the Old World's architecture. Thus Roosevelt championed the national park movement that his friend John Muir was promoting.

But Roosevelt also had the aggressive instincts of a hunter and warrior. He perceived wilderness as a virile adversary whose conquest built men's—and a nation's—character; he therefore favored the *wise use* of resources and land development advocated by Muir's colleague and eventual adversary, Gifford Pinchot, who was head of the Forest Service. It is tempting to see in Roosevelt's complex character contradictory elements of the American mind that are still engaged in the current version of the debate over land use.

When the state of California ceded its stewardship of Yosemite to the federal government in 1906, under the urging of Muir, and the national park system was launched, it became customary, under the 1906 Antiquities Act, for presidents to set aside by law certain richly endowed geographical areas as exempt from development. At a conference on the conservation of natural resources held at the White House on May 13, 1908, Roosevelt spoke with prescient insight about the importance of using natural resources in moderation. He states:

> We have become great because of the lavish use of our resources and we have just reason to be proud of our growth. But the time has come to inquire seriously what will happen when our forests are gone, when the coal, the iron, the oil, and the gas are exhausted, when the soils shall have been still further impoverished and washed into the streams polluting the rivers, denuding the fields, and obstructing navigation. These questions do not relate only to the next century or to the next generation. It is time for us now as a nation to exercise the same reasonable foresight in dealing with our great natural resources that would be shown by any prudent man in conserving and wisely using the property which contains the assurance of well-being for himself and his children.[21]

At the cusp of the twentieth century it was clear to many Americans that the vast and diverse geography of America offered inexhaustible resources such as coal, trees and fresh water. Roosevelt could not have foreseen the capitalist overreach that would exploit and threaten to exhaust those resources while polluting the environment; nevertheless, his prophecy about what will happen without the exercise of "reasonable foresight" has come to pass.

The debate eventually tilted from preservation and conservation to unchecked consumption of the natural world through a virtually unregulated capitalism generated by an unregulated use of fossil fuels. This accelerating imbalance is destabilizing the planet.

Two recent examples of this acceleration are the executive orders signed by the current president on April 26 and April 28, 2017. The former approves a review of the allocation of national monuments and parks with the intent of mining more than 100,000 acres of protected land for fossil fuels. The latter rescinds President Obama's protection of federal waters and extends offshore drilling in the Arctic and Atlantic Oceans as well as certain marine sanctuaries. The orders (which can be reversed by a future president) challenge the long legacy of presidential protection of designated lands and are an abrogation of the rights of the American people to enjoy public lands and waters maintained by the National Wilderness Preservation System. This agency protects nearly 110 million acres in forty-four states and Puerto Rico. More than half the total acreage is situated in Alaska and includes the Arctic National Wildlife Refuge.

THREE MENTORS FOR THE ECOZOIC ERA

The efforts of three prominent eco-pioneers in American history who have sought to guide a developing nation towards policies that protect treasures of the natural landscape, even as resources are developed for human use, can serve as mentors for today's activists all over the world who are fighting to defend environmental protection by reversing a deep pattern of exploitation. The ideas of Henry David Thoreau, John Muir and Aldo Leopold influenced the historical debate over land use as each man attempted, in his own unique way, to bring balance to the issue. The contributions of these eco-pioneers exemplify Arnold Toynbee's premise regarding the growth of civilizations. In *A Study of History* Toynbee argues that creative, visionary people serve as "a leaven in the lump of ordinary humanity."[22] These individuals, he says, are able to successfully respond to a challenge with creative solutions rather than adhere to the more narrowly defined status quo. Through their vision and persistence they lift their societies to more refined cultural achievements. These cultural pioneers are also the movers and shakers of Kuhn's paradigm shifts. It could be argued that this quality of person represents the moral leadership we need today in order to navigate our way out of the ecological crises caused by human-induced climate change.

Thoreau teaches us that an authentic relationship to the natural world is formed through the practice of awareness and a frugal lifestyle. He provides a practical philosophy to live by. Muir inspires us to fight for the rights of all species and for the being which is Nature herself, motivated by love. He embodies a spiritual vision of man's connection to the natural world. Leopold appeals to the scientist-artist in all of us, that combination of character traits that creates an ecological science capable of attaining a balance between preserving, conserving and developing the natural world.

All three eco-pioneers were influenced by the spiritual potency of America's native-born spirituality—Transcendentalism. The aim of Transcendentalism was to transcend the world, both natural and man-made. But paradoxically the most direct heavenly route for transcendentalists was immersion in the natural world. This nature mysticism required an attentive surrender to the peace, solitude and beauty of Nature. Voiced by Emerson, Thoreau and other members of the Concord group, the transcendental vision passed into Muir's psyche and even affected Leopold who was the first ecologist to perceive and write about the planet as a living organism—a premise advocated today by deep ecologists such as John Seed and biologists such as James Lovelock.

Henry David Thoreau (1817–1862)

In 1845 Thoreau left Concord to lead a hermit's life in the woods around Walden Pond. He stayed there for two years, two months, and two days. His choice was an early experiment in adopting a lifestyle of self-sufficiency and minimal possessions. Thoreau occupied a simple, self-built cabin, sparsely furnished. He cultivated a small vegetable garden to satisfy a spartan diet. Thoreau's intention was to learn from Nature her secret wisdom. Nature was the teacher and he the willing pupil. To be receptive to her wisdom Thoreau chose not the language of books but natural sounds, sights and smells to which he gave full attention. The townspeople thought he was daft and lazy, an unproductive member of a burgeoning nation of commerce and industry. Thoreau writes in *Walden* (1854):

> I did not read books the first summer; I hoed beans. Nay, I often did better than this. There were times when I could not afford to sacrifice the bloom of the present moment to any work, whether of the head or hands. . . . I sat in my sunny doorway from sunrise til noon, rapt in a revery, amidst the pines and hickories and sumachs, in undisturbed solitude and stillness, while the birds sing around or flitted noiseless through the house, until by the sun falling in at my west window, or the noise of some traveller's wagon on the distant highway, I was reminded of the lapse of time. I grew in those seasons like corn in the night.[23]

Two important lessons that Thoreau learned from Nature were the art of sensory awareness and a simple lifestyle. The first lesson showed him how to penetrate and participate in the oneness of life through being present to the moment. Like Native Americans, his spiritual kin, Thoreau perceived Earth not as "'a dead, inert mass; it is a body, has a spirit, is organic.'"[24] He felt himself part of a living whole of "'vast alliances and universal relatedness.'"[25] For example, Thoreau writes of a delightful encounter with a swarm of toads who, in early spring, were copulating in the muddy pools that dotted a meadow through which he was walking barefoot. As they hopped excitedly around his legs he felt a euphoric sense of vital cosmic energy and writes: "'I was thrilled to my spine and vibrated to it.'"[26]

In *Walden* Thoreau speaks of his motivation in leaving the provincial, predictable town life. He wants "to live deliberately, to front only the essential facts of life and not, when I came to die, discover that I had not lived. I did not want to live what was not life."[27] Thoreau is equating life with living deliberately. What does Thoreau mean by this? He explains himself by recommending that we "spend one day as deliberately as Nature."[28] *Deliberate* means *conscious*. Nature is always conscious, always sensorily awake and present. By contrast man is beset with mental distractions; he succumbs to mental slumber. "Our life is frittered away by detail," says Thoreau, and we are constantly "thrown off the track by every nutshell and mosquito's wing that falls on the rails."[29] Thoreau uses the industrial metaphor of the train, and the intercontinental railroad then occupying society's attention, to highlight man's inventive capacity; yet this gift goes awry when man forgets to be present to his life and, instead, resembles the *sleepers* or cross boards that make up the train track. It takes real effort to awaken out of the habit of mechanical living. But Nature, says Thoreau, teaches us to stay awake. He writes: "To be awake is to be alive. I have never yet met a man who was quite awake. How could I have looked him in the face? We must learn to reawaken and keep ourselves awake by a conscious endeavor."[30]

The second lesson that Thoreau gained from his guru Nature was the reminder that accumulation of and attachment to possessions—including property—diminishes a man's stature. Nature is frugal and disciplined. She doesn't waste time or energy on non-essentials. Man can learn these virtues by imitating Nature: "Simplicity, simplicity, simplicity! I say, let your affairs be as two or three and keep your accounts on your thumbnail."[31] One could argue that the modern concept of *sustainability* originated with Thoreau.

Thoreau argued that as immigrants from a tame, culturally unimaginative and torpid Europe, Americans were apt to suffer the same cultural fate if they lose contact with wild Nature—the source of moral vigor and inspiration. They would also become susceptible to the lesser instinct of material acquisitiveness, reducing the natural world from source of life to resource for man.

Indeed, Thoreau feared that "'for one that comes with a pencil to sketch or sing, a thousand come with an axe or rifle.'"[32] But for all his idealism Thoreau was also a realist. He may have berated his countrymen for being workaholics but he himself had to work periodically at his family's pencil factory to make ends meet. He believed, however, that human beings enhance their civilized lives by periodic sojourns in the wilderness of Nature where they are invited to enter their own interior wilderness through contemplation. Thoreau enjoins his countrymen to conquer this inner frontier and be "'the Lewis and Clark of your own streams and oceans; explore your own higher latitudes.'"[33] We Americans can acknowledge this advice every time we go hiking, camping, and visiting our national parks and monuments.

John Muir (1838–1914)

John Muir was the son of sturdy Scottish stock, his father a religious zealot who immigrated to the Wisconsin frontier with his two sons and daughter in 1849. John was eleven when they arrived. By day he helped with the tough work of clearing land and establishing a farm; by night he learned the Bible by heart. Muir endured frequent whippings by his severe Calvinist father who was following the child-rearing custom of the old country. Muir's father viewed the natural world in utilitarian terms—as an object which, through human use, became praiseworthy in God's view. Muir opposed this philosophy early on, believing that Nature had a value in and of itself. Nature praised the Creator through its very existence. For Muir the Book of Nature had as much to teach as Biblical scriptures. At the age of 22 Muir entered the intellectual atmosphere of the University of Wisconsin where his prodigious mental capacities were awakened. He especially took to the study of botany and geology, but these sciences were fleshed out and deepened by a spiritual affinity with the transcendentalist ideas of Thoreau and Emerson.

After two and a half years Muir exchanged the academic life for the life of a vagabond. He said he wanted to enroll in another type of university—the University of Wilderness. Before venturing into the wild Muir took a temporary job at Osgood, Smith and Co., the nation's largest manufacturer of carriage parts, located in Indianapolis. This choice was prompted by Muir's early success with inventions. As a young boy he made himself a violin and later, on the farm, whittled scraps of wood to make a self-setting rotary saw. Muir could have earned a partnership at the company for his inventive and organizational skills, but a freak on-the-job accident nearly blinded him. He decided then that the outdoors was his calling and he set out on a thousand mile walk to South America by way of Florida. On the way he contracted a malarial sickness, changed his itinerary and, in 1868, reached California by steerage ship. When asked upon arrival in San Francisco where he wanted to go he replied: "'any place that is wild.'"[34]

It was April and a profusion of golden flowers greeted Muir's entrance into Yosemite Valley. "And from the eastern boundary of this vast golden flowerbed" writes Muir, "rose the mighty Sierra, miles in height, and so gloriously colored and so radiant, it seemed not clothed with light, but wholly composed of it, like the wall of some celestial city."[35] Muir the mystic had come home. Now his life's mission of rapturous communion with the natural world could truly begin. He would spend many solitary hours exploring Yosemite's geography, describing in his journal through word and drawing every detail of his newfound acquaintance with the area's flora and fauna. He writes of such walks in the wilderness as serving both scientific and contemplative aims. Luckily he was able to earn his daily bread right there in the valley, working as a carpenter for Jeremiah Hutchins and his tourist hotel—an operation which would eventually be prohibited by new laws governing national parkland.

Muir possessed a broad intelligence. On the one hand his acute observational skills and scientific knowledge provided a backdrop for precise empirical study. On the other, Muir's creative, intuitive gifts and spiritual fervor illuminated his writing. His articles in various magazines ignited in the American psyche a love for the natural world. Through the lyricism of his prose he redefined wilderness as God's paradise, a refuge and reflection of divinity. His relationship to wildlife was egalitarian, recalling Native American animism. Contemplating an encounter with a bear he writes: "Bears are made of the same dust as we, and breathe the same winds and drink the same waters. A bear's days are warmed by the same sun, his dwellings are overdomed by the same blue sky, and his life turns and ebbs with heart-pulsings like ours, and was poured from the same First Fountain."[36]

Muir was fearless in his desire to lose his small identity by merging into all of God's wonders. He stood atop Yosemite Falls, leaning into the cascading water to experience its crashing power. He climbed a tree during a fierce storm and swayed with the branches to experience the power of the Almighty. Muir came to be reputed as America's wild man, "a voice calling in the wilderness" amidst cathedrals of rock and tree, "prepare ye the way of the Lord."[37] Tourists would come to Yosemite to see the wonders that Muir wrote about and, if they were lucky, to get a glimpse of the seer of the Sierra himself.

In 1890 Muir pressured the state of California to increase the 10 square miles of the Yosemite preserve to two million acres. In 1892 the Sierra Club, America's first environmental organization, was born with John Muir as its first president.

Aldo Leopold (1887–1945)

The last of the triumvirate of eco-pioneers, Aldo Leopold, brought scientific legitimacy to the efforts of Thoreau and Muir. Leopold made the study of the natural world a science—the science of ecology. Leopold's concepts of a *land ethic* and an *ecological conscience* developed out of an early attraction to the solitary wildernesses of Wisconsin where alone with his dog at daybreak he reveled in walking the one hundred twenty acres of his "worldly domain" and beyond, asserting: "It is not only boundaries that disappear, but also the thought of being bounded . . . and solitude, supposed no longer to exist in my county, extends on every hand."[38] Like Muir, he loved to observe wildlife—his 'tenants' as he would refer to them—and he journaled on the habits of geese and carp, woodcocks and wrens, oaks and birches. Also like Muir, Leopold personalized his encounters, lending to wild creatures human attributes. During a spring flood he observes:

> The enthusiasm of geese for high water is a subtle thing, and might be overlooked by those unfamiliar with goose-gossip . . . Unlike the geese and the carp, the terrestrial birds and mammals accept high water with philosophical detachment. . . . Meadow-mice paddle ridgeward with the calm assurance of miniature muskrats. . . . Everywhere are rabbits, calmly accepting quarters on our hill which serves, in Noah's absence, for an ark.[39]

A graduate of the Yale School of Forestry in 1908, Leopold took a position in the Forest Service of Arizona and New Mexico which at that time were still territories. He became aware of the quickly diminishing number of big game, fish and waterfowl. In response Leopold organized local hunters and fishermen—of which he was one—into associations to protect game animals. In a newspaper article distributed by one of these groups Leopold revealed ideas which would later express his philosophy: the rights of all wild creatures to life and the obligation of humans to respect those rights by not overstepping their power over other animate beings.

As his view of the natural world clarified in his mind—and his heart—Leopold abandoned his gun and fishing pole. Perhaps this change of heart can be traced to an incident that occurred during Leopold's trek to the White Mountain in Arizona. This mountain was the habitat of deer, coyotes—and wolves. Guns in tow he and his friends made their way to a high rimrock where, while eating lunch, they watched the flow of a turbulent river below. Out of the river suddenly emerged a female wolf shaking the water from her fur, followed by her grown pups who began to play on the bank. Leopold recalls the excitement felt by himself and his friends as they aimed their rifles downhill and let off shot after shot. In this moment of shame he experiences an epiphany that transforms his life into a crusade to protect the rights of all species as members of an interconnected web—Earth's ecosystem. He writes:

> We reached the old wolf in time to watch a fierce green fire dying in her eyes. I realized then and have known ever since, that there was something new to me in those eyes—something known only to her and to the mountain. I was young then, and full of trigger-itch; I thought that because fewer wolves meant more deer, that no wolves would mean hunters' paradise. But after seeing the green fire die, I sensed that neither the wolf nor the mountain agreed with such a view. Since then I have lived to see state after state extirpate its wolves.[40] [This slaughter continues.]

Whereas American progress had been measured as a conquest of wilderness converted to economic use, Leopold made a plea for a new land policy that would reverse this idea by redefining a progressive American culture as one that valued and preserved the remaining wilderness. Leopold argued on two fronts: first, the environment of wilderness produced the vigorous cultural institutions that Americans enjoy; and second, preserved wilderness is a pristine model of a healthy ecosystem that can be studied and emulated in such domains as agriculture.[41] Wilderness has an underlying order; it is not chaotic. That order is now known as *ecosystem*. Bound by the ecological laws of interconnectedness and reciprocity each species in an ecosystem plays a role that benefits the whole while securing its own survival. Beyond these reasons, said Leopold, is the ethical argument. We have a moral duty, said Leopold, to protect the rights of all living organisms of the living Earth. With prophetic voice Leopold asserts in *A Sand County Almanac*: "We abuse land because we regard it as a commodity belonging to us. When we see land as a community to which we belong, we may begin to use it with love and respect."[42]

Ecologically sound policy and action depend upon a change in thinking, a shift in worldview. After all, says Leopold, though technology gives human beings the "'whip-hand over nature'" we must remember that we are "'only fellow-voyageurs with other creatures in the odyssey of evolution.'"[43] If we sicken the soil and water, the birds and animals, we sicken ourselves.

WILDERNESS AT RISK

In Paria Canyon Vermillion Cliffs Wilderness in Arizona the endangered California condor—the largest bird in North America with a wingspan of 11 feet—soars over the red-striped rock formations. This mighty bird along with other wild creatures such as jaguars, grizzlies, and black bear find refuge in wilderness areas. So long as the Endangered Species Act and the Wilderness

Act remain as legislative givens such animals and birds, and their habitats, are protected. However, the old ambivalence about land use continues to pose friction between developers and environmentalists.

Wilderness protection began as an antidote to America's unchecked hunger for development. Champions of the wilderness continue to speak out. Writing in a 2014 commemorative edition of the magazine *Sierra* honoring the fiftieth anniversary of the Wilderness Act, Kenneth Brower—son of David Brower whose persistent efforts, along with Howard Zahniser, paved the way for passage of the bill—urges Americans to reclaim the wilderness idea as an experiential process that elevates human lives. He refers to a letter sent to his father by novelist Wallace Stegner in 1960 which says: "'We simply need that wild country available to us even if we never do more than drive to its edge and look in. For it can be a means of reassuring ourselves of our sanity as creatures, a part of the geography of hope.'"[44]

This vision of a place untouched by humans yet a source of nourishment by simple proximity is now under siege in perhaps the most famous of America's national parks—the Grand Canyon. Over the nearly one hundred years of the canyon's existence as a national park there have been attempts to invade and tame this landmark site. In 2007 a precedent was set when a skywalk

Figure 9.2. California condor by Dominique Medici.
Used with the permission of Dominique Medici.

was constructed on the western rim by developers in collaboration with the Hualapai tribe. Now these same developers have proposed a one billion dollar plan featuring a gondola that would cross the Grand Canyon at the eastern rim, carrying visitors down 1.4 miles to the canyon floor where a variety of attractions like an elevated river walk, restaurant and Indian cultural center would be constructed on a portion of Navajo land located at the Confluence—a place where the green water of the Colorado River meets and merges with the turquoise water of the Little Colorado River. This area has long been considered sacred ground by Hopi, Zuni and Navajo tribes. Within the Navajo nation a controversy brews as to whether to allow a commercial project to desecrate this hallowed site. At the gondola hub a complex of stores, restaurants, trailer park and elite hotels called the Grand Canyon Escalade development would accommodate tourists and provide jobs for local people including Native Americans. Meanwhile, at the South Rim, in the small town of Tusayan, the town council (packed by supporters of developers) have approved construction of thousands of new homes plus three million square feet of commercial space. Both developments threaten the already endangered Colorado River by disturbing the groundwater supply. As David Uberuaga, the park superintendent, states: "We have the protections of the National Park Service Act, the act that created the Grand Canyon, the Clean Water Act. All that body of law, and I still spend most of my time protecting the place, day in and day out. Everybody wants to make a buck off the canyon."[45]

An environmental group is fighting back by proposing a 1.7 million-acre enlargement of protected land called the Grand Canyon Watershed National Monument—an umbrella ecosystem that would include adjoining Kaibab Plateau and Kanab Creek. The group's intent is to preserve groundwater, habitat and natural beauty while preventing mining in uranium rich areas.

Native Americans are not the only people who perceive the Grand Canyon as sacred space. At the sight of such majesty, tourists use words like *cathedral, tabernacle,* and *shrine* to describe what they see. Standing on the rim, looking out and down, one's eyes trace more than a mile of red and yellow layers of rock that display a lineage of seventeen million centuries into the past. That is more than a third of the life of this planet. One feels awe and a humbling sense of one's own miniscule existence. Words from the Book of Job come to mind, as if they reverberated in the chasm: "Where wast thou when I laid the foundation of the earth?" asks God of his servant Job. "Declare, if thou hast understanding."[46]

In 1903 President Theodore Roosevelt stood on the South Rim and delivered a speech in which he enunciated the idea of the Grand Canyon as a public treasure, to be forever held in trust for and by the American people. He recommended that Americans ". . . keep this great wonder of nature as it now is. I hope you will not have a building of any kind, not a summer cottage, a hotel, or anything else, to mar the wonderful grandeur, the sublimity, the great loneliness and beauty of the canyon. Leave it as it is. You cannot improve on it. The ages have been at work on it, and man can only mar it."[47]

Wilderness is wild, untamed, open, free—free to roam, expand itself, reproduce and diversify itself. Man has always been either attracted to or afraid of the wild—both the outer and the inner wildness; and man, as part of Nature, possesses a wild streak. In the twenty-first century man's wildness is to be feared because he expands himself in ways he should not. Nature has a sense of measure and knows the limits of her laws. By instinct she acts to regulate and balance. If a forest is too thick it thins itself. If a species is overpopulated it controls its birthrate. If humans remain wild without self-regulation, and without humility, they threaten themselves and the planet. Nature, says Lovelock, detests the unnatural. How are we to become natural again? Voices from the past and present say: be reconciled in mind and heart to the natural world; reawaken, as children from sleep, and remember the "ancient mother-love."[48] Herein lies the taming of the beast.

We have come to a fork in the road of human cultural evolution. Humanity has arrived at a transitional point in which a new life-affirming paradigm is challenging the existing paradigm that shows severe signs of dysfunction. Applying Kuhn's theory of revolutionary change, this moment in time has the earmarks of a possible paradigm shift. A worldview that renews the feeling of connectedness to all life generates this shift. The adoption of such a worldview depends, however, upon an awakening to the ancient bond between man and Nature. This awakening is born of awareness, of mindfulness.

The prominent Hindu sage, Sri Aurobindo, taught that the next step in human development is the rediscovery of self-awareness.[49] He calls this awareness *Supermind*. As the human being becomes more aware, more conscious, Nature also advances towards a realization of her hidden divinity; the two trajectories are in tandem. The dualistic paradigm that arrested this natural movement by separating spirit from matter and then elevating matter as the only reality is, says Aurobindo, based on a falsehood. Spirit evolves through and within matter into a full measure of bliss when being present and being one with all life forms is the aim and delight of living. The cultivation of awareness is the key to making the right choice that ushers in the Ecozoic Era.

Jung's principle of synchronicity can be instructive as the clash between two mindsets—anthropocentric and ecocentric—escalates. Synchronicity proposes that events are not solitary occurrences ruled by linear cause and effect but arise non-linearly out of a network of relationships. Thus, instances of synchronicity can serve as teachers for they mirror inner archetypal patterns in the collective unconscious that are manifesting in the outer world. According to physicist F. David Peat these instances are of special import during periods of individual or cultural transformation. The first quarter of the twenty-first century may be one such period of transformation, but its compass stretches beyond the individual and even the collective; its impact is planetary. Two contrary and intensifying inner energy patterns confront each other. One pattern displays negative, destructive qualities like greed and selfishness that produce outer damage to the Earth displayed in synchronous events like the melting of glaciers, weather extremes, topsoil depletion, air and water pollution, and species extinctions. These phenomena interconnect, reflecting the deeper issue of global warming and climate change due to fossil fuel extraction and use. The other inner energy pattern displays constructive qualities of compassion and remembrance of wholeness which produce harmonious developments like conservation of resources, preservation of species, organic sustainable farming, alternative energies, green building and intentional communities based in self-sufficiency and service to the wider community. One such intentional community is the 400-acre organic Hawthorne Valley Farm in Ghent, New York. As a model of the power of living by a philosophy of interconnectedness, the farm attracts farmers, artisans, teachers, and young people who gather to "'cultivate a soil of fertility for new thinking.'"[50]

Environmental activists continue to feed the constructive cultural energy pattern while corporate control of industry, government and the military define the destructive pattern. In spiritual terms a war between the gods and the demons is being waged; in the secular language of psychology, a battle is underway in the human psyche between Eros and Thanatos. The journey home to the Primal Matrix requires an embrace of Eros.

Chapter Ten

Coming Home

A Change of Mind and Heart

We know what we are, but know not what we may be

—Ophelia, *Hamlet* IV:1

A collective shift to an ecocentric paradigm requires a fundamental revolution of thought that dislodges habitual cultural patterns based in egoism and the narrow use of mental faculties known as technological mind. Coming home to Earth as maternal provider, and to our true selves as caretakers of the Garden, will require a change of mind and heart that dismantles an unsustainable global cultural system whose lifeblood is the fossil fuel industry and agribusiness. This system is subjecting all species, including *Homo sapiens*, to perpetual degradation. For example, in a 2015 study by the Institute for the Developing Mind at Children's Hospital in Los Angeles researchers tested the blood and urine of 40 mothers in the third trimester of pregnancy as well as the urine of their children. They found high levels of PAH (polycyclic aromatic hydrocarbon) compounds, a form of air pollution caused by the burning of fossil fuels. Researchers concluded that a mother's prenatal exposure to PAHs is linked to changes in the fetus' brain structure that can result in intellectual and behavioral difficulties, such as ADHD, in childhood.[1]

The practices of agribusiness are also endangering public health. For example, the current administration has refused to accept the EPA's recommendation that the agricultural use of chlorpyrifos—a virulent pesticide—be banned. This pesticide—a product of the Dow Chemical Company, generous donor to President Trump's inaugural festivities—belongs to a class of chemicals which Nazi Germany used to make nerve gas. Chlorpyrifos has been found to cause damage to the human brain. It is linked to reduced IQ, attention disorders, and stunted motor development in children.[2]

A Darwinian struggle to define *the survival of the fittest* is upon us. The word *fit* refers to adaptations which are favorable to survival. The current ecological crisis is symptomatic of a maladaptive cultural system that has spread worldwide. The 'world war' now being waged against the planet cannot be won; it is a lose-lose situation. The effort to regain health as a global society will require a collective remembrance of our ancestral knowledge of interconnectedness and the commitment to manifest that principle through sustainable actions.

In advance of the 2015 Paris conference on global warming Pope Francis released a papal encyclical entitled *Laudato Si'* (*Praise Be To You*). Demonstrating a command of the scientific data the Pope characterizes climate change as a "global problem with grave implications: environmental, social, economic, political."[3] He continues: "The urgent challenge to protect our common home includes a concern to bring the whole human family together to seek sustainable and integral development."[4] By *integral* the Pope is referring to the principle of integral ecology which advocates a balance between economic development, to satisfy basic human needs, and environmental protection. When, for example, Lake Tanganyika in Africa warms up to the extent that fish, a main staple of food for the poor, die, then the interlocked system of poverty and global warming is exposed.

Only a deep structural change in thinking can create a new ethos of sustainability that can be implemented in our cultural institutions. This change begins as a personal awakening and then spreads into communities through education, breaking up the old but persistent rationalist framework of modernity that delivered the discoveries, as well as the handicaps, of the Scientific and Industrial Revolutions. This new understanding of reality will have new premises; as Kuhn states: "The transition from a paradigm in crisis to a new one . . . is far from a cumulative process, one achieved by an articulation or extension of the old paradigm. Rather it is a reconstruction of the field from new fundamentals, a reconstruction that changes some of the field's most elementary theoretical generalizations. . . ."[5]

The ascendancy of an ecocentric worldview would change cultural values by placing *biophilia* at the forefront of such 'new fundamentals.' In this final chapter the new fundamentals that guide our way forward will be explored: specifically, biophilia as a cultural mindset, the integration of male and female energies in society (if we see from wholeness we will see wholeness), and sustainability as principle and practice. It will be argued that systemic change can be effected if and when individuals gain awareness of the gravity of planetary signs of imbalance and join together in solidarity to confront the defenders of the status quo by speaking truth to power. When we fuse ourselves to the Earth in mind and heart, realizing *this is my body,* we will be home.

LESSONS IN BIOPHILIA

In his book *Voluntary Simplicity* Duane Elgin presents a life cycle of four stages of civilizational change in industrial societies. The stages align with Arnold Toynbee's theory of historical growth, effulgence, and decay. Using the analogy of the four seasons these stages are High Growth (spring), Full Blossoming (summer), Initial Decline (fall), and Breakdown (winter). Elgin adopts Toynbee's argument that a civilization that has shown remarkable cultural and technological achievements will start to disintegrate when the failure to respond to severe challenges in an enlightened way leads to complacency, denial and inaction. He applies this scenario to the shift in the 1990s by industrial nations, including the United States, to a condition of systems breakdown—Stage IV (winter). Elgin cites some of the intertwined ecological problems that are metastasizing like a cancer around the globe including a destabilized climate, widespread deforestation, and toxic pollution. While no one person is to blame, says Elgin, we all participate in prolonging a worldview which now threatens all existence.

Elgin sets out three possible outcomes of civilizational breakdown: *collapse*—ecological challenges are ignored and solutions delayed precipitating the sickening and death of the whole biotic community; *stagnation*—people deny or try to stave off ecological disaster by propping up the status quo which may produce authoritarian regimes to keep order; people rely on bioengineering for new food sources and genetic engineering to deal with disease outbreaks[6]; and *revitalization*—grass-roots organizations of a decentralized society recognize the gravity of environmental damage and, through sophisticated tools of mass communication, a courageous spirit and a willingness to "break the cultural hypnosis of consumerism," stimulate the global citizenry to share and enact visions of a sustainable future.[7]

In order for revitalization to be the chosen outcome in this 'winter' stage there needs to be a quickened 'winter of discontent' that establishes what Elgin calls a "new common sense."[8] Elgin cites the cultivation of awareness as the critical element that propels a conscious decision to change course towards sustainability. He writes:

> Citizens of the earth must see themselves as part of a tightly interdependent system rather than as isolated individuals and nations. With a witnessing consciousness or observer's perspective, citizens cultivate the detachment [from ego] that

enables us to stand back, look at the big picture, and make the hard choices and trade-offs that our circumstances demand.[9]

This new vision of ourselves as citizens of the earth, with the responsibilities implied in that role, is the reawakening of biophilia in the human psyche. In *Earth in Mind,* David Orr describes the evolutionary selection of biophilia as an integral component of the human mind. He writes:

> . . . in the long gestation of humankind we acquired an affinity for life, earth, forests, water, soils, and place—what E. O. Wilson calls biophilia. We ought not to look first to our technological cleverness or abstractions about progress of one kind or another, but rather to the extent and depth of our affections, which set boundaries on what we do and direct our intelligence to better or worse possibilities. The possibility of affection for our children, place, posterity, and life is in all of us. It is part of our evolutionary heritage.[10]

Indeed, ecologist Carl Safina, who studies the behavior of animals in the wild, insists that all mammals share a spectrum of emotions including fear, pain, anxiety, aggression, contentment, and even empathy due to "shared brain structures and shared chemistries, originated in shared ancestry. They are the shared feelings of a shared world." [11] Altruism appears to be an adaptive behavior that not only serves a utilitarian purpose by eliciting a return act of kindness but it also makes us feel good. Empathy is the healthy, natural response even down to the chemistry in the brain which releases oxytocin when the feeling of relationship to others is activated. Elephants, for example, will readily help their companions—as when a researcher saw an elephant put food into the mouth of another elephant whose trunk was injured. Even rats show empathy for their fellows in distress. When, in an experiment, rats were given a choice to free fellow rats imprisoned in a cage or be given chocolate they first freed the prisoners and then shared the treat!

This instinctual acknowledgement of a shared existence surfaces any time we look into the eyes of a pet cat or dog and see the same consciousness that lights our own eyes. Indeed, the empathetic response is shown to be trans-species. Safina relates the example of a bonobo in an English Zoo who caught a starling. The keeper pleaded with the bonobo to release the bird. In response the bonobo climbed a tree, wrapped her legs around the trunk to free her hands and, spreading the bird's wings with care, sent the bird into flight.

Have we human beings closed ourselves off from our most basic feelings for other sentient beings—and even from each other? In southern Africa children are traditionally taught to practice a philosophy called *ubuntu* which translates as *I am because we are.* An anthropologist decided to test this enculturated behavior. He put a basket of fruit some distance away, instructed a group of children to run to the basket; whoever got there first would win the fruit. The children joined hands and ran together. When they arrived at the basket they sat down together and shared the fruit.

New research in cognitive neuroscience is exploring the capacity of mind to induce higher states of consciousness that trigger an experience of unity not only with other human beings but also with other sentient beings. Using new measuring techniques like fMRI brain imaging researchers are finding a holistic interplay between cognitive (psychological), affective (emotional) and neurological (biological) parts of the human mind-body. Although there is a tendency in some neuroscientific research to reduce all human thought and emotion to neural circuitry some studies are yielding intriguing results which suggest that compassion for a suffering Earth is a natural response that registers in the brain. Several empathy studies merit brief comment.

Empathy is defined as the ability to take on the perspective of the 'other' and thus feel what he or she feels. In a paper published in the *Journal of Neuroscience*, September 2013, scientists at the Max Planck Institute for Human and Cognitive Brain Sciences reported that their research shows that in human relationships empathy is a natural response to another person's distress. The empathetic response is chemically triggered in parts of the cerebral cortex including the anterior insula and the right supramarginal gyrus. An egocentric response is also activated at these cortical sites and serves as a neurological mechanism to distinguish one's own ego from other egos. Both responses—egocentric and empathetic—are innate. Scientists discovered that when the empathetic area of the brain is not working properly narcissistic impulses take over with a psychopathological result. However, when the supramarginal gyrus is in proper working order it recognizes when the natural empathy accorded the 'other' is not operating and will autocorrect itself to promote the neural circuitry of empathy.[12]

This study coincides with another study published in the *Journal of Environmental Psychology*, September 2013, by Kim-Pong Tam, a researcher at the Hong Kong University of Science and Technology.[13] In order to extend empathy studies beyond human relationships and measure a person's response to distress occurring in the natural world Tam's study added a construct he calls *dispositional empathy with nature* (DEN). Using questions from Davis's (1983) Interpersonal Reactivity Index Tam found that people who feel a connection with Nature, especially viewed as a sentient force, possess a dispositional empathy which steers them into efforts to conserve the environment. Females were more likely to show this empathy. Tam supports empathy training in schools so that children grow up with a strong feeling for environmental conservation.

Finally, a study conducted in March 2008 at the Center for Healthy Minds at the University of Wisconsin-Madison by R. J. Davidson and Antoine Lutz shows that empathy is not only natural but can be taught—a proposal which gels with Tam's outlook.[14] Sixteen Tibetan Buddhist monks with experience in loving kindness meditation and sixteen controls with no meditation training were hooked up to machines that recorded brain scans. The control group were taught the meditation process two weeks before the experiment. As the meditating subjects focused loving kindness on loved ones and then were instructed to extend that feeling towards all beings their meditation was interrupted periodically by sounds, some neutral, some designed to evoke empathy—such as a baby crying. The scans in both groups showed the activation of regions in the frontal cortex that have to do with empathy—particularly the insula and temporal parietal juncture. Although the empathetic responses were quicker and more profound in the monks' brain scans Davidson and Lutz concur that the experiment showed that empathy can be elicited and taught and that the brain's plasticity offers the possibility of training in order to extend empathetic responses from personal to social to planetary dimensions.

Since the advent of science rationality has been the touchstone of cultural progress. Yet poisoning one's habitat is an irrational act. Such irrationality suggests that instinct has been numbed, that the animal in us is hibernating and that the function of reason itself has been misconstrued. Feminist philosopher Sara Ruddick argues that the association of reason with the male gender and scientific achievement disregards *maternal thinking* which, in combining attention (a cognitive faculty) and love, is a higher form of reason. This "attentive love" or *Love's Reason*, as Ruddick calls this blend of mind and heart, is essential to caring for a child and, by extension, caring for the Earth.[15] In order to evolve beyond the anthropocentric paradigm, therefore, we must cultivate a more holistic use of human cognitive faculties that goes beyond rationality to include imagination, intuition, and emotional intelligence which is the ability to recognize and share emotions (closely aligned with empathy). The synthesis of head and heart, of intellect and emotion, elevates both reason and empathy as the guiding principles of intelligent action. As David Orr contends, "Science without passion and love can give us no reason to appreciate the sunset, nor can it give us any purely objective reason to value life. These must come from deeper sources."[16]

When we re-cognize ourselves as members of the Earth community then we realize that "nothing is itself without everything else."[17] This simple truth—as formulated by Brian Swimme and Thomas Berry in *The Universe Story*—is illustrated in a graphic way:

An unborn grizzly bear sleeps in her mother's womb. Even there in the dark with her eyes closed, this bear is already related to the outside world. She will not have to develop a taste for blackberries or for Chinook salmon. When her tongue first mashes the juice of the blackberry its delight will be immediate. . . . In the very shape of her claws is the musculature, anatomy and leap of the Chinook. The face of the bear, the size of her arm, the structure of her eyes, the thickness of her fur—these are dimensions of her temperate forest community. The bear herself is meaningless outside this enveloping web of relations.[18]

The authors conclude that, from an ecocentric perspective, it is obvious that "the well-being of the Earth is primary. Human well-being is derivative."[19]

TOWARDS WHOLENESS

Human beings are poised to enter a new age of healing and regeneration if we choose to create an *Ecozoic Era*. According to Thomas Berry human cultural evolution proceeds by the conscious transmission of a downward flow of energy from the spiritual realm into the material world. Unlike biological evolution, which involves a mechanical process of natural selection through mutations that give adaptive advantage to certain individuals and species, cultural choice is conscious. If we are to move into an Ecozoic Era a critical mass of human beings must reawaken to their filial bond with the living Earth. This remembrance happens at the spiritual level and subsequently stimulates the fashioning of a mental framework to fit that insight—in other words, an ecology of mind—which in turn is the impetus to reconstruct cultural institutions. Technology is then used to heal, protect and feed the planet and all species.

When this vertical dimensional shift triggers horizontal social change human culture is reformed and transformed. Anima mundi is revisited and reconfigured to reflect an original egalitarian design in which all species are perceived as related and ensouled. A new translation of the Act of Contrition is written as we humans do penance, through ecologically sound action, for all the harm we have inflicted on the Earth community.

Such a cultural florescence depends upon an integration of energies that spurs a high level of creative activity. One way to speak of these energies is to differentiate them as male and female. Each individual—and by extension, the collective body of society—displays a certain gestalt of male and female energies. Gender in part determines the energy balance with women exhibiting more female energy and men more male energy as the norm. In Taoism these energies are known as *yin* (female) and *yang* (male). Taoism teaches that a primordial energy—*ch'i*—split into two complementary energies as the

Figure 10.1.   Yin yang symbol.
Converted to svg by Gregory Maxwell.

universe unfolded. Yin is inner, spiritual, dark, receptive, soft and fluid as water; yang is outer, worldly, light, active, hard as a mountain. Yang's power is forcefulness and fortitude; yin's power is the capacity to yield. Each energy is contained within its complementary partner.

In Jungian psychology a balancing of these two energies (known as *animus* and *anima*) in the individual person is viewed as necessary for healthy individuation. The fifteenth century Renaissance could be viewed as an historical example of the cultural benefit of balancing yin and yang. By integrating stunning works of art by master artists with the intellectual revival of Platonic studies the Renaissance achieved an organic connection between outer creative achievements (yang) and the interior philosophical/spiritual work (yin) that inspired them.

The arc of Western history shows a magnification of male energy with female energy taking a subordinate, counter-cultural role. Moreover, a corruption and distortion of both energies came to identify life-giving, peaceful female energy with the dark art of witchcraft and wild, adversarial Nature, while male energy, associated with reason and the intellectual achievements of the Scientific and Industrial Revolutions, was co-opted for the suppression of women and minorities, the waging of war and ruthless domination of the natural world. With the ascent of a rational, linear, materialistic and competitive worldview in the West male energy has produced a world in disequilibrium because the female intuitive/emotional, non-linear, subtle and cooperative counterpart has been excluded.

Jung gave us a way to restore psychological equilibrium in his excavation of certain powerful archetypes held in the collective unconscious. One such image that can draw all humanity together is Nature as the Great Mother Goddess. This maternal, divinized image of Earth, prominent in myths of diverse cultures, undergirded the ethos of tribal societies and agrarian societies of the ancient Middle East and formed the anima mundi of medieval thought. Legends of an earlier age of peace—the Garden of Eden and Atlantis, for example, and the veneration bestowed on the *Queen of Heaven, Creatress,* and *Mother of Heaven and Earth*—honorific names inscribed on ancient Mesopotamian tablets—indicate a cultural preference for what cultural historian Riane Eisler calls the *partnership model* of society. This pacifist model characterized pre-patriarchal cultures where adulation of female energy was the norm. The Mother Goddess was she who gave humans the arts of civilization: agriculture and the domestication of plants and animals, spirituality, healing, prophecy, craftwork, law and justice. Queen Isis of Egypt as goddess of the universe is said to have appeared to her devotee, Lucius Apulcius, and spoken thus:

'I am she that is the natural mother of all things, mistress and governess of all the elements, the initial progeny of worlds, chief of the powers divine, queen of all that are in hell, the principal of them that dwell in heaven, manifested alone and under one form of all the gods and goddesses. At my will the planets of the sky, the wholesome winds of the seas, and the lamentable silence of hell are disposed; my name, my divinity is adored throughout the world, in divers manners, invariable customs, and by many names.'[20]

Poet and feminist writer Adrienne Rich notes that when a patriarchal cosmology replaced the Earth Mother the primal female force was banished "to a purely 'chthonic' or tellurian presence, represented by darkness, unconsciousness and sleep."[21] A Greek myth foreshadows this change: Persephone, daughter of the Earth Goddess Demeter, is required to join her abductor Hades in the underworld for half a year because she tasted the food of the dead—pomegranate seeds—while in his clutches. The modern era placed her in the underworld permanently.

In *The Chalice and the Blade* Riane Eisler examines the historical rise of a dominator model of society which supplanted the partnership model. The dominator model, a manifestation of male energy, idolized the gods of war and proselytized male supremacy. Starting as early as the Neolithic era, Kurgan (Indo-European) invasions swept across prehistoric Europe, amassing wealth and power through conquest. This shift in social dynamics occurred, says Eisler, after a period of "system disequilibrium or chaos [when] there was a critical bifurcation point out of which an entirely different social system emerged."[22] She connects her cultural analysis to the work of scientists such as physical chemist Ilya Prigogine who studied how a far-from-equilibrium biological system undergoing stress reaches a bifurcation point where it either uses its ability to *self-organize* at a 'higher' level of order or move further towards fragmentation and replacement. In evolutionary theory this fragile point of bifurcation relates to the emergence of more complex forms of life through chance mutations. Living systems, for example, either adapt to crisis and move to a more adaptive level of organization or suffer extinction. For example, when the oxygen produced by photosynthesis filled the atmosphere to the point of threatening to kill off the vegetal world, animals evolved that could breathe oxygen.

Self-organization resembles *autopoiesis*—the property of each life form, from cells to galaxies, to maintain a unique integral identity. In discussing autopoiesis Thomas Berry states that this identity or self is the power of a life form to fulfill its particular creative role in cosmogenesis. Lovelock's Gaia Hypothesis asserts this idea as well. Berry gives the example of the autopoiesis of a star who "organizes hydrogen and helium and produces elements and light. This ordering is the central activity of the star itself. That is, the star has a functioning self, a dynamic of organization centered within itself."[23]

Cultural systems can also lose equilibrium, reach a bifurcation point, and regain equilibrium through self-organization. It is evident that humanity has made choices that contradict its role in cosmogenesis. We have precipitated the far-from-equilibrium system we now experience. Our task must be to reorganize according to the dictates of our true 'self.' Indeed, Eisler points out that cultural evolution, unlike biological evolution, is a matter of choice. According to the choices made a culture may break down, but it may also generate novel structures because the underlying energy network from which the system arose may emerge to refashion it. For Eisler, human dimorphism—male and female sexes—has always posed a basic constraint on the possible paths of cultural transformation—as, for example, whether social organization is egalitarian or hierarchical, peaceful or warlike.

The word *evolution* connotes a movement to a higher (i.e., better) level of order, but this, says Eisler, is a faulty premise. Thus the dominator model, born of disequilibrium, was not necessarily an evolutionary improvement. In certain aspects it produced social and technological advances but some of the uses to which technology has been designed have put cultural evolution into jeopardy. Eisler argues that the dominator model, which still grips modern culture, is less evolved than earlier partnership societies which, while less technologically and socially advanced, were more evolved in quality of life and attunement to Nature.

Eisler concludes that the replicative code that once replaced a partnership model with a dominator model can be recalibrated; indeed, we are now facing a cultural bifurcation point where the opportunity to replace the dysfunctional dominator model with a modern version of the partnership model is ripe. In other words, the time for a paradigm shift has arrived. But will the corrosive and divisive tenets of the male dominator model that represent *wétiko*—racism, misogyny, neocolonialism, economic inequality and environmental exploitation—be rejected in sufficient force to propel society into an Ecozoic Era? The human species possesses a brain with the flexibility and lack of narrow specialization that primes it for an evolutionary move. Humans can change their thinking and behavior in response to compelling feedback. In order to move from technologies of destruction to life-enhancing technologies, says Eisler, it is essential that a new adaptive change occur in the collective mind that favors integration of the positive frequencies of male and female energies.

In *The Passion of the Western Mind*, Richard Tarnas comes at the problem of disequilibrium from another angle. By tracing the trajectory of Western thought Tarnas uncovers a long-standing historical split in the Western worldview between Romantic and Enlightenment thinking—between humanism and science, between unity with nature and exploitation of nature. The historical tension between these two streams of thought—identified with female and male energies respectively—has decelerated the evolutionary move towards wholeness which, Tarnas argues, is nevertheless the goal of the Western mind. Tarnas contends that while the predominance of male energy was a necessary evolutionary stage that ignited achievements in science and industry the aggressive side of male energy was also unleashed, buttressed by the Cartesian vision of man as destined to coerce and drive the 'machine' of Nature. This destructive side of male energy now threatens planetary health and must yield, says Tarnas, to the healing powers of female energy. This return recalls Glendinning's depiction of the Primal Matrix which is rediscovered when the trauma of separation is rejected and the underlying unity of all life forms is realized.

The Hindu epic tale, the *Ramayana*, tells of the marriage of the hero, Prince Rama, to the chaste heroine Sita. When Sita is kidnapped by the evil Ravana Rama enlists the help of the clever monkey god, Hanuman (who represents reasoning mind), to rescue his beloved so that their harmonious union can be reestablished. Even in Western fairy tales the prince and princess 'live happily ever after'—after the obstacles to their union are overcome.

SUSTAINABILITY AS A LIFESTYLE

Sustainability is the ability to sustain life. Nature is naturally sustainable through processes of homeostasis that are maintained through the intelligent

actions of all living creatures working together in obedience to the two ecological laws of interconnectedness and reciprocity. Even as individual lives
are continually sacrificed through the natural mechanisms of eater and eaten
the duty of the individual is to serve life, even in death. The cardinal virtue
of sustainability is temperance—an old-fashioned, theologically tinged word
that needs to reenter the human vocabulary. The Great Economy of Nature
requires an understanding by human beings that less is more, that resources
must be used wisely to satisfy basic needs of all living creatures, that the
'enough point' must be recognized and obeyed in commerce, and that ways
to conserve energy and limit waste depend upon temperance. *Wétiko*—the
Western worldview of conquest and domination—must be replaced by cooperation and mutual nurturance at local, national and international levels in
order to avoid pushing Nature beyond her capacity for regeneration.

Such a worldview is not new. The recognition of harmony and intimacy
with Nature, characteristic of the Romantic temperament of poets like Wordsworth and philosophers like Thoreau, ran parallel, though subordinate, to the
scientific worldview that desacralized Nature and made her man's adversary.
Ironically it was modern physics that reinstated the Romantic impulse by
discovering the mystery of interrelationships at the subatomic level.

Lovelock offers an imaginative reconciliation between human destiny and
Gaia's evolutionary path. He writes:

> The evolution of homo sapiens, with his technological inventiveness and his
> increasingly subtle communications network, has vastly increased Gaia's range
> of perception. She is now through us awake and aware of herself. . . . This
> new interrelationship of Gaia with man is by no means fully established; we
> are not yet a truly collective species, corralled and tamed as an integral part of
> the biosphere, as we are as individual creatures. It may be that the destiny of
> mankind is to become tamed so that the fierce, destructive and greedy forces
> of tribalism and nationalism are fused into a compulsive urge to belong to the
> commonwealth of all creatures which constitutes Gaia.[24]

In order to bring humanity to this renewed fellowship with the Earth a
new *sustainable thinking* is necessary. Sustainable thinking is equated with
ecology of mind. In his book *Voluntary Simplicity* Duane Elgin describes the
underlying mental shift that translates ecology of mind into a life of *voluntary
simplicity*. Elgin explains: "To live more voluntarily is to live more consciously. . . . To live more simply is to live in harmony with the vast ecology
of all life. It is to live with balance—taking no more than we require and, at
the same time, giving fully of ourselves. To live with simplicity is by its very
nature a 'life-serving' intention."[25]

Living consciously refers to mindfulness, to directing the mind to rest in awareness from which right action can arise. Living consciously also refers to being aware of the tendency of mind to be deflected into imaginings that have nothing to do with the present moment. Human history has shown that the emotional loss of kinship with the Earth has been a study in mental distraction and overweening desire. Yet the invitation to mindful living is ever here. Certainly Thoreau's sojourn at Walden Pond is a model of Elgin's advice.

In the biblical parable of the prodigal son the father (symbolizing God, though Father-Mother is a more accurate reading of divinity) acquiesces to his younger son's request that his inheritance be given to him in advance. The younger son leaves home and "wastes his substance in riotous living."[26] Destitute and alone he awakens, 'comes to his senses,' and realizes that in squandering his inheritance and in rejecting the nurturing energy of home and family he has lost himself. He returns to his father, penitent. We human beings are poised to see and reclaim the looming loss of our inheritance—the abundance of Earth—if we wake up in time, turn around, and head home. Thomas Merton describes such a revolutionary turn in consciousness as *metanoia* which means *turning around*. Man leaves the divine center of his being; this departure, says Merton, is sin. But he can retrace that path and return to the center.

As the separate self dissolves, says Ken Wilber, its inner identity—the Higher or "Eco-Noetic Self"—is revealed.[27] This Higher Self communes with the natural world because it knows that there is no outside or inside. Love is the connecting energy. Wilber writes:

> Molecules awoke one morning to find that atoms were inside them, enfolded in their very being. And cells awoke one morning to find that molecules were actually inside them, as part of their very being. And you might awake one morning and find that nature is a part of you literally internal to your being. You are not a part of nature, nature is a part of you. And for just that reason, you treat nature as you would treat your lungs or your kidneys. A spontaneous environmental ethics surges forth from your heart, and you will never again look at a river, a leaf, a deer, a robin, in the same way.[28]

A unique community model of sustainable living is the village of Ashton Hayes, England—population of about 1,000 strong. Inspired ten years ago by a lecture on the dangers of climate change at a literary gathering in Wales, former journalist and hydrologist Garry Charnock decided to do something to reduce the carbon footprint of his village. Garry wanted to help create the first English carbon-neutral village so he talked up the idea with neighbors, using a light touch—no 'finger-pointing' was his motto, just set an example by your actions and have fun while becoming sustainable. The fact that Ashton

Hayes is an up-scale, well-educated village may be an important factor because most villagers were already primed for action by their awareness of the gravity of a rapidly warming planet. It also turned out that the decision early on by villagers that they wanted to do this makeover themselves, without political interference from parliamentary representatives, strengthened their resolve. This apolitical tactic kept the community from being divided by any personal political allegiances. Enthusiasm spread and pretty soon the rich and the not so rich started changing their habits. Residents placed photovoltaic solar panels on their roofs, including a communal project that placed solar panels on the primary school roof. A new playing field was built with a solar-powered pavilion next door to house a community café. Villagers installed triple-glazed windows in their houses for better insulation, planted vegetable gardens, erected cisterns to catch rainwater, and began using clotheslines instead of dryers. One of their leisure activities is meeting together for wine and cheese at the homes of the rich who seem to enjoy hosting these parties. The villagers recently celebrated their tenth anniversary of energy-efficient living and community building. Not only have they achieved a 24 percent cut in greenhouse emissions but they have also come to realize—as do a number of towns and cities around the globe who are now imitating Ashton Hayes—that it does 'take a village' to turn the world green.[29]

A SUSTAINABLE ECONOMY

An ecology of mind based in voluntary simplicity will facilitate the practical solutions for healing the planet. This new mindset ignites sustainable actions. Let us look at two important signs of a sustainable lifestyle: a sustainable economy and a sustainable education.

In order to make the capitalist system sustainable policies would need to be put in place that restore the original balance of the capitalist design to reflect an appreciation of communal as well as individual needs, service as well as profit-making, and cooperation as well as competition. Corporate and financial institutions would need to submit to tough regulations to correct the growing disparity in wealth while economic opportunity would expand to all citizens. The aim would be to reinstate de Tocqueville's formula for a healthy capitalist democracy: *self-interest well understood.* Spearheaded by human ingenuity the double-barreled shotgun of fossil fuels and agribusiness would be replaced with Nature's renewables: energies of the sun and wind and organic sustainable agriculture. As Gabe Brown, North Dakota farmer and spokesman for sustainable practices, remarks: "'The greatest roadblock to solving a problem is the human mind and having to unlearn all the things that you thought were true.'"[30] This 'unlearning' releases the mind's creative potential and plants "the seeds of nurture capitalism."[31]

In their book *for the common good* Herman Daly and John Cobb examine ways to incorporate a communal aspect into the creation of a self-sufficient national economy that encourages thriving local economies in balance with international trade. Small businesses and labor need protection, say the authors, particularly from outsourcing which is tied to the narrow profit-making motive. They argue that as a nation moves towards self-sufficiency it will be necessary to increase competitiveness among American companies and also encourage decentralization of production and control. As renewable energy sources become more affordable, for example, investment in their development becomes a more profitable venture, making capitalist competition a positive influence in the transition from fossil fuels to renewables. New long-term batteries will not only power electric cars and public transportation but also integrate sun and wind into electrical grids by storing electricity and releasing it when needed. Public enthusiasm for electric cars shows in the fact that the stocks of Tesla, with its new affordable Model 3 electric sedan, have risen substantially, surpassing both Ford and GM.

William E. Baker, president emeritus of WNET and author of *Leading With Kindness* presents research that shows a correlation between inspirational managers, who practice integrity and kindness, and sustainable business growth. An example of such a business leader is Hamdi Ulukaya, founder and CEO of Chobani. Hamdi is a Turkish immigrant (he calls himself a refugee) who came to America penniless, with no relatives stateside to help him. He built Chobani from scratch with a vision to produce the kind of nutritious, delicious yogurt he remembered from his Turkish upbringing. Chobani is now America's most popular Greek yogurt. Hamdi is the prototype success story of the American Dream, but he does not claim the rewards just for himself. He believes in sharing the wealth. In 2016 he stunned the food industry by promising his employees shares worth up to 10 percent of the company when it is sold or goes public. From the start Hamdi set employee salaries above the minimum wage, established a 401(k) program for his workers, and provided healthcare benefits.[32]

If, as the above example shows, capitalism can be tamed and redirected towards a balance of profit and service it may begin to resemble Buddhist economics which is based in self-sufficiency, sustainability and collaboration. As founder of the International Network of Engaged Buddhists, Sulak Sivaraksa of Thailand offers a new economic vision that brings the Buddhist and Western capitalist theories together in a syncretistic, hybrid form. Sivaraksa's activism focuses on practical work at the local level—such as the building of roads, houses and schools by communities—and a disavowal of capitalist excesses and inequalities. In his book *Seeds of Peace* Sivaraksa identifies major flaws in consumerist capitalism that include the 'think big' strategy of development in which Western agribusiness companies usurp Southeast Asian farmlands, urban sweatshops degrade work and workers, and neocolonialist corporations exploit and impoverish local people. He suggests an economic middle way that blends Western materialist ingenuity and competition with traditional indigenous models that (1) value a fair distribution of wealth within a local community and (2) honor Earth's plenty by mandating a sustainable lifestyle based in moderation—an important Buddhist tenet. Sivaraksa states that development of this new economic model requires a new type of education that focuses on inner cultivation of *the four abodes* of Buddhism: equanimity, loving kindness, compassion, and sympathetic joy (being happy rather than jealous when another person experiences happiness). These four disciplines are cultivated through mindfulness. Industrial-technological advances need not be eliminated, says Sivaraksa. What needs to be eliminated is the selfishness which hinders the development of a new work ethic that values cooperating with others rather than getting ahead of others.

Creating a sustainable economy involves a number of inventive practices. Two of these practices, green building and strategies for energy efficiency, attest to the power of human ingenuity.

Green Building

Ecologically sound architectural and building criteria—green building—is one of several important practical solutions to human-induced climate change. For the individual home, the suburban office, and the commercial and residential buildings that line our city streets, green building has the potential to conserve resources by the use of materials that do not damage the environment and by achieving energy efficiency through renewable sources.

Green Building initiatives are cropping up all over the world. Many of these structures are LEED certified. LEED stands for Leadership in Energy and Environmental Design. Developed by a non-profit organization, the U.S. Green Building Council (USGBC), LEED sets criteria for sustainable building worldwide—from design and construction to operation and maintenance. New York City passed one of the nation's first green building laws in 2005—Local Law 86—which requires that any new construction using a certain amount of city funding must be LEED certified. The first green residential tower in the nation was the Solaire in Battery Park City, New York City. In downtown Pittsburgh the Tower at PNC Plaza, which opened in 2015, is so green it even exceeds LEED standards.

A green building is one that, ideally, uses construction materials that have a high thermal mass but low embodied energy. High thermal mass means that the interior temperature is held constant. This constancy, which delivers a 'tight envelope,' can be achieved by the use of natural insulation materials with high R-value (resistance to heat loss). These materials include straw bale, cob, adobe, and newer green materials like cellulose which is 100 percent recycled paper, eco-fiberglass (made from recycled bottles and sand instead of glass so it lacks formaldehyde), and soy or castor based spray foam. Even your old recycled and shredded denim jeans provide suitable insulation.

Embodied energy refers to the amount of energy from fossil fuels used in the manufacturing and transport of materials. Sometimes a compromise is made to get high thermal mass even if the material used has high embodied energy. Concrete, for example, has high embodied energy but provides excellent thermal mass. The owner of the straw bale home displayed in the photo decided to use concrete as his interior flooring.

Another important ingredient in green building is passive solar design. In order to take advantage of sunlight, particularly in northern climes, a house

Figure 10.2.   Strawbale construction on a home in New Paltz, New York.
Courtesy of James Yastion.

is positioned to face south with family rooms like kitchen and living room placed in this quadrant. Windows are ample and double or triple glazed. Overhangs provide shade in the summer. A radiant heat system of pipes through which heated water flows can be put underneath the downstairs flooring. If the flooring is concrete—as in the case of the straw bale home—the concrete convects the heat to the surface so that even in winter one can walk barefoot comfortably—no slippers needed.

Some green homes are heated with a geo-thermal heat pump installed outside the house. Pipes are laid horizontally or vertically four to six feet under the frost line. The pump facilitates absorption of the Earth's constant heat (a mean temperature of 50 to 60 degrees) as the water flows into the house. For even better energy efficiency geo-thermal may be combined with solar panels on the roof to create a geosolar system. In some commercial buildings a green (or living) roof of vegetation planted over a waterproofing membrane serves multiple functions including absorption of rain water (some roofs even have small ponds to store greywater), insulation, habitat for wildlife, and reduction of air pollution as the plants drink in CO_2—of particular relevance in urban areas. Not to be discounted is the aesthetic pleasure of viewing a green roof, especially in a city where the most pervasive material is concrete.

Energy Efficiency

Farseeing CEOs of businesses such as PepsiCo, UPS, Walmart and Siemens are taking responsibility to make their corporations more energy efficient. Their reasoning for going green is two-fold. By reducing their companies' carbon footprints they are fulfilling their role as good citizens. They are also making a profitable market decision because they foresee a future economy based in renewable energy. For example, Joe Kaeser, chief executive of Siemens, a global manufacturer of high-speed trains, MRI machines and wind and gas turbines, stated in 2015 that the company was ready to invest more than $110 million to make their worldwide offices, factories, and a company fleet of roughly 45,000 vehicles energy efficient. New buildings will be LEED certified. To compensate for carbon emissions that are unavoidable Siemens will buy clean power in the form of carbon credits from organizations committed to green practices.[33]

Hal Harvey, advisor to major companies on energy policy, cites the drop in the cost of alternative energies as a major reason for the uptick in corporate energy efficiency. The cost of solar energy, for example, has dropped more than 80 percent since 2008.[34] Thanks to new technology, says Harvey, "'a clean future now costs less than a dirty one.'"[35] In fact, scientists have recently discovered by accident a chemical reaction through nanotechnology that turns carbon dioxide into ethanol. A two-for-one bargain is struck: companies can make profits by using the biggest polluting substance to run vehicles and power plants while helping to combat climate change.

Energy Vision is an example of a company that has found a way to create energy efficiency by converting organic waste into fuel, thereby reducing global warming. Founded and chaired by Joanna D. Underwood, Energy Vision is dedicated to promoting a positive type of natural gas called Renewable Natural Gas (RNG). RNG is not a fossil fuel like the natural gas procured through hydrofracking of shale deposits. It does consist mainly of methane, but RNG is made from the methane gases emitted by decomposing organic waste that rots in landfills, polluting the air. Compared to 400,000 tons of methane emitted into the atmosphere from the natural gas industry each year, 11.5 million tons of methane are released into the atmosphere from unprocessed waste and municipal wastewater.[36] "Virtually every country in the developed and developing worlds is drowning in waste—from homes, from farms, from businesses," says Underwood, "so the feedstock for making RNG fuel is EVERYWHERE, a brand new great energy resource and climate change solution."[37]

By harnessing methane gas worldwide and converting it into a virtually carbon-free fuel using anaerobic digesters the new product—RNG—can be used for all kinds of energy needs, including heating and transportation. Underwood argues that RNG, when used to fuel trucks and buses, reduces net greenhouse gas emissions by 80 percent to 115 percent when compared with gasoline or high-carbon diesel driven vehicles.[38] This means that each vehicle running on RNG is not only meeting but is exceeding the goal set by the Paris Agreement to cut greenhouse gases 80 percent (from 2005 levels) by 2050. "This is no futuristic pipe dream; it's happening now," says Underwood.[39] A number of cities in the United States including Sacramento, Santa Monica, and Los Angeles are outfitting their transit buses and refuse trucks with RNG. And companies like UPS are coming on board the RNG wagon as well to fuel their delivery vehicles.

A SUSTAINABLE EDUCATION

The problem that we face in establishing a wider affiliation with the Earth community is the fact that many of us still see the world from the narrow lens of anthropocentrism. In order to broaden this lens and create an ecologically healthy world two primary subjects must be introduced into our educational system: biophilia and sustainability. Loving life depends upon the perception of life. The awakening of an *emotional* identification with the creatures of the natural world accompanies a *mental* recognition that all living forms have the right to exist and that no one form can divorce itself from the whole. When biologist Barbara McClintock encourages her Harvard students to "live your way into each plant organ until you attain 'a feeling for the organism'" they are being encouraged to connect to the web of life emotionally as well as intellectually.[40] David Orr urges academia to reshape education by promoting ecological literacy. Through a "biophilia revolution," says Orr, a new age of enlightenment can be attained.[41]

According to psychologist Daniel Goldman, two intelligences—rational and emotional—spring from the same neurological root in the neocortex. The neocortex in turn develops out of a more primitive emotional storehouse of experience lodged in the limbic system which itself grows out of the olfactory lobe that investigates the world by means of the oldest animal sense—smell. This original role of the senses suggests the primacy of sensory awareness— and the origin of our connection with the natural world. Emotional intelligence operates in social learning and expresses itself as empathy. The positive evolution of human society, says Goldman, depends on the harmonizing and proper use of these two 'minds.' This balancing act—a characteristic of the new paradigm—can be achieved through education.

The teaching of biophilia engenders a cultural ethos, or set of values, based in sustainability which in turn becomes the backbone of a sustainable society. As students connect to the web of life they are simultaneously attracted to the idea of voluntary simplicity which is the root practice of a sustainable lifestyle. In fact, college students at a growing number of campuses are becoming actively involved in the experience of running a campus sustainably—from purchasing more nutritious, locally grown food for dining options to more efficient energy use, water conservation, and waste management. Thus the college or university becomes a living laboratory in the study and practice of ecological design and sustainability. For example, Warren Wilson College, a private university in Asheville, North Carolina, has a unique educational vision that, for over half a century, has been a model of sustainable facilities, practices and course offerings such as a broad-based major in environmental studies. Its innovative Green Walkabout is a hands-on educational adventure in sustainable living that explores such practices as green building and sustainable agriculture. By forming a College Triad of rigorous academics, experiential learning through campus work projects, and community service the college has sought to follow the findings of the 1983 Brundtland Commission which recommended that education in sustainable development must address the interwoven strands of poverty, overpopulation and environmental deterioration.[42]

As early as pre-school the mind can be awakened to both biophilia and sustainability. Teachers can encourage their students to re-cognize the natural world as subject and partner rather than object and adversary. This mental-emotional orientation is best achieved through experiential learning and the outdoor classroom. The teacher is aided by the fact that the young child's innate affinity with Nature is easily nurtured; there are no mental filters that label the soil, plants and animals as objects for human utilitarian purposes.

Maria Montessori's educational system, for example, was an early experiment in experiential education. She believed that the child is a "spiritual embryo" who should be protected from more traditional curriculums that stuff information into the child's head instead of removing obstacles from the special being that the child is.[43] By furnishing the child with playwork that develops a sensory hands-on connection to living beings, like plants or objects made of natural material, Montessori believed that the child could be guided in a favorable direction so that when he or she takes on the work of the adult—transformation of the environment—that work would be done with care and compassion.

David Sobel is an educator at Antioch University New England who pioneered place-based (experiential) education, especially in regards to nourishing the child's connection to the natural world. Sobel argues that a commitment to environmental conservation begins in the cultivation of empathy which should be an important focus in early childhood education. In his 1996 publication "Beyond ecophobia: Reclaiming the heart in nature education," Sobel advises educators to explore with children the natural environment and encourage them to identify with the perspective of an animal or tree, for example, to experience that life form. Although today's educational objectives prioritize 'a computer for every child in the classroom' it is well to consider the pedagogy of John Dewey who said that *secondary experience* cannot substitute for *primary experience*; the former impoverishes the creative imagination and encourages mediocrity.

Aldo Leopold credits his own empathetic understanding of life to a self-taught education that awakened both the intellect of a scientist and the affections of a poet. He writes of his own outdoor classroom in *A Sand County Almanac*: "Every farm woodland, in addition to yielding lumber, fuel, and posts, should provide its owner a liberal education. This crop of wisdom never fails, but it is not always harvested."[44]

One of the lessons Leopold learned was the capacity of a river to display the artistry usually reserved for human beings. As his description reveals, the river was, for him, a subject, not an object. He writes:

I know a painting so evanescent that it is seldom viewed at all, except by some wandering deer. It is a river who wields the brush, and it is the same river who, before I can bring my friends to view his work, erases it forever from human view. . . . Like other artists, my river is temperamental; there is no predicting when the mood to paint will come upon him, or how long it will last.[45]

The current American educational system joins other cultural institutions in upholding the outdated anthropocentric paradigm as legitimate and normal. The mechanistic paradigm, honed by the Scientific and Industrial Revolutions, prevails. Students are turned out like products for careers in the global economy. This corporate business model which turns the world into a marketplace of individual ambition, monetary success, and material gratification delivered by technological mind is a far cry from Plato's *paideia*—the Greek liberal arts education which cultivated a kaleidoscope of cognitive faculties— rational, empirical, intuitive, emotional, aesthetic, imaginative and moral—in order to prepare citizens to maintain a virtuous, well-ordered society that reflected the cosmic order. By contrast, the aim of education today contains, as Orr points out,

> a hidden curriculum that says that human domination of nature is good . . . that all knowledge, regardless of its consequences, is equally valuable; that material progress is our right. As a result we suffer a kind of cultural immune deficiency anemia that renders us unable to resist the seductions of technology, convenience, and short-term gain.[46]

The duty of an educational institution is to reflect and faithfully pass on to successive generations the accumulated knowledge of human endeavor. In policy and practice, however, the dominant cultural paradigm is also reflected and passed on. Even so, an educational institution possesses a built-in escape valve through which it can serve as a nucleus of dissent and change. Innovative teaching methodologies often originate within a school's walls and, especially at the college level, the four year hiatus from social norms creates a liminal atmosphere that encourages free thinking and gives rise to countercultural agendas that can affect the body politic, such as the wave of campus demonstrations for civil rights and against the Vietnam War in the 1960s and 1970s.

In a 2015 online essay, "Higher Education and the Promise of Insurgent Public Memory," author Henry A. Giroux warns that critical dissent and civic debate, by which university faculty and students held power accountable in the public sphere in the 1960s, are being challenged by a resurgent neoliberal capitalist agenda which has adopted the sentiments of the 1971 Powell Memo. This document demonized universities as places that created anti-democratic, anti-free enterprise intellectuals. Giroux cites John Dewey who warned in the 1930s about the growing influence of a corporate mentality which was endangering democracy by proselytizing "a mental and moral corporateness for which history affords no parallel." [47] It is imperative, Dewey argued, that democracy "'be reborn in each generation and education is its midwife.'"[48]

In the formation of an educational system for the Ecozoic Era the core curriculum courses in biophilia and sustainability will need an underlying discipline. That discipline is mindfulness training. Biophilia manifests as empathy; empathy is grounded in mindfulness—in being present and aware of one's surroundings. When we are fully present to the 'other' that 'other'—be it plant, animal or human—becomes a subject with whom I, as subject, commune. Mindfulness closes the gap between observer and observed, inciting a natural empathy for what is being explored. Goethe, who was a botanist as well as a poet and playwright, called this type of scientific inquiry "'delicate empiricism'" because it "makes itself utterly identical with the object."[49]

Jon Kabat-Zinn, a pioneer in mindfulness research, introduced mindfulness practice in 1979 to chronically ill patients at University of Massachusetts Medical Center as a method for stress reduction. Since then MBSR (Mindfulness-Based Stress Reduction) has been adopted in hospitals and medical schools worldwide. Kabat-Zinn has expanded his work into the field of education, arguing that mindfulness training helps children deal with distraction and stress by improving attention skills that accompany cognitive and social-emotional learning. As their ability to stay mindful increases children experience more equanimity and self-confidence.[50]

It is disconcerting that awareness—the trans-species instinct for survival—must now be taught. That this is so indicates how far we human beings have digressed from our elemental nature. Mindfulness practices are being introduced into higher education under the umbrella term *contemplative pedagogy*. Arthur Zajonc, physics professor at Amherst College and former director of the Center for Contemplative Mind in Society, speaks of contemplative pedagogy as a necessary inclusion in the college curriculum to stimulate personal and cultural transformation. He writes: "Parallel with the study of their major and the mastery of marketable skills, students long for a forum that can address their inner or spiritual concerns thoughtfully and deeply. If we are to educate the whole human being, then these dimensions of their nature cannot be forgotten." [51]

A restructuring of our educational system will enable teachers and parents to provide a new, life-enhancing enculturation process from cradle through college. Children will be taught to think about the natural world as their extended self and their lives will be shaped by a commitment to keep that world healthy through responsible action. As a torch is held and passed on to successive runners at the start of the Olympic Games so successive generations will carry the light of sustainability into the future.

FUSION WITH THE EARTH: THIS IS MY BODY

In her book, *Models of God: Theology for an Ecological, Nuclear Age*, Protestant theologian Sallie McFague argues that references in Christian theology to God as monarch and king mirror the authoritarian, patriarchal worldview which, in displacing an earlier reverence for Mother Earth as the embodiment of primal female energy, now places humanity at the precipice of ecological and nuclear disaster. According to McFague the outdated male triumphalist image of the Godhead must be revised by imagining new names for God such as Mother, Lover, and Friend. These fresh perceptions of God can shift energy from control and power towards love and compassion. The Earth is God's body, says McFague. When human beings abuse the Earth they profane God's body. This profanity is the essence of sin.

From the Buddhist perspective all beings are connected by a common essence—the *buddha-nature*. As Thich Nhat Hanh puts it, all life forms *interare*. We humans are made of non-human elements—sun, rain, air and earth. When humans interfere in the planet's operation the freedom of every being to be its essential self is disturbed. In order to guarantee freedom to all life forms the natural response of human beings must be compassion and non-violence.

The monastic order that Thich Nhat Hanh founded is called the Tiep Hien Order, the Order of Interbeing. *Tiep* means *to be in touch*; *hien* means *the present time*. Only in the present moment, and only through mindfulness, can we be in touch with Mother Earth and our fellow creatures. A simple way of connecting to the Earth is the practice of mindful walking. Thich Nhat Hanh writes:

> We are children of the Earth. We rely on her for our happiness, and she relies on us also. Whether the Earth is beautiful, fresh and green, or arid and parched depends on our way of walking. When we practice walking meditation beautifully we massage the Earth with our feet and plant seeds of joy and happiness with each step. Our Mother will heal us and we will heal her.[52]

To be in touch with other organisms assumes that we sense ourselves as embodied. But a hallmark of the modern cultural trauma is the feeling of disembodiment, of living exclusively in the mind which is usually experienced as a chaotic place in the head. This disconnection between mind and body is captured in a Zen story. A man on horseback is racing through a town. Another man who stands by the side of the road watches the rider as he passes and calls out: 'Where are you going in such a hurry?!' The rider, wild-eyed and breathless, shouts back, 'I don't know; ask my horse!'

Sensory perception is a mind-body process that connects us with our own bodies and the bodies around us. Touch, for example, provides immediate information which can deepen into hands-on knowledge unless the mind is trapped in thoughts which disengage it from the present moment. An 'absent' mind weakens the power of sensory perception which relies on awareness to fully operate. Take for example the life form called *tomato*. What is involved in *knowing* a tomato? I can gain partial knowledge by reading a book about tomatoes. But until I hold a tomato, smell and taste it, I cannot begin to know what a tomato is. A further dimension of knowledge is added when the tomato is grown in a garden that I till and plant. Each day I watch the life journey of the tomato unfold, from seedling in the loamy earth to a leafy plant to the appearance of little yellow flowers that, if pollinated, become pale green buttons that grow in size to deep green globes. Then one day a blush of orange appears, and, in time, the tomato ripens into a deep red plumpness. The slightly acrid smell of the stem joint from which the tomato is separated at picking time, the feel of the tomato in the palm of my hand with its smooth skin, warmed by the sun, touching my skin, and finally the release of its sweet juices into my mouth—all of these mind-body sensations become clues to the mystery of a tomato's identity, even as they affect and modulate the sense of my own identity by virtue of the relationship which has been cultivated.

By re-entering our own bodies consciously we simultaneously re-enter the body of the Earth. As this expansion is felt we are emboldened to say: this is my body. The heart opens; we feel an affinity for all beings. The experience of fusion with the Earth rescues us from self-imposed exile and elicits an intimation of a larger force at work. In the words of Wordsworth we become aware of

> . . . a presence that disturbs me with the joy
> Of elevated thoughts: a sense sublime
> Of something far more deeply interfused,
> Whose dwelling is the light of setting suns,
> And the round ocean and the living air,
> And the blue sky, and in the mind of man;
> A motion, and a spirit, that impels
> All thinking things, all objects of all thought,
> And rolls through all things. Therefore am I still
> A lover of the meadows and the woods,
> And mountains; and of all that we behold
> From this green earth. . . .[53]

The collective level of awareness that keeps the mind-body in conscious relationship with the outer world, and thereby prepared to make wise decisions in regards to the environment, lags behind our advancements in material comforts and technological expertise. The energy of awareness—our foremost source of power—is being misdirected and sacrificed to something manufactured. This developmental imbalance may be the greatest danger to human and planetary survival.

How is this imbalance corrected? By re-sensitizing ourselves to the natural world so that we consciously see, hear, taste and touch the sensory delicacies of the moment. The sudden delight that accompanies such a moment of pure presence leaps out of a poem by Mary Oliver called "Blackwater Pond." She writes:

> At Blackwater Pond the tossed waters have settled
> after a night of rain.
> I dip my cupped hands. I drink
> a long time. It tastes
> like stone, leaves, fire. It falls cold
> into my body, waking the bones. I hear them
> deep inside me, whispering
> *oh, what is that beautiful thing*
> *that just happened?*[54]

It is possible to be present, right now. . . . Relax the body . . . let the senses take in the sounds . . . sights . . . and smells around you. As your attention widens notice the quieting of the mind, the absence of thought. Notice too the absence of ego. If ego were the experiencer fear would inhibit expansion—fear of diminishment. When ego is quiescent there is just presence meeting other forms of presence. Rest for a moment in this expanding presence. . . .

Nature is always present. She invites us to roam (in presence) her fields and forests where she will teach us that it is natural to be present, to be whole. As Muir discovered: "'I only went out for a walk and finally concluded to stay out till sundown, for going out, I found, was really going in.'"[55]

When we human beings realize that the inner and the outer are the same then we will see that the outer sickness inflicted on the Earth reflects our own inner sickness. We will then seek healing for the inner and the outer body. Healing comes from a commitment to true principles. Mahatma Gandhi called this power *satyagraha*. Also translated as *soul force*, *satyagraha* literally means *clinging to truth*. Gandhi taught that a truthful member of society is one who advocates social justice and is willing to suffer in his or her own person to conquer the adversary through non-violent means. Non-violence preserves one's inner dignity. The truth to which one clings will in time break through injustice which must yield to the supreme power of truth.

The fight for climate justice must follow this same philosophy. The overriding principle that guides humanity towards a major cultural shift that will cure the ecological crisis is the truth of interdependence. We are one Earth family. A passion to uphold this truth and a commitment to persevere in the struggle to realize a healthy, just and compassionate world is incumbent upon

each of us. Regardless of the seeming strength of those who oppose this Great
Work the power of a truthful principle is infectious; it rallies its guardians to
turn the cultural tide towards an Ecozoic Era.

HOMECOMING

All living beings have homes. Some homes are on land; some are in or near
water; some are up in the trees. Home is where a creature lives, reproduces,
and finds protection. The mud wasp builds a house that looks like a turban
made out of mud; it hangs from a tree branch. Bears live in caves where they
hibernate in winter. The gopher tortoise joins the rabbit and groundhog in her
choice of home, burrowing into the dark earth. She even shares her home with
strangers when a sudden storm or predator requires a quick place of refuge.
Humans also make houses, many of which start out as holes in the ground
where foundations are set on footings that will support the final structures.

All of us live on Earth as our common home. Yet this home now labors to
retain equilibrium because of human folly. We are one family, yet we humans
behave as if we are separate from and better than our kin. We move through
the routines of the day mechanically, as if the house we live in is not on fire,
even though the flames are licking at our heels. To use a sports metaphor, the
clock is running out and we may have to go into overtime where anything
can happen.

Each day we are called to a more conscious life. Just as the child is sum-
moned to supper by his mother as dusk approaches and playtime must end,
so the Earth Mother calls us home with every sunrise and sunset. As David
Abram puts it,

An eternity we thought was elsewhere now calls out to us from every cleft in
every stone, from every cloud and clump of dirt. To lend our ears to the drip-
ping glaciers—to come awake to the voices of silence—is to be turned inside
out, discovering to our astonishment that the wholeness and holiness we'd been
dreaming our way toward has been holding us all along. . . .[56]

In the following poem Rainer Maria Rilke expresses the longing we have
all felt to belong to a greater identity. Sometimes this longing for completion,
for communion, for wholeness overwhelms us as it did Rilke when he wrote:

Ah, not to be cut off,
Not through the slightest partition
Shut out from the law of the stars.
The inner—what is it?

> If not intensified sky,
> Hurled through with birds and deep
> With the winds of homecoming.[57]

We are in fact already home. That's the good news. We are already part of a great communion. As human beings we have a unique capacity to remember, to be aware, to contemplate this unity. If ever there was a time to use that capacity it is now.

Appendix One

Pausing: A 2–3 minute exercise in sensory awareness

1. Sitting in a comfortable but erect position, *let the body relax* from the crown of the head to the soles of the feet. Let bodily tensions dissolve . . . feel the loosened energy flow down into the floor and into the Earth where it will be received and recycled. . . . (allow time) Also release any mental tensions in the form of ideas and preoccupations.
2. Using the sense of *touch*, become aware of the body as a whole . . . feel the feet in contact with the floor, feel the clothes on the skin, the air passing across the face; aware of your breathing, let it deepen . . .
3. Using the sense of *sight*, let the eyes receive the images in your immediate surroundings; be aware of color and form without naming or commenting on what is seen; just see and know that seeing is taking place . . .
4. Using the sense of *smell*, breathe in the scents around you; smell and know that you are smelling . . .
5. Using the sense of *taste*, notice whatever taste may linger in the mouth and know that you are tasting . . .
6. Continuing to relax the body, aware through the senses of touch, sight, smell and taste, open up the listening . . . listen to all the sounds which surround you . . . let this listening extend to the furthest sound without strain or comment . . . these sounds are arising from silence . . . rest in the deep silence from which the sounds arise and into which they recede . . .
7. *Resting in simple awareness* by means of the senses, feel the sense of self, of wholeness, extend into your surroundings. . . . Let imagined boundaries dissolve. . . . If a thought, daydream, image or feeling pulls the attention away from being-present and you awaken to this momentary distraction just redirect the attention to any one of the five senses and the connecting circuit of healing energy between body, mind and heart will be restored.

Appendix Two
Loving Kindness Meditation

1. Sit quietly and connect your heart with basic goodness and love. . . .
2. Recollect a vivid moment of happiness from your life. Recall the details and sensations, the place and people of this event. Try to renew this feeling in your heart and let it fill you completely. Think or say: "May I be happy, may I be healthy, may I live with ease." Rest in this feeling for a few minutes.
3. Recollect a relationship with a person or animal who is close and dear to you. Visualize his or her face or remember a situation in which you were together. Let the energy of loving kindness fill you. Send your love to this person or animal. Think or say: "May you be happy, may you be healthy, may you live with ease." Rest in this feeling for a few minutes.
4. Recollect someone about whom you have neither a strong positive or negative feeling: a 'neutral' person. Send the flow of loving kindness energy from your heart to the heart of this neutral person. Think or say: "May you be happy, may you be healthy, may you live with ease." Rest in this feeling for a few minutes.
5. Recollect someone with whom you have a difficult relationship or negative feelings. Send the flow of loving kindness energy from your heart to the heart of this difficult person. Think or say: "May you be happy, may you be healthy, may you live with ease." Rest in this feeling for a few minutes.
6. Radiate loving kindness to all beings, thinking or saying "May everyone, everywhere, be happy, healthy and may they live with ease." Rest the mind in silence for a few minutes.

[Loving Kindness Meditation is used by permission of the MA Contemplative Education program at Naropa University, Boulder, CO]

Notes

PREFACE

1. Alan Watts, *The Book: On the Taboo Against Knowing Who You Are* (New York: Vintage Books, 1989), 9.

CHAPTER 1

1. Lauren Tierney, "The grim scope of 2017's California wildfire season is now clear. The danger's not over," *The Washington Post*, January 4, 2018, https://www .washingtonpost.com/graphics/2017/national/california-wildfires-comparison/
2. Organizations such as Homes for the Homeless operate on the principle that settling into something as personal and self-affirming as 'my home' precedes finding a job. Temporary housing is available as parents receive practical skills that prepare them for jobs while their children participate in programs for educational enrichment.
3. Peter Berger, Brigitte Berger and Hansfried Kellner, *The Homeless Mind* (New York: Vintage Books, 1974), 184.
4. Peter Berger, Brigitte Berger and Hansfried Kellner, *The Homeless Mind*, 195.
5. Abraham Lincoln, "Abraham Lincoln Quotes," Goodreads, accessed May 1, 2018, https://www.goodreads.com/author/quotes/229.Abraham_Lincoln.
6. See J. W. Kirchner, "The Gaia Hypothesis: Fact, Theory, and Wishful Thinking," *Climatic Change* 52, 291–408.
7. This is the title of Robert F. Kennedy's book *Crimes Against Nature* (New York: Harper Collins, 2004).
8. Edwin Way Teale, ed., *The Wilderness World of John Muir* (New York: Mariner Books/Houghton-Mifflin, 2001), 311.
9. *The Essential Rumi*, trans. Coleman Barks with John Moyne, A. J. Arberry, and Reynold Nicholson (New York: HarperSanFrancisco, 1996), 112–113.

10. Thomas Merton, *Conjectures of a Guilty Bystander* (Garden City, NY: Image/ Doubleday, 1968), 85. Thomas Merton lived during the turbulent 1960's. He became renowned as a proponent of the reforms of Vatican II, particularly the injunction that the Church revive its contemplative tradition and build sanguine relationships with other religions. Through his prolific writings and participation in interreligious dialogue Merton influenced Christians and non-Christians to heal their divisions by finding common ground.

11. Huston Smith, *The World's Religions* (New York: HarperCollins, 1961), 174.

12. David Kinsley, *Ecology and Religion* (Upper Saddle River, NJ: Prentice Hall, 1995), 77.

13. Chinese religions fuse mind and heart. This makes sense: what we feel reflects what we think and vice-versa.

14. Kent Nerburn, ed., *The Wisdom of the Native Americans* (New York: MJF Books, 1999), 4.

15. Jerry Mayer and John P. Holms, *bite-size einstein* (New York: St. Martin's Press, 1996), 10.

16. Simone Weil, *The Need For Roots* (New York: G. P. Putnam's Sons, 1952), 43.

17. See James Gorman, "Lizards That Can't Get Lost," *The New York Times*, July 7, 2015, D4.

CHAPTER 2

1. Fritjof Capra, *The Tao of Physics* (Boston: Shambhala, 1991), 319.

2. Smithsonian Institution, Ocean Portal Team, "Gulf Oil Spill," accessed May 13, 2018, ocean.si.edu/gulf-oil-spill.

3. Hannah Arendt was a German-born citizen of Jewish ancestry who escaped Germany during the Holocaust and came to America where she became a renowned political theorist. Her first book, *The Origins of Totalitarianism*, earned her instant acclaim as an influential political thinker. She rejected the label 'philosopher' with which some accorded her. She believed that human beings have a responsibility to use their intellect practically by publically voicing their disdain for forms of authoritarianism, especially in the political sphere. The phrase *banality of evil* is used in the title of her book on Adolf Eichmann.

4. The director of the National Institute of Mental Health (NIMH), Dr. Thomas Insel, in a blog posted on Feb. 5, 2014, said that in 2010 (the most recent statistics available) more than 38,000 Americans died by suicide. Suicide is the tenth leading cause of death for people of all ages and a disturbing second cause of death for young people ages 25–34. While deaths from heart disease and cancer, for example, are declining suicide rates have not decreased despite intervention strategies.

5. The World Bank, "The World Bank: Understanding Poverty," accessed May 3, 2018, www.worldbank.org/en/topic/poverty/overview. According to the World Bank, the number of people living in extreme poverty remains unacceptably high

even though that number has decreased from 1.85 billion in 1990. Half of the poor live in Sub-Saharan Africa.

6. Justin Gillis and Nadja Popovich, "The US. Is the Biggest Carbon Polluter in History. It Just Walked Away From the Paris Climate Deal," June 1, 2017, www.nytimes.com/interactive/2017/06/01/climate/us.

7. "Air Pollution in China," Facts and Details, accessed May 4, 2018, factsand details.com/china/cat10/sub66/item392.html.

8. Nida Najar and Hari Kumar, "Pray for Shade: Heat Wave Sets a Record in India," May 20, 2016, www.nytimes.com/2016/05/21/world/asia/india-heat-wave.html

9. The squiggles record the dips and rises in CO2 due to decaying leaves in the fall, when more CO2 is released into the atmosphere, and leafing of trees in the spring.

10. Climate Central, "The 10 Hottest Global Years on Record," January 18, 2018, www.climatecentral.org/gallery/graphics/the-10-hottest-global-years-on-record.

11. Union of Concerned Scientists, "The Planet's Temperature is Rising," November 17, 2016, https://www.ucsusa.org/global-warming/science-and-impacts/science/temperature-is-rising.

12. NASA, "Global Climate Change: Vital Signs of the Planet, Ice Sheets," accessed May 4, 2018, https://climate.nasa.gov/vital-signs/ice-sheets.

13. Michael D. Lemonick, "East Coast Faces Rising Seas From Slowing Gulf Stream," February 12, 2013, www.climatecentral.org/news/east-coast-faces-rising-seas-from-slowing-gulf-stream-15587.

14. Laura Parker, "Ocean Trash: 5.25 Trillion Pieces and Counting, but Big Questions Remain," *National Geographic,* January 11, 2015, https://news.national geographic.com/news/2015/01/150109-oceans-plastic-sea-trash-science-marine-debris. See also follow-up article by Laura Parker, "A Whopping 91 percent of Plastic Isn't Recycled," *National Geographic,* July 19, 2017, https://news.nationalgeographic .com/2017/07/plastic-produced-recycling-waste-ocean-trash-debris-environment/.

15. Carl Sagan, *Pale Blue Dot* (New York: Random House, 1994), 9.

16. Jason Bosher, "Hydrocarbons: Caught between the ozone and a hard place," *Alive,* updated April 24, 2015, https://www.alive.com/lifestyle/hydrocarbons/.

17. An example of state governments as vanguards in the effort to reduce carbon emissions is the Regional Greenhouse Gas Initiative or REGGI, a group of nine Eastern and New England states whose governors have succeeded in promoting substantial reductions in emissions from big power plants since 2009.

18. Rob Sargent, "President Obama's Renewable Energy Legacy," Environment America Blog, January 10, 2017, https://environmentamerica.org/blogs/environment -america-blog/ame/president-Obama's-renewable-energy-legacy.

19. "The Global Commission on The Economy and Climate," IMF-WB annual meetings, October 8, 2014, www.worldbank.org/content/dam/Worldbank/document/ WEurope/2014/IMF-global-commission-economy-climate.pdf.

20. "2017 is set to be in top three hottest years, with record-breaking extreme weather," Global Climate Change, NASA, www.climatechange.nasa.gov.

21. The 2017 National Climate Assessment shows that from 1901 to 2016 a global annually averaged increase in surface air temperature approximated 1.8 Fahrenheit

(1.0 Celsius) making this the warmest period in the modern era. A precipitous rise in ozone, a pollutant in the lower atmosphere, is also of concern. See U.S. Global Change Research Program, "Fourth National Climate Assessment," https://www.globalchange.gov/nca4.

22. Kelly Levin, "World's Carbon Budget to be Spent in Three Decades," World Resources Institute, September 27, 2013, www.wri.org/blog/2013/09/world's-carbon-budget-be-spent-three-decades.

23. Thomas Merton, *Conjectures of a Guilty Bystander* (Garden City, NY: Doubleday/Image, 1968), 43. Giono helped to inspire the ecological movement. His book *The Man Who Planted Trees* is a classic story of one man's effort to reforest a bleak landscape.

24. *Tao Te Ching*, trans. Stephen Mitchell (New York: HarperCollins, 1988), 29.

25. William McDonough and Partners website, www.mcdonoughpartners.com/design-approach/.

26. Bill McKibben, *The End of Nature* (New York: Random House, 2006), 41.

27. Bill McKibben, *The End of Nature*, 50.

28. Chellis Glendinning, *My Name is Chellis and I'm in Recovery from Western Civilization* (Gabriola Island, Canada: New Catalyst Books, 2007), 100.

29. Lydia Saad, "Half in U.S. Are Now Concerned Global Warming Believers," Gallup, March 27, 2017, news.gallup.com/poll/207119/half-concerned-global-warming-believers.aspx.

30. Robert Jay Lifton, "Our Changing Climate Mind-Set," *New York Times Sunday Review*, October 8, 2017, 10.

31. Implied in the anthropocentric perspective is the association of *anthropos* with the male gender. Woman's identity is perceived as appended to man's identity.

32. Carl R. Rogers, *On Becoming a Person* (Boston: Houghton Mifflin Company, 1995), 104.

33. Charles E. Tart, *Open Mind, Discriminating Mind: Reflections on Human Possibilities* (San Francisco: Harper & Row, 1998), 163.

34. Charles E. Tart, *Open Mind, Discriminating Mind: Reflections on Human Possibilities*, 163.

35. Charles E. Tart, *Open Mind, Discriminating Mind: Reflections on Human Possibilities*, 162.

36. Robert Ornstein, ed., *The Nature of Human Consciousness* (New York: Viking Press, 1974), 318.

37. David Abram, *Becoming Animal* (New York: Vintage Books, 2010), 38.

38. David Abram, *Becoming Animal*, 124.

39. Robert Ornstein, ed., *The Nature of Human Consciousness* (New York: Viking Press, 1974), 323.

40. *The Ten Principal Upanishads*, trans. Shree Purohit Swami and W. B. Yeats (London: Faber and Faber, 1970), 19.

41. Paul Ehrlich, "Eco-Catastrophe!" in *The Natural World—Chaos and Conservation*, ed. Cecil E. Johnson (New York: McGraw-Hill, 1972), 67.

CHAPTER 3

1. Adobe is one of the oldest, most durable building materials. It is made of clay, sand, water and fibrous material like straw.

2. Justin Gillis, "Rise in Carbon Defies Slowing of Emissions," *The New York Times*, July 27, 2017, A6.

3. *An Ecology of Mind, Millennium, Tribal Wisdom and the Modern World*, New Vision Media Ltd. 1992. Narrated by David Maybury-Lewis. Produced by Adrian Malone and Richard Meech.

4. *An Ecology of Mind, Millennium, Tribal Wisdom and the Modern World.*

5. Abrahm Lustgarten, "Unplugging the Colorado River," May 20, 2016, https://www.nytimes.com/2016/05/22/opinion/unplugging-the-colorado-river.html.

6. See Center for Climate and Life, Columbia University, Tag: Park Williams, "Warming Climate is Deepening California's Drought," August 20, 2015, climateandlife.columbia.edu/2015/08/20/warming-climate-is-deepening-California-drought/

7. David Suzuki, with Amanda McConnell & Adrienne Mason, *The Sacred Balance: Rediscovering Our Place in Nature* (Vancouver, BC: Greystone Books, 2007), 88.

8. *The Ten Principal Upanishads*, trans. Shree Purohit Swami and W. B. Yeats (London: Faber and Faber, 1970), 89.

9. Indries Shah, *Tales of the Dervishes* (New York: E. P. Dutton, 1967), 21.

10. The barnacle's story is told by biologist Rachel Carson in her book *The Edge of the Sea.*

11. U.S. Geological Survey, "Ocean Warming Affecting Florida Reefs," September 9, 2014, https://www.usgs.gov/news/ocean-warming-affecting-florida-reefs. The USGS report cites a trend in Florida water temperatures which have warmed by nearly 2 degrees F. in the last several decades.

12. David Abram, *Becoming Animal* (New York: Vintage, 2010), 129.

13. *Tao Te Ching*, trans. Stephen Mitchell (New York: HarperCollins, 1988), 39.

14. E.E. Cummings, *Complete Poems 1913–1962* (New York: Harcourt Brace Jovanovich, 1972), 663. From "I thank you God for most this amazing," *Complete Poems of ee cummings*, © 1968 Harcourt Brace Javanovich. Reprinted by permission of Liveright/W. W. Norton & Company.

15. Edwin Way Teale, ed., *The Wilderness World of John Muir* (Boston: Mariner Books/Houghton Mifflin Company, 2001), 315.

16. Edward Connery Lathem, ed., *The Poetry of Robert Frost*, Copyright © 1928, 1969 by Henry Holt and Company (New York: Henry Holt and Company,1969), 251.

17. Joanna Macy, *Widening Circles* (Gabriola Island, BC: New Society Publishers, 200), 2–3.

18. Peter Reich, "Explainer: how much carbon can the world's forests absorb?", The Conversation, June 11, 2013, https://theconversation.com/explainer-how-much-carbon-can-the-worlds-forests-absorb14816.

19. Tia Ghose, "Fog Decline threatens California's Towering Redwoods," *Wired*, February 15, 2010, www.wired.com/2010/02/fog-decrease-threatens-coastal-redwoods/.

20. Amanda Rhoades, "Bark Beetle Infestation Continues to Threaten Tahoe-Truckee Forests," *Truckee Sun*, June 24, 2017, https://www.truckeesun.com/news/environment/bark-beetle-infestation-continues-to-threaten-tahoe-truckee-forests/.

21. This statistic and the rest of the paragraph's data can be found at Rainforest Facts, accessed May 8, 2018, www.rain-tree.com/facts.htm#.Wv#1GqQvypo.

22. National Geographic, Rain Forests, www.nationalgeographic.com/environment/habitats/rain-forests/.

23. Rainforest Facts, www.rain-tree.com/facts.htm#.Wv#GqQvypo.

24. ENI School Energy and Environment, Soil Formation, accessed May 8, 2018, www.eniscuolo.net/en/argomento/soil/soil-formation/how-long-does-it-take-to-form/ In temperate climates it takes from 200 to 400 years.

25. Julia Butterfly Hill, *The Legacy of Luna* (New York: HarperCollins, 2000), 8. Copyright © 2000 by Julia Butterfly Hill. Excerpt reprinted by permission of HarperCollins Publishers.

26. In *The Last Hours of Ancient Sunlight* author Thom Hartmann uses the term to refer to the forgetting by modern 'younger' cultures of the wisdom of indigenous 'older' cultures and the desecration of their land.

27. Jared Diamond, *Collapse: How Societies Choose to Fail or Succeed* (New York: Penguin. 2006), 425.

28. LuAnn Dahlman, "Climate Change: Global Temperature," NOAA, September 11, 2017, https://www.climate.gov/news-features-understanding-climate-change/.

29. Thomas Friedman, "A Lack of Water Set the Stage for Revolution in Syria," *The New York Times Sunday Review:* May 19, 2013, pp. 1, 3.

30. Elizabeth Kolbert, *The Sixth Extinction, An Unnatural History* (New York: Henry Holt and Co., 2014), 16.

31. Brainy Quote, John Adams Quotes, accessed March 15, 2016. www.brainyquote.com/quotes/john_adams_134175.html.

32. Center for Biological Diversity, The Extinction Crisis, www.biologicaldiversity.org/programs/biodiversity/elements_of.../extinction_crisis/.

33. Kenneth Brower, "Reclaiming Wilderness," *Sierra*, July/August 2014, 31.

34. David S. Wilcove and Lawrence L Master, "How many endangered species are there in the United States?", JSTOR *Frontiers in Ecology and the Environment*, vol. 3, no. 8, October 2005, https://www.jstor.org/stable/3868657?seq=1#page_scan_tab_contents.

35. Scott Coleman, "UA study: species can't evolve fast enough to adjust to climate change," *Tucson Sentinel*, July 12, 2013, https://www.tucsonsentinet.com/local/report/071213_climate_change_study/ua-study-species-cant-evolve-fast-enough-adjust.

36. Edward O. Wilson, *The Diversity of Life* (Cambridge, MA: Belknap Press of Harvard University Press, 1992), 344.

37. Edward O. Wilson, *The Diversity of Life*, 342.

38. Albert Schweitzer, *Reverence for Life* (New York: Harper & Row, 1969), 116.

CHAPTER 4

1. Chellis Glendinning, *My Name is Chellis and I'm in Recovery from Western Civilization* (Gabriola Island, BCV, Canada: New Catalyst Books, 2007), 126.

2. Chellis Glendinning, *My Name is Chellis and I'm in Recovery from Western Civilization*, 101.

3. *The Essential Rumi*, trans. Coleman Barks with John Moyne, A. J. Arberry, Reynold Nicholson (New York: HarperSan Francisco, 1996), 142. From the poem "Childhood Friends".

4. Chellis Glendinning, *My Name is Chellis and I'm in Recovery from Western Civilization*, (Gabriola Island, BCV, Canada: New Catalyst Books, 2007), 140–41.

5. Chellis Glendinning, *My Name is Chellis and I'm in Recovery from Western Civilization*, 134.

6. Chellis Glendinning, *My Name is Chellis and I'm in Recovery from Western Civilization*, 138.

7. Chögyam Trungpa, *Shambhala: the Sacred Path of the Warrior* (Boston: Shambhala, 1988), 103.

8. Erich Fromm, *The Sane Society* (Greenwich, CT: Fawcettt Publications, 1967), 40.

9. Erich Fromm, *The Sane Society*, 127.

10. In the film *A Guide to Walking Meditation* Thich Nhat Hanh uses this phrase attributed to the Buddha.

11. Eckhart Tolle, *A New Earth* (New York: Dutton, 2005), 45.

12. Eckhart Tolle, *A New Earth*, 14. In ecological terms, the egoic mind must dissolve because it disobeys the two universal laws of interdependence and reciprocity. Tolle's equation of egoic behavior with insanity recalls Fromm's analysis.

13. Eckhart Tolle, *A New Earth*, 21–22.

14. Eckhart Tolle, *A New Earth*, 21.

15. Eckhart Tolle, *A New Earth*, 19.

16. Daniel Quinn, *Ishmael* (New York: Bantam, 1992), 166.

17. Thomas Merton, *The New Man* (New York: Noonday Press, 1993), 112–113.

18. Thomas Merton, *The New Man*, 118–119.

19. Ken Wilbur, *Up From Eden* (Wheaton, Ill.: Quest Books, 1996), 48.

20. Ken Wilbur, *Up From Eden*, 17.

21. Tom Brown, Jr. *Awakening Spirits* (New York: Berkley Books, 1994), 99. Excerpt from *Awakening Spirits: A Native American Path to Inner Peace, Healing, and Spiritual Growth* by Tom Brown Jr., copyright © 1994 by Tom Brown Jr.. Used by permission of Berkley, an imprint of Penguin Publishing Group, a division of Penguin Random House LLC. All rights reserved. Any third party use of this material, outside of this publication, is prohibited. Interested parties must apply directly to Penguin Random House LLC for permission.

22. John Mansley Robinson, *An Introduction to Early Greek Philosophy* (Boston: Houghton-Mifflin, 1968), 95.

23. Plato, *Timaeus and Critias*, trans. Desmond Lee (New York: Penguin Books, 1979), 67.

24. Loren Eiseley, *The Invisible Pyramid* (New York: Scribner's, 1970), 70.

25. Henry David Thoreau, *Walden* (New York: Fall River Press, 2008), 33.

26. *King James Bible*, Psalm 8:4–5.

27. In *Utriusque Cosmi* Fludd explores the relationship between the two worlds: the microcosm of earthly life and the macrocosm of the universe which includes the divine realm. This relationship is also known as the hermetic metaphor: as above, so below. It appears that Fludd views Jesus as the point of intersection between the two worlds, the link by whom unity is realized.

28. Beldon C. Lane, *Landscapes of the Sacred* (Baltimore: John Hopkins University Press, 2002), 148.

29. Theodore Roszak, *The Voice of the Earth* (Grand Rapids, MI: Phanes Press, 2001), 142.

30. Theodore Roszak, *The Voice of the Earth*, 143.

31. David Kinsley, *Ecology and Religion* (Upper Saddle River, NJ: Prentice-Hall, 1995), 111.

32. Richard Tarnas, *The Passion of the Western Mind* (New York: Ballantine Books, 1991), 290.

33. Brian Swimme & Thomas Berry, *The Universe Story: From the Primordial Flaming Forth to the Ecozoic Era—A Celebration of the Unfolding of the Cosmos* (New York: HarperCollins, 1994), 230. Copyright © 1992 Brian Swimme.

34. Carolyn Merchant, *The Death of Nature* (New York: HarperCollins, 1989), 169.

35. Carolyn Merchant, *The Death of Nature*, 169.

36. *King James Bible*, Genesis 1:28.

37. Note the similarity between Descartes' view and the Protestant valuation of the individual's direct access to God.

38. Christopher Biffle, *A Guided Tour of Rene Descartes' Meditations*, trans. Ronald Rubin (Mountain View, CA: Mayfield, 2001), 53.

39. Richard Tarnas, *The Passion of the Western Mind* (New York: Ballantine Books, 1991), 279.

40. A pivotal figure of the late Middle Ages who would influence the way the nascent discipline of science would be taught was William of Ockham (1287–1347). An English philosopher and Franciscan friar, Ockham drove Aristotle's focus on matter to its extreme by positing the only reality as that which is observable, quantifiable and devoid of transcendent qualities. Ockham's reductionist approach, known as nominalism, slices off the *meta* from *physical*, rejecting Thomas Aquinas' argument that metaphysical truths about God can be inferred by contemplation of Nature. Known as *Ockham's razor*, this 'law of parsimony' was applied to the scientific method. It favors simple theories rather than complex ones that are difficult to test empirically. In effect, this materialist perspective which objectifies and de-animates Nature won out and was joined at the hip by Cartesian dualism when Descartes placed Nature/body in a separate, subordinate and confrontational position to Man/mind. Historical progress would be measured henceforth by the ability of human beings to know and control Nature through science and technology.

CHAPTER 5

1. Thom Hartmann, *The Last Hours of Ancient Sunlight* (New York: Three Rivers Press, 2004), 33.

2. Thom Hartmann, *The Last Hours of Ancient Sunlight*, 32.

3. This phrase was coined by English philosopher Herbert Spencer and then used by Charles Darwin in *On the Origin of Species* to describe the mechanism of natural selection.

4. Korten discusses this attitude in *The Great Turning: from Empire to Earth Community.*

5. E. F. Schumacher, *A Guide for the Perplexed* (New York: Harper & Row, 1977), 41.

6. E. F. Schumacher, *A Guide for the Perplexed*, 44.

7. E. F. Schumacher, *A Guide for the Perplexed*, 53–54.

8. Brainy Quote, Mahatma Gandhi Quotes, accessed May 9, 2018, https://www.brainyquote.com/quote/mahatma_gandhi_104952.

9. In Bill McKibben, *The End of Nature* (New York: Random House, 2006), 67.

10. Christopher Ricks, ed. *The Oxford Book of English Verse* (New York: Oxford University Press, 1999), 328.

11. Christopher Ricks, ed. *The Oxford Book of English Verse*, 328.

12. Eckhart Tolle, *A New Earth* (New York: Dutton, 2005), 47–48.

13. T. S. Eliot, *Collected Poems 1909-1962* (Orlando, FL: Harcourt Brace Jovanovich, 1991), 157.

14. Alexis de Tocqueville, *Democracy in America* (Chicago: University of Chicago Press, 2000), 502.

15. Alexis de Tocqueville, *Democracy in America*, 515.

16. Alexis de Tocqueville, *Democracy in America*, 587.

17. Alexis de Tocqueville, *Democracy in America*, 663.

18. Alexis de Tocqueville, *Democracy in America*, 663.

19. Erich Fromm, *The Sane Society* (New York: Fawcett World Library, 1967), 190.

20. Erich Fromm, *The Sane Society*, 188.

21. A form of George's progressive tax, aimed at leveling the economic playing field, has been instituted in Denmark where higher taxes are seen as investments in quality of life. The Danes' sense of well-being makes Denmark one of the happiest countries in the world. See Meik Wiking, "Why Danes Happily Pay High Rates of Taxes," January 20, 2016, https://www.usnews.com/news/best-countries/articles/2016-01-20/why-danes-happily-pay-high-rates-of-taxes/.

22. In Erich Fromm, *The Sane Society,* (New York: Fawcett World Library, 1967), 191.

23. In Erich Fromm, *The Sane Society*, 191.

24. Erich Fromm, *The Sane Society*,129–130.

25. Erich Fromm, *The Sane Society*, 143.

26. Erich Fromm, *The Sane Society*, 168.

27. Erich Fromm, *The Sane Society*, 168.

28. Erich Fromm, *The Sane Society,* 124. Fromm would add television, computers, iPhones and the Internet to the list were he alive today.

29. Erich Fromm, *The Sane Society*, 115.

30. Erich Fromm, *The Sane Society*, 193.

31. Erich Fromm, *The Sane Society*, 192.

32. Erich Fromm, *The Sane Society*, 161.

33. In Thomas Merton, *Conjectures of a Guilty Bystander* (New York: Doubleday Image, 1967), 23.

34. John Paul II, *On Human Work, Laborem Exercens* (Washington, D.C.: United States Catholic Conference, 1981), 20–21.

35. John Paul II, *On Human Work, Laborem Exercens*, 32.

36. John Paul II, *On Human Work, Laborem Exercens*, 27.

37. Marshall Sahlins, *Stone Age Economics* (Chicago: Aldine-Atherton Inc., 1972), 1.

38. Oxfam Briefing Paper, "An Economy for the 1 percent," January 18, 2016, https://www.oxfam.org/files/file_attachments/bp210-economy-one-percent-tax

39. Thomas Merton, *Conjectures of a Guilty Bystander* (Doubleday Image, 1968), 75–76.

40. Thomas Merton, *Conjectures of a Guilty Bystander*, 76.

41. Thomas Merton, *Conjectures of a Guilty Bystander*, 77.

42. Herbert Marcuse, *One Dimensional Man* (Boston: Beacon Press, 1964), 177–178.

43. Herbert Marcuse, *One Dimensional Man*, 84.

44. Ken Wilber, *A Brief History of Everything* (Boston: Shambhala Publications, 1996), 268.

45. Ken Wilber, *A Brief History of Everything*, 267.

46. Neoliberalism is linked to the post-Marxist world system or dependency theory of Immanuel Wallerstein and others who argue that the exploitation of developing and less developed or periphery countries by powerful industrialized core nations exhibits the 'highest' (most predatory) stage of capitalism.

47. Naomi Klein, *The Shock Doctrine: The Rise of Disaster Capitalism* (New York: Metropolitan Books, Henry Holt and Co., 2007), 23.

48. Naomi Klein, Analysis by Gypsy Perry, www.norcalbeat.com/shock_doctrine .htm

49. Naomi Klein, *This Changes Everything* (New York: Simon & Schuster, 2014), 20–21.

50. Naomi Klein, *This Changes Everything*, 21.

51. David Abram, *Becoming Animal* (New York: Vintage Books, 2010), 62.

52. E. F. Schumacher, *Small is Beautiful* (New York: HarperPerennial, 1973), 156.

CHAPTER 6

1. EIA, Frequently Asked Questions, https://www.eia.gov/tools/faqs/faq.php?id =77&t=11.

2. Union of Concerned Scientists, Car Emissions and Global Warming, https://www.ucsusa.org/clean-vehicles/car-emissions-and-global-warming.

3. "Oil Consumption in North America," maps.unomaha.edu/Peterson/funda/ sidebar/oilconsumption.html

4. Jeffrey Sachs, 'Forecasts,' *The New York Times*, September 23, 2014, D3.

5. Felicity Barringer, "Climate Change Will Disrupt Half of North America's Bird Species, Study Says," *The New York Times*, September 9, 2014, A14.

6. Sindya N. Bhanoo, "Honeybees Show Evidence of Insecticide," *The New York Times*, July 28, 2015, D4.

7. Jonah Engel Bromwich, "Insecticide Can Cut Bee Sperm Count by Nearly 40 percent, Study Finds," *The New York Times*, July 28, 2016, A16.

8. Seth Borenstein, "Honeybee Die-Off Threatens Food Supply," Associated Press, May 2, 2007, www.washingtonpost.com/wp-dyn/content/article/2007/05/02/AR2007050201413_pf.html.

9. While the fossil fuel industry is worldwide, this chapter will focus on the United States. Some European nations, such as Germany and Denmark, are ahead of the US in weaning themselves from fossil fuels, while China now exceeds the United States in pollution due to their expansion of coal-firing plants.

10. Jeffrey S. Dukes, "Burning Buried Sunshine: Human Consumption of Ancient Solar Energy," Springer Link, November 2008, volume 61, https://link.springer.com/article/10.1023/A:1026391317686.

11. Dave Pollard, "Population: A Systems Approach," How to Save the World, February 6, 2004, https://howtosavetheworld.ca/2004/02/06/population-a-systems-approach/.

12. EIA, Frequently Asked Questions, "What is US electricity generation by energy source?", accessed May 9, 2018, www.eia.gov/tools/faqs/faq.php?id=427&t=3.

13. EIA U.S. Energy Information Administration, "Coal Explained. Where Our Coal Comes From," accessed May 9, 2018, https://www.eia.gov/energyexplained/index.php?page=coal_where.

14. Appalachian Voices, "Ecological Impacts of Mountaintop Removal," accessed May 9, 2018, appvoices.org/end-mountaintop-removal/ecology/.

15. "EPA Response to Kingston TVA Coal Ash Spill," accessed May 14, 2018, https://www.epa.gov/tn/epa-response-kingston-tva-coal-ash-spill.

16. 10 NEWS, "Lawsuit claims 100+ new cases of dying, sick Kingston coal ash spill workers," March 29, 2018, https://www.wbir.com/article/news/crime/lawsuit/claims.

17. EPA, "History and Response Timeline," accessed May 14, 2018, https://www.epa.gov/dukeenergy-coalash/history-and-response-timeline.

18. On February 16, 2017 an executive order was signed by President Trump that allows coal companies to dump coal debris into streams. This order is part of a larger effort by Republican lawmakers to loosen EPA environmental regulations.

19. James Hansen, "The Enemy of the Human Race," *Sierra*, May-June, 2009, 41.

20. Steve Hawk, "The Cost of Coal," *Sierra,* November/December 2012, 29.

21. Ground Truth Trekking, "Mercury from Coal," May 5, 2013, www.groundtruthtrekking.org/Issues/AlaskaCoal/CoalMercury.html.

22. Leonardo Trasande, Clyde Schechter, Karla A. Haynes, Philip J. Landrigan, "Applying Cost Analyses to Drive Policy that Protects Children," The New York Academy of Sciences, October 5, 2006, https://nyaspubs.onlinelibrary.wiley.com/doi/abs/10.1196/annals.1371.034.

23. Statista, "Number of offshore rigs worldwide as of January 2018 by region," accessed May 14, 2018, www.statista.com/statistics/279100.

24. Tribune wire report, "Federal data: As oil production soars, so do pipeline leaks," *Chicago Tribune*, accessed May 9, 2018, www.chicagotribune.com/news/ nationworld/ct-oil-pipeline-leak-20150522-story.html.

25. Mary Pipher, "Lighting a Spark On the High Plains," *The New York Times* Op-Ed, April 18, 2013, A27.

26. Mary Pipher, "Lighting a Spark On the High Plains," A27.

27. David Treuer, "An Indian Protest for Everyone," *The New York Times*, November 27, 2016, SR5.

28. John Schwartz, "Norway will Divest From Coal in Push Against Climate Change," *The New York Times*, June 5, 2015, https://www.nytimes.com/2015/06/06/ science/norway-in-push-against-climate-change-will-divest-from-coal/.

29. Larry Elliott, "World Bank to end financial support for oil and gas extraction," *The Guardian*, December 12, 2017, https://www.theguardian.com/business/2017/ dec/12/uk-banks-join-multinationals-pledge-come-clean-climate.

30. Anthony R. Ingraffea, "Gangplank to a Warm Future," *The New York Times*, July 29, 2013, A17.

31. Fiona Harvey, "Rapid rise in methane emissions in 10 years surprises scientists," *The Guardian*, December 12, 2016, https://www.theguardian.com/environment/2016/ dec/12/.

32. EIA, Today in Energy, "Hydraulically fractured wells provide two-thirds of U.S. natural gas production," May 5, 2016, https://www.eia.gov/todayinenergy/detail .php?id=26112.

33. Statistics on fracking come from the *Human and Ecological Risk Assessment*; *Proceedings of the National Academy of Sciences* study, and *Nature* groundwater study; reprinted from *The Nation* in *Mother Earth News*. Shelley Stonebrook, "Fracking and Our Food Supply," *Mother Earth News*, 2013, 19.

34. Shelley Stonebrook, "Fracking and Our Food Supply," *Mother Earth News*, 2013, 19.

35. Thuy Ong, "Norway will spend 13 million to upgrade its doomsday seed vault," The Verge, February 26, 2018, https://www.theverge.com/2018/2/26/17052690/.

36. Walt Whitman, *Leaves of Grass* (New York: Barnes & Noble Books, 2004), 58.

37. Michael Pollan, *The Omnivore's Dilemma* (New York: Penguin, 2006), 126.

38. Michael Pollan, *The Omnivore's Dilemma*, 127.

39. David Suzuki, with Amanda McConnell and Adrienne Mason, *The Sacred Balance: Rediscovering Our Place in Nature* (Vancouver, B.C.: Greystone Books, 2007), 120.

40. Wendell Berry, *Home Economics* (New York: Farrar, Straus and Giroux, 1987), 72–74.

41. David Suzuki, with Amanda McConnell and Amanda Mason, *The Sacred Balance: Rediscovering Our Place in Nature* (Vancouver, BC: Greystone Books, 2007), 145.

42. Robert Sanders, "Pesticide atrazine can turn male frogs into females." *Berkeley News*, March 1, 2010, news.berkeley.edu/2010/03/01/frogs/.

43. Helena E. Virtanen, Annika Adamsson, "Cryptorchidism and endocrine disrupting chemicals," *Molecular and Cellular Endocrinology*, volume 355, Sci-

ence Direct, May 22, 2012, https://www.sciencedirect.com/science/article/pii/S0303720711006782.

44. Brainy Quote, Franklin Roosevelt Quotes, accessed May 10, 2018, https://www.brainyquote.com/search_results?q=Franklin%20Roosevelt.

45. FEW Resources.org, "Losing Ground," https://www.fewresources.org/soil-science-and-society-were-running-out-of-dirt.html.

46. Mark Bittman, "Now This Is Natural Food," *The New York Times*, October 23, 2013, A29.

47. *The Ten Principal Upanishads,* trans. Shree Purohit Swami and W. B. Yeats, (London: Faber and Faber, 1970), 89.

48. Brainy Quote, Franklin Roosevelt Quotes, accessed May 10, 2018 https://www.brainyquote.com/search_results?q=Franklin%20Roosevelt.

49. Abraham Joshua Heschel, *Moral Grandeur and Spiritual Audacity: Essays*, ed. Susannah Heschel (New York: Farrar, Straus and Giroux, 1966), 328.

CHAPTER 7

1. Cyanobacteria use energy from sunlight to convert water and carbon dioxide into food. Because they are mostly found in the deep seas cyanobacteria need to capture every bit of light energy by means of sophisticated antennae. Their chemical processes of conversion are not fully understood by scientists. Their ability to harvest light is being studied by solar-panel manufacturers who want to raise the efficiency level of solar cells. A recent report in the journal *Molecular Biology and Evolution* by Dr. Tanai Cardona and colleagues points to a key gene in cyanobacteria which supports evidence that oxygen-making photosynthesis arose about one billion years earlier than was previously thought. (see "Ever Green," *The New York Times Science Times,* April 21, 2015, D1).

2. Thomas Berry, *The Great Work* (New York: Bell Tower, 1999), 82.

3. John (Fire) Lame Deer and Richard Erdoes, *Lame Deer, Seeker of Visions* (New York: Pocket Books, 1994), 113.

4. Marcus Aurelius, *Meditations* (New York: Penguin Books, 1964), 73.

5. Parker J. Palmer and Arthur Zajonc with Megan Scribner, *The Heart of Higher Education: A Call to Renewal* (San Francisco: Jossey-Bass, 2010), 26.

6. John Mansley Robinson, *An Introduction to Early Greek Philosophy* (Boston: Houghton-Mifflin, 1968), 9.

7. F. David Peat, *Synchronicity,* (New York: Bantam Books, 1987), 55.

8. F. David Peat, *Synchronicity,* 16.

9. Zoologist Wayne Potts has studied this phenomenon. He argues that flocks of birds synchronize their movements not to follow a leader or copy their neighbors because the reaction time required is too fast and sudden for this kind of deliberate motion. Instead, the birds 'anticipate' a change in the direction of flight and the new motion spreads throughout the flock like a wave. He calls his theory *the chorus line hypothesis*. See Wayne K. Potts, "The chorus-line hypothesis of manoeuvre coordination in avian flocks," *Nature* 309, May 24, 1984, 344–345.

10. T. S. Eliot, *Collected Poems 1909–1962* (Orlando, FL: Harcourt Brace Jovanovich, 1991), 177.

11. Fritjof Capra, *The Tao of Physics* (Boston: Shambhala, 1991), 80.

12. Meister Eckhart, *Selected Writings,* trans. Oliver Davies (New York: Penguin Books, 1994), 123.

13. Meister Eckhart, *Selected Writings,* 129.

14. Thomas Berry, *The Great Work* (New York: Bell Tower, 1999), 5–6.

15. James Gorman, "Focusing on Fruit Flies, Curiosity Takes Flight," *The New York Times,* October 08, 2013, D1.

16. Lewis Thomas, *The Lives of a Cell* (New York: Bantam, 1975), 3.

17. Lewis Thomas, *The Lives of a Cell,* 2.

18. Wikipedia, Apoptosis, https://en.wikipedia.org/wiki/Apoptosis

19. Science Daily, "Children with autism have mitochondrial dysfunction, study finds," University of California-Davis Health System, November 30, 2010, https://www.sciencedaily.com/releases/2010/11/101130161521.htm.

20. David Abram, *Becoming Animal* (New York: Vintage, 2010), 61.

21. Gary Snyder, "Grace", *Co-evolution Quarterly,* vol 43 (Fall 1984), 1.

22. Gary Snyder, "Grace", *Co-evolution Quarterly,* 1.

23. *King James Bible,* Genesis 3:19.

24. *The Ten Principal Upanishads,* trans. Shree Purohit Swami and W.B. Yeats (London: Faber and Faber, 1970), 69.

25. Stephen A. Forbes, "Lake as a Microcosm," in *Readings in Ecology,* ed. Edward Kormondy (Upper Saddle River, NJ: Prentice-Hall, 1965), 168.

26. Stephen A. Forbes, "Lake as a Microcosm," in *Readings in Ecology,* ed. Edward Kormondy, 169.

27. Stephen A. Forbes, "Lake as a Microcosm," in *Readings in Ecology,* ed. Edward Kormondy, 170.

28. Stephen A. Forbes, "Lake as a Microcosm," in *Readings in Ecology,* ed. Edward Kormondy, 170.

29. Brainy Quote, Marcus Tullius Cicero Quotes, https://www.brainyquote.com/authors/marcus_tullius_cicero

30. Natalie Angier, "The Lives of Sociable Spiders," *The New York Times,* May 13, 2014, D1-2. The self-sacrifice of the parents provokes an inquiry into whether these social insects are displaying a genetic basis for altruism—a theory developed by evolutionary biologist William Hamilton that inspired Richard Dawkins' controversial book *The Selfish Gene* (selfish in the sense that the gene works to secure survival of one's offspring).

31. Geneticists have determined that chimps and humans share roughly 98 percent of their genetic make-up. With this fact in mind environmental groups worldwide have been lobbying nations for laws to protect our primate 'cousins.' In 2008, a successful outcome was achieved in Spain when the environmental committee of the Spanish Parliament voted to support the Great Ape Project, founded by animal rights advocate Peter Singer and Italian philosopher Paola Cavalieri, by granting legal rights to great apes. These rights forbid the use of torture, abuse and even death in the treatment of great apes because they are members with humans of what Cavalieri calls a

"'community of equals.'" Donald G. McNeil, Jr., "When Human Rights Extend to Nonhumans," *The New York Times*, July 13, 2008, 3.

32. Western culture favors a bilineal/bilateral form of descent rather than a unilineal pattern. Tracing one's family tree is an acknowledgement that each side of the family exerts equal influence.

33. Marcel Mauss, *The Gift* (New York: W. W. Norton, 1990), 22–23.

34. The Hudson Valley, in upstate New York, is a region of apple orchards, dairy farms and agricultural farms. Most of those farms that practice organic, sustainable farming have formed CSAs. Residents invest in a CSA by buying shares to help the farmer succeed; they receive a portion of the harvest of vegetables according to their financial contribution.

35. Drew Dellinger, "MLK's Cosmology of Connectedness—Christmas Eve 1967," posted 12/26/12, https://drewdellinger.org/pages/blog/679/.

36. Abraham Heschel, *Moral Grandeur and Spiritual Audacity: Essays*, ed. Susannah Heschel (New York: Farrar, Straus & Giroux, 1966), 322.

37. *The Ten Principal Upanishads*, trans. Shree Purohit Swami and W. B. Yeats, (London: Faber and Faber, 1970), 15.

38. A survey conducted by The National Institute on Drug Abuse (NIDA) in 2010 showed that 1 in 9 young people (11.4% of youth, ages 12–25) use prescription drugs like Vicotin and OxyContin nonmedically. See "Prescription Drug Abuse: Young People at Risk," https://www.drugabuse.gov/related-topics/trends-statistics/infographics/.

39. *Tao Te Ching*, trans. Stephen Mitchell (New York: HarperCollins, 1988), 51 (second stanza)

40. Mary Oliver, *New and Selected Poems* (Boston: Beacon Press, 1992), 181.

CHAPTER 8

1. Bill Plotkin, *Nature and the Human Soul* (Navato, CA: New World Library, 2008), 50. Copyright © 2008 by Bill Plotkin.

2. St. Bonaventure, *The Soul's Journey into God*, trans. Ewert Cousins (New York: Paulist Press, 1978), 100. This saying is attributed by St. Bonaventure to the mystic Alan de Lille.

3. *King James Bible*, Psalm 19:1, 4.

4. J. Philip Newell, *The Book of Creation* (New York: Paulist Press, 1999), xxv.

5. David Kinsley, *Ecology and Religion* (Upper Saddle River, NJ: Prentice-Hall, 1995), 47-48.

6. *King James Bible*, Matthew 13:13.

7. See Appendix 1 for a generic practice in sensory awareness called *pausing*.

8. David Abram, *Becoming Animal* (New York: Vintage Books, 2010), 271.

9. David Abram, *Becoming Animal,* 271.

10. David Abram, *Becoming Animal,* 272.

11. Clifford Geertz, *The Interpretation of Cultures* (New York: Basic Books, 1973), 129.

12. Paul Radin, *Primitive Man as Philosopher* (New York: Dover Publications, 1957), 274. Terms like *primitive* and *savage* were commonly given to native peoples in the 19th c. These terms expressed the cultural worldview of colonial powers like Britain and Spain who thought that natives were inferior to 'civilized' Europeans. Anthropologists—even those who argued that indigenous peoples have the same mental capacities as the rest of mankind, like Radin and Malinowski—were still enculturated into the language and to some extent the bias of their time.

13. Colin Turnbull, *The Forest People* (New York: Simon and Schuster, 1968), 272. The pygmies are one of the oldest indigenous peoples on the planet; they live in the Congo region of Africa. As with another ancient people, the San Bushmen of southern Africa, the encroachment of Western industrialized 'development' is threatening to displace this native people from the ancestral forest home where their culture formed.

14. David Kinsley, *Ecology and Religion* (Upper Saddle River, NJ: Prentice-Hall, 1995), 49.

15. *The Geeta: The Gospel of the Lord Shri Krishna*, trans. W. B. Yeats and Purohit Swami (London: Faber and Faber, 1973), 60.

16. Thich Nhat Hanh, *The Long Road Turns to Joy: A Guide to Walking Meditation* (Berkeley, CA: Parallax Press, 1996), 88.

17. David Suzuki and Peter Knudtson, *Wisdom of the Elders* (New York: Bantam Books, 1992), 204.

18. David Suzuki and Peter Knudtson, *Wisdom of the Elders*, 204.

19. It is interesting that Tibetan Buddhist monks also use sand painting as a healing tool.

20. David Suzuki and Peter Knudtson, *Wisdom of the Elders* (New York: Bantam Books, 1992), 205.

21. The history of the Aborigines, one of the most archaic extant human groups on the planet, has been traced, through genetic studies, to Africa and thence to South Asia up to 75,000 years ago. After interbreeding with Denisovan peoples of South Asia (descendants of the Neanderthal race) and peoples of Papua New Guinea, the Aborigines finally arrived and settled in Australia.

22. Paula Gerber, "Aboriginal people are still denied full citizenship," ABC News, October 31, 2012, www.abc.net.au/news/2012-11-01/gerber—-aboriginal -citizenship/4344704.

23. W.E.H. Stanner, "Religion, Totemism and Symbolism" in *A Reader in the Anthropology of Religion*, ed. Michael Lambek (Malden, MA: Blackwell Publishing, 2008), 85.

24. David Suzuki and Peter Knudtson, *Wisdom of the Elders* (New York: Bantam Books, 1992), 161.

25. David Suzuki and Peter Knudtson, *Wisdom of the Elders*, 163.

26. W. E. H. Stanner, "Religion, Totemism and Symbolism" in *A Reader in the Anthropology of Religion*, ed. Michael Lambek (Malden, MA: Blackwell Publishing, 2008), 86.

27. There are other religious systems, such as Hindu Vedanta, which also claim that the entrance of a soul into a physical embryo defines the human person.

28. This interview takes place in the rainforest at the base of Gulaga volcanic mountain, sacred site of Dream Time for the Yuin, New South Wales, Australia. See www.globalaloneness.org.

29. www.globalaloneness.org

30. Bill Plotkin, *Nature and the Human Soul* (Novato, CA: New World Library, 2008), 39. Copyright © 2008 by Bill Plotkin.

31. Bill Plotkin, *Nature and the Human Soul*, 31.

32. Bill Plotkin, *Nature and the Human Soul*, 31.

33. Sandra Ingerman, *Medicine for the Earth: How to Transform Personal and Environmental Toxins* (New York: Three Rivers Press, 2000), 131. Excerpt from *Medicine for the Earth: How to Transform Personal and Environmental Toxins* by Sandra Ingerman, copyright © 2000 by Sandra Ingerman. Used by permission of Harmony Books, an imprint of the Crown Publishing Group, a division of Penguin Random House LLC. All rights reserved. Any third party use of this material, outside of this publication, is prohibited. Interested parties must apply directly to Penguin Random House LLC for permission.

34. Theodore Roszak, *The Voice of the Earth, An Exploration of Ecopsychology* (Grand Rapids, MI: Phanes Press, 2001), 321.

35. Theodore Roszak, *The Voice of the Earth*, 321.

36. *The Complete Poetical Works of William Wordsworth* (Boston: Houghton-Mifflin, 1904), 91. From "Lines Composed a Few Miles Above Tintern Abbey."

37. Roderick Nash, *Wilderness and the American Mind* (New Haven: Yale University Press, 1982), 127.

38. Edwin Way Teale, ed., *The Wilderness World of John Muir* (Boston: Mariner Books/Houghton Mifflin Company, 2001), 313.

39. David Orr, *Earth in Mind* (Washington, DC: Island Press, 2008), 163.

40. Kurt Vonnegut, *A Man Without a Country* (New York: Seven Stories Press, 2005), 56.

41. Roderick Nash, *Wilderness and the American Mind* (New Haven: Yale University Press, 1982), 140.

42. Bill Plotkin, *Nature and the Human Soul* (Navato, CA: New World Library, 2008), 122. Copyright © 2008 by Bill Plotkin. This description of a child's affinity with animals and plants is reflected in the Native American concept of a power animal or plant that is discovered through a vision or dream. This guardian spirit provides strength of body and mind to the human being according to the primary power which that animal or plant possesses.

43. Richard Louv, *Last Child in the Woods* (Chapel Hill: Algonquin Books, 2005), 103.

44. Richard Louv, *Last Child in the Woods*, 56.

45. Richard Louv, *Last Child in the Woods*, 33–34.

46. Richard Louv, *Last Child in the Woods*, 131.

47. See Louv's support group website www.childrenandnaturenetwork.org

48. Christopher M. Bache, *Dark Night, Early Dawn* (Albany, NY: State University of New York Press, 2000), 4.

49. *Millennium, Tribal Wisdom and the Modern World: (4) An Ecology of Mind,* New Vision Media Ltd. 1992. Narrated by David Maybury-Lewis. Produced by Adrian Malone and Richard Meech.

50. James Gorman, "Finding Zen in a Patch of Nature," *The New York Times Science Times,* October 23, 2012, D4.

51. Abraham Joshua Heschel, *Moral Grandeur and Spiritual Audacity: Essays,* ed. Susannah Heschel (New York: Farrar, Straus & Giroux, 1966), 308.

52. *Srimad Bhagavatam, The Wisdom of God,* trans. Swami Prabhavananda (New York: G.P. Putnam's Sons, 1968), 190.

CHAPTER 9

1. Ralph Waldo Emerson, *Nature, Addresses and Lectures* in *Complete Works of Ralph Waldo Emerson* (Boston: Houghton-Mifflin, 1903), 10.

2. Thomas H. Johnson, ed., *The Complete Poems of Emily Dickinson* (New York: Little, Brown and Co., 1960), 385.

3. Arnold J. Toynbee, *A Study of History, Abridgement of Volumes I-VI* by D. C. Somervell (New York: Oxford University Press, 1946), 206–207.

4. *The Great Work* is the title of Thomas Berry's book (New York: Bell Tower, 1999).

5. Thomas Berry, *The Great Work* (New York: Bell Tower, 1999), 91–92.

6. Bill McKibben, *The End of Nature* (New York: Random House, 2006), 182–183.

7. Rachel Carson, *Silent Spring* (Boston: Mariner Books/Houghton Mifflin, 2002), 99–100.

8. Rachel Carson, *Silent Spring,* 277.

9. Fritjof Capra, *The Tao of Physics* (Boston: Shambhala, 1991), 319.

10. A holistic use of mind in terms of the brain refers to a balanced use of the scientifically discovered aptitudes identified with the right and left brain hemispheres.

11. *The Essential Rumi,* trans. Coleman Barks (New York: HarperSanFrancisco, 1996), 281.

12. Robert C. Orenstein, ed., *The Nature of Human Consciousness* (New York: Viking Press, 1974), xiii.

13. Jerry Mayer and John P. Holms, *bite-size Einstein* (New York: St. Martin's Press, 1996), 10.

14. Gerald Holton, "'What, precisely, is 'thinking?' Einstein's answer" in *Einstein: A Centenary Volume,* ed. A. P. French (Cambridge, MA: Harvard University Press, 1979), 161.

15. Pagan Kennedy, "Want to be a genius? Think like a 94-year-old," *Tampa Bay Times,* April 10, 2017, 4P.

16. Thomas Kuhn, *The Structure of Scientific Revolutions* (Chicago: University of Chicago Press, 1996), 129.

17. Thomas Kuhn, *The Structure of Scientific Revolutions,* 113.

18. Thomas Kuhn, *The Structure of Scientific Revolutions,* 78.

19. Thomas Kuhn, *The Structure of Scientific Revolutions*, 117.

20. Edwin Way Teale, ed., *The Wilderness World of John Muir* (Boston: Mariner Books/Houghton Mifflin Company, 2001), 315, 318.

21. Theodore Roosevelt, "Wilderness Makes Men New" in *The Natural World—Chaos and Conservation*, ed. Cecil E. Johnson (McGraw-Hill, 1972), 30.

22. Arnold J. Toynbee, *A Study of History: Abridgement of Volumes I-VI* by D. C. Somervell (New York: Oxford University Press, 1987), 215.

23. Henry David Thoreau, *Walden* (New York: Fall River Press, 2008), 105–106.

24. David Kinsley, *Ecology and Religion* (Upper Saddle River, NJ: Prentice-Hall, 1995), 143.

25. David Kinsley, *Ecology and Religion*, 143.

26. David Kinsley, *Ecology and Religion*, 144.

27. Henry David Thoreau, *Walden* (New York: Fall River Press, 2008), 85.

28. Henry David Thoreau, *Walden*, 91.

29. Henry David Thoreau, *Walden*, 91.

30. Henry David Thoreau, *Walden*, 84–85.

31. Henry David Thoreau, *Walden*, 86.

32. Roderick Nash, *Wilderness and the American Mind* (New Haven: Yale University Press, 1982), 92.

33. Roderick Nash, *Wilderness and the American Mind*, 89.

34. Edwin Way Teale, ed., *The Wilderness World of John Muir* (Boston: Mariner Books/Houghton Mifflin Company, 2001), 100.

35. Edwin Way Teale, ed., *The Wilderness World of John Muir*, 100.

36. Edwin Way Teale, ed., *The Wilderness World of John Muir*, 313

37. *King James Bible*, Luke 3:4.

38. Aldo Leopold, *A Sand County Almanac* (New York: Oxford University Press, 1987), 41.

39. Aldo Leopold, *A Sand County Almanac*, 24.

40. Aldo Leopold, *A Sand County Almanac*, 130.

41. The Land Institute in Salina, Kansas farms its crops sustainably by mimicking the resilience of perennial prairie grasses.

42. Aldo Leopold, *A Sand County Almanac* (New York: Oxford University Press, 1987), viii.

43. Roderick Nash, *Wilderness and the American Mind* (New Haven: Yale University Press, 1982), 195–196.

44. Kenneth Brower, "Reclaiming Wilderness," *Sierra*, July/August 2014, 29.

45. Adam Nagourney, "Where 2 Rivers Meet, Visions for Canyon Clash," *The New York Times* December 04, 2014, A24.

46. *King James Bible*, Book of Job 38:4.

47. Patricia O'Toole, ed. *In the Words of Theodore Roosevelt: Quotations from the Man in the Arena* (Ithaca: Cornell University Press, 2012), 128. www.amazon.com/Words-Theodore-Roosevelt-Quotations-Arena-ebook/dp/B009GJQGEK/ref=mt_kindle?-encoding.

48. Edwin Way Teale, ed., *The Wilderness World of John Muir* (Boston: Mariner Books/Houghton Mifflin Company, 2001), 311.

49. Sri Aurobindo and the Mother are co-founders of the worldwide spiritual organization Integral Yoga.

50. Holly Tarson, "Utopic Uprising," *Edible Hudson Valley*, Fall 2013, 18.

CHAPTER 10

1. Children's Hospital Los Angeles, "Prenatal Exposure to Common Air Pollutants Linked to Cognitive and Behavioral Impairment", March 25, 2015, https://www .chla.org/press-release/prenatal-exposure-common-air-pollutants-linked-cognitive -and-behavioral.

2. Earthjustice, "Chloropyrifos: the toxic pesticide now harming our children and environment," accessed May 14, 2018, https://earthjustice.org/features/what/you -need-to-know-about-chlorpyrifos.

3. Pope Francis, *On Care For Our Common Home: The Encyclical Letter 'Laudato Si'* (New York: Paulist Press, 2015), 21.

4. Pope Francis, *On Care For Our Common Home: The Encyclical Letter 'Laudato Si'*, 13.

5. Thomas S. Kuhn, *The Structure of Scientific Revolutions* (Chicago: University of Chicago Press, 1996), 84, 85.

6. This reaction is endemic to technopolies.

7. Duane Elgin, *Voluntary Simplicity* (New York: Quill, 1993), 189. It is interesting to compare Elgin's stages of cultural change with Jared Diamond's delineation of various cultural responses to crisis (see chapter 3).

8. Duane Elgin, *Voluntary Simplicity* (New York: Quill, 1993), 176.

9. Duane Elgin, *Voluntary Simplicity*, 187.

10. David Orr, *Earth in Mind* (Washington, D.C.: Island Press, 2004), xiv.

11. Carl Safina, *Beyond Words* (New York: Henry Holt and Company, 2015), 34.

12. G. Silami, C. Lamm, C. C. Rugg, T. Singer, "Right Supramarginal Gyrus Is Crucial to Overcome Emotional Egocentricity Bias in Social Judgments," *Journal of Neuroscience*, September 25, 2013, www.jneurosci.org/content/33/39/15466.

13. Kim-Pong Tam, "Dispositional empathy with nature," *Journal of Environmental Psychology*, v. 35, September 2013, 92-104, repository.ust.hk/ir/Record/ 1783.1-58869.

14. Center For Healthy Minds, "Study Shows Compassion Meditation Changes the Brain", March 25, 2008, www.centerhealthyminds.org/news/study-shows -compassion-meditation-changes-the-brain. Appendix II offers a practice in loving kindness meditation.

15. Sara Ruddick, *Maternal Thinking*, (Boston: Beacon Press, 1995), 115, 3.

16. David Orr, *Earth in Mind* (Washington, D.C.: Island Press, 2004), 32.

17. Brian Swimme & Thomas Berry, *The Universe Story: From the Primordial Flaming Forth to the Ecozoic Era—A Celebration of the Unfolding of the Cosmos* (New York: HarperCollins, 1993), 77. Copyright © 1992 Brian Swimme.

18. Brian Swimme & Thomas Berry, *The Universe Story*, 77–78.

19. Brian Swimme & Thomas Berry, *The Universe Story*, 243.

20. Joseph Campbell, *The Masks of God: Primitive Mythology* (New York: Penguin, 1976), 56.

21. Adrienne Rich, *Of Woman Born* (New York: W. W. Norton, 1976), 109.

22. Riane Eisler, *The Chalice and the Blade* (New York: HarperCollins, 1995), 60.

23. Brian Swimme & Thomas Berry, *The Universe Story: From the Primordial Flaming Forth to the Ecozoic Era—A Celebration of the Unfolding of the Cosmos* (New York: HarperCollins, 1992), 75. Copyright © 1992 Brian Swimme.

24. J. E. Lovelock, *Gaia: A New Look at Life on Earth* (Oxford: Oxford University Press, 1979), 148.

25. Duane Elgin, *Voluntary Simplicity* (New York: Quill, 1993), 157–158.

26. *King James Bible*, Luke 15:13.

27. Ken Wilber, *A Brief History of Everything* (Boston: Shambhala, 1996), 202.

28. Ken Wilber, *A Brief History of Everything*, 204.

29. Titiana Schlossberg, "An English Village Leads a Climate Revolution," *The New York Times*, August 22, 2016, A1.

30. Erica Goode, "Movement to Spare the Plow," *The New York Times*, March 10, 2015, D1, 4.

31. Kathryn Shattuck, "An Effort to Add a Key Ingredient to the Slow Food Movement: Investor Money," *The New York Times*, May 5, 2013. This is the philosophy of 'slow money' investors who financially support the Slow Food Movement. Begun in Italy in 1986 the Slow Food Movement strives to promote traditional and regional cuisine using local products farmed organically. Slow food restaurants are committed to high quality food and leisurely meals.

32. Stephanie Strom, "At Chobani, It's Not Just the Yogurt That's Rich," *The New York Times*, April 27, 2016, www.nytimes.com/2016/04/27/business/a-windfall-for-chobani-employees-stakes-in-the-company...

33. Siemens, The Magazine, "Siemens aims for CO2 neutral operations by 2030," December 4, 2015, https://www.siemens.com/customer-magazine/en/home/cities/CO2-neutral-by-2030.html.

34. Ryan Whitwam, "We could be headed for a solar power renaissance as costs keep dropping," Extreme Tech, December 19, 2016, https://www.extremetech.com/extreme/241300-headed-solar-power-renaissance-costs-keep-dropping.

35. Thomas Friedman, "Mr. Trump, Help Heal The Planet," *The New York Times*, November 16, 2016, A27.

36. Energy Vision, NGT News, "Energy Vison Touts RNG, Honors Nat-Gas Transport Leaders," accessed May 12, 2018, https://impactbioenergy.com/wp-content/uploads/2017/01/NGT-News-2016.pdf.

37. Joanna Underwood, email message to author, January 27, 2017.

38. Joanna Underwood, email message to author, January 27, 2017.

39. Robert B. Catell and Joanna D. Underwood, "How Garbage Trucks Can Drive a Green Future," *The New York Times* August 19, 2016, accessed March 14, 2017, http://energy-vision.org/new-york-times-rng-garbage-trucks/.

40. Parker J. Parker and Arthur Zajonc, *The Heart of Higher Education* (San Francisco: Jossey-Bass, 2010), 113.

41. David Orr, *Earth in Mind* (Washington, D.C.: Island Press, 2004), 145.

42. The vision statement of Warren Wilson College is a powerful call to sustainable living and communal cooperation. It reads "We acknowledge that a complex web of economic, social, cultural, spiritual and environmental factors determine the well-being of our community. We recognize our power as individuals, and in community, to influence these complex, interdependent relationships. We strive to make responsible decisions that take into account the multiple dimensions of sustainability in order to ensure quality of life now and for generations to come," www.warren -wilson.edu/sustainability. Every year Sierra magazine prints an issue that celebrates the top 'coolest' colleges of that year. Warren Wilson College is always on that list.

43. Maria Montessori, *The Secret of Childhood*, trans. M. Joseph Costelloe (New York: Ballantine Books, 1966), 34.

44. Aldo Leopold, *A Sand County Almanac* (New York: Oxford University Press, 1987), 73.

45. Aldo Leopold, *A Sand County Almanac*, 51.

46. David Orr, *Earth in Mind* (Washington, D.C.: Island Press, 2004), 32.

47. Henry A. Giroux, "Higher Education and the Promise of Insurgent Public Memory," accessed March 7, 2015, www.truth-out.org/news/item/29396.

48. Henry A. Giroux, "Higher Education and the Promise of Insurgent Public Memory."

49. Parker J. Parker and Arthur Zajonc, T*he Heart of Higher Education* (San Francisco: Jossey-Bass, 2010), 107.

50. Among important research centers that are evaluating mindfulness training are the Center for Healthy Minds, founded by Richard J. Davidson, professor of psychology at University of Wisconsin-Madison, and UCLA's MARC (Mindful Awareness Research Center). Davidson's research in contemplative neuroscience shows that contemplative disciplines such as mindfulness re-structure the brain, enhancing mental and emotional health. MARC offers classes in mindfulness meditation, provides teacher training to introduce mindfulness to children from Pre-K through Grade 12, and fosters research correlating mindfulness practice with health benefits.

51. Parker J. Parker and Arthur Zajonc, *The Heart of Higher Education* (San Francisco: Jossey-Bass, 2010), 117.

52. Thich Nhat Hanh, *The Long Road Turns to Joy* (Nyack, NY: United Buddhist Church, 1996), 15.

53. *The Complete Poetical Works of William Wordsworth* (Boston: Houghton-Mifflin, 1904), 92. Excerpt is from "Lines Composed a Few Miles above Tintern Abbey."

54. Mary Oliver, *New and Selected Poems* (Boston: Beacon Press, 1992), 226.

55. Edwin Way Teale, ed., *The Wilderness World of John Muir* (Boston: Mariner Books/Houghton-Mifflin, 2001), 311.

56. David Abram, *Becoming Animal* (New York: Vintage Books, 2010), 180–181.

57. *Ahead of All Parting: The Selected Poetry and Prose of Rainer Maria Rilke,* trans. Stephen Mitchell (New York: Penguin Modern Library Series, 1995), 191.

Index

About the Author

Lyla Yastion obtained a PhD in Anthropology from SUNY-Albany and has taught anthropology and religious studies at the college level for eighteen years. She is the author of *Pause Now: Handbook for a Spiritual Revolution*. Besides her work as an educator and author she is a reiki master with training in shamanic healing and mindfulness-based stress reduction.